Contents

Chapter 1

Chapter 2

Chapter 3

Ethical and Responsible Sourcing

[L4M4]
Core
Study Guide

Level 4
Diploma in Procurement
and Supply

Printed and distributed by:
The Chartered Institute of Procurement & Supply, Easton House, Easton on the Hill, Stamford, Lincolnshire PE9 3NZ

info@cips.org
www.cips.org

ISBN: 978-1-86124-291-4

A CIP (Catalogue in Publication) catalogue record for this publication is available from the British Library.

All facts are correct at time of publication.

Authors: Katie Jarvis-Grove FCIPS Chartered Procurement and Supply Professional and Michael Miles

First published in 2019 by CIPS

Editorial and project management by Haremi Ltd.
Typesetting by York Publishing Solutions Pvt. Ltd., INDIA
Index by LNS Indexing.

Chapter 4

Your qualification

CIPS qualifications are regulated internationally to ensure we offer a recognised, professional standard in procurement and supply. CIPS Level 4* Diploma in Procurement and Supply is a vocationally related professional qualification. Formal recognition is included within the regulatory frameworks of an increasing number of countries such as the UK (England, Wales and Northern Ireland), UAE (including Dubai) and Africa (including Zambia). Further information on this recognition and the details of corresponding qualifications levels for other international qualifications frameworks are detailed on our website. CIPS members can have the confidence in our regulated qualifications, which reliably indicate the standard of knowledge, skills and understanding that you, as a learner, are required to demonstrate.

A step up from the Level 3 Advanced Certificate in Procurement and Supply Operations, the Level 4 Diploma in Procurement and Supply is a stepping stone to study on the CIPS Level 5 Advanced Diploma in Procurement and Supply. The content has been written using the CIPS Procurement and Supply Cycle as its focus, which presents a cyclical process of key steps faced by those procuring goods or services. The Diploma offers the most common entry route to the profession and should be used by learners to develop a professional 'tool box' which learners can apply in the practical environment and further develop at Levels 5 and 6.

In this way successful learners will possess transferable workplace skills, developing their operational and tactical abilities as they strive for managerial roles and responsibilities. It is aimed at those in the profession who have procurement and supply activity at the heart of their role. Learners will be expected to provide advice and guidance to key stakeholders on the performance of organisational procedures and processes associated with procurement and supply and will aspire to manage developments in and improvements to the related functions. Transferable skills are those such as communication, teamwork, and planning and completing tasks to high standards, all enable the learner to add value to the organisation.

Entry level — Level 2 Certificate in Procurement and Supply Operations

Entry level — Level 3 Advanced Certificate in Procurement and Supply Operations

Highest Entry level — Level 4 Diploma in Procurement and Supply Operations

Level 5 Advanced Diploma in Procurement and Supply

Level 6 Professional Diploma in Procurement and Supply

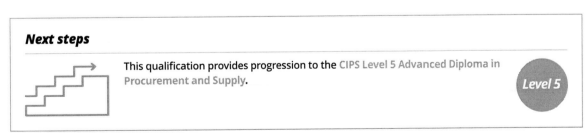

Next steps

This qualification provides progression to the CIPS Level 5 Advanced Diploma in Procurement and Supply.

Level 5

* Refers to levels within the UK RQF. Other regulatory bodies may have different corresponding levels

Based on the Tactical competency level of CIPS Global Standard

Guide to qualification content

What will I study?

Eight CORE modules make up 60 required credits

60 Credits required for completion

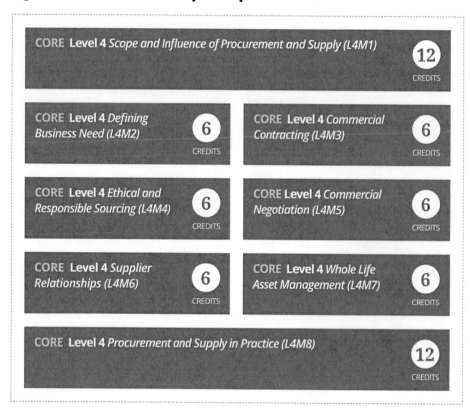

CORE **Level 4** *Scope and Influence of Procurement and Supply (L4M1)* — **12** CREDITS

CORE **Level 4** *Defining Business Need (L4M2)* — **6** CREDITS

CORE **Level 4** *Commercial Contracting (L4M3)* — **6** CREDITS

CORE **Level 4** *Ethical and Responsible Sourcing (L4M4)* — **6** CREDITS

CORE **Level 4** *Commercial Negotiation (L4M5)* — **6** CREDITS

CORE **Level 4** *Supplier Relationships (L4M6)* — **6** CREDITS

CORE **Level 4** *Whole Life Asset Management (L4M7)* — **6** CREDITS

CORE **Level 4** *Procurement and Supply in Practice (L4M8)* — **12** CREDITS

Who is it for?

This qualification is the essential toolkit for anyone planning a career in procurement and supply. Developed and written using the Procurement and Supply cycle** as its focus, it is at the same level as the first year of an undergraduate degree course. It is suitable for those in operational roles or those managing or supervising the procurement and supply function who want to develop their career and work towards MCIPS Chartered Procurement and Supply Professional.

What will I learn?

You will learn about making procurement and supply happen within an organisation, and you will be equipped with an essential range of knowledge and tools that you can apply immediately in your workplace. Learn how to apply practical, theoretical and technical knowledge, gain a clear understanding of procurement and supply and develop the ability to address complex, non-routine problems.

On completion, you will be able to analyse, interpret and evaluate relevant information and ideas and have an informed awareness of differing perspectives and approaches within the profession. You will also be able to review the effectiveness and appropriateness of methods, actions and results.

Entry requirements

This is the only entry point onto our Diploma qualifications. A minimum of at least two A-levels (or international equivalent) or a CIPS Level 3 Advanced Certificate qualification is required. Alternatively, you will need a minimum of two years' relevant experience in a business environment.

Credit values

To gain a qualification you are required to complete a total number of credits. This is a way of quantifying the required number of study hours. 1 credit is equivalent to 10 hours of study. Each module is given a credit value of 6 or 12 credits.

Total credits required for completion **60**

* *The Procurement cycle is the cyclical process of key steps when procuring goods or services.* www.cips.org/en-gb/knowledge/procurement-cycle/

About our exams and your study commitments

Objective Response exam format (OR)

OR

These questions allow you to select a response from a list of possible answers. You will find these types of exams across all our qualifications levels and they are marked by computer and then moderated by CIPS examiners.

Constructed Response exam format (CR)

CR

These questions require you to create or 'construct' a response to the question such as an essay or case study. You will find this type of exam in our diploma level qualifications and they will be marked by subject expert examiners.

Your total qualification time (TQT)

600 TQT HRS

The TQT indicates the overall number of guided learning hours, additional self-study and assessment time that is required.

Guided learning hours (GLH)

250 GLH HRS

It is expected that you will undertake 250 GLH. The definition of guided learning hours is: 'A measure of the amount of input time required to achieve the qualification. This includes lectures, tutorials and practicals, as well as supervised study in, for example, learning centres and workshops'.

Self-study requirement (SSR)

335 SSR HRS

Additionally, we recommend that you also commit to at least 335 SSR hours. This includes wider reading of the subject areas and revision to give yourself the best preparation for successfully achieving the qualification.

Total exam time

15 HRS

All the modules in CIPS qualifications are assessed by an examination.

How to use this book

Welcome to this study guide for Ethical and Responsible Sourcing. It contains all the information needed to prepare you for the assessment in this module.

This study guide follows the order of the module specification and each chapter relates to one of the learning outcomes below. You can also see the assessment criteria for each learning outcome.

Learning outcome 1

By the end of this chapter, you will be able to define sourcing and outsourcing, and identify the entire process in relation to procurement.

Learning outcome 2

By the end of this chapter, you will understand the processes that can be used to analyse potential external suppliers and how to carry them out effectively.

Learning outcome 3

By the end of this chapter, you will understand the compliance issues that buyers may face when sourcing from within different sectors, and with suppliers on an international scale.

Learning outcome 4

By the end of this chapter, you will understand more about the responsibilities of a procurement professional in terms of ethical and responsible sourcing.

Book features

Throughout this book there are a number of features to aid your learning and simplify your revision. Take a look at the different features you will find in the book below.

Glossary
These are the key terms and their definitions

Remember This information is important, so you should make a note of it.	
Check These revision questions give you a chance to check you understand the content in this chapter.	
Apply These tasks give you a chance to test out your knowledge and understanding.	
Recap This information will summarise sections from previous chapters.	

Case study — These case studies will relate the content you have learned to real-world examples.

Recommended reading These books can give you more understanding on the subject.	

Link to CIPS knowledge where members will be able to access additional resources to extend your knowledge, plus links to online eLearning content including videos, audio and interactive quizzes to recap and test your knowledge and understanding.

End of chapter assessments

At the end of each chapter in the book there is a set of exam-style questions to prepare you for your assessment.

End of Chapter Assessment

IDENTIFY

1 The National Health Service (NHS) in the UK is an example of an organisation from which sector?

a. Public

b. Private

c. Third

d. Primary

Ethical and Responsible Sourcing
[L4M4]

C

CORE MODULE

CIPS GLOBAL
STANDARD
6.4 • 6.5 • 11.3

OR

OBJECTIVE
RESPONSE EXAM

1.5

HRS

EXAM DURATION
HOURS

60

HRS

MODULE
LEARNING
TIME

6

CREDITS

Module purpose

On completion of this module, learners will be able to explain the options and associated processes available for sourcing with external suppliers. They will also examine the legal and ethical impact and the implications of corporate social responsibility, on the final sourcing decision.

Module aim(s)

In any organisation, a significant element of procurement and supply activity is based around decisions to internally conduct activity or to source from an external supplier. Hence, the selection of the correct external suppliers is a vital contributor to overall organisational success. This module enables personnel with roles in procurement and supply to formulate selection criteria and sourcing strategies to ensure that the organisation will make the correct choice of external suppliers. It explains options for sourcing, and examines the key processes that can be applied to the analysis of potential external suppliers and to ensure the development of ethically and socially responsible sourcing agreements.

Credit value

CHAPTER 1
Understand options for sourcing requirements from suppliers

Learning outcome

By the end of this chapter, you will be able to define sourcing and outsourcing, and identify the entire process in relation to procurement.

Chapter overview

1.1 Identify the sourcing process in relation to procurement

You will understand:

- Definitions of sourcing and outsourcing
- Make or buy decisions
- Strategic and tactical sourcing costs and benefits of outsourcing
- Outsourcing non-core and core work or services
- Supplier pre-qualification or criteria for supplier appraisal
- Vendor or supplier performance management
- Risks in outsourcing
- The market development and growth of outsourcing
- Regulations affecting employees' terms of employment

1.2 Differentiate between approaches to the sourcing of requirements from suppliers

You will understand:

- Single, dual and multiple sourcing arrangements
- The use of tendering; open, restricted and negotiated approaches to tendering
- Direct negotiations with suppliers
- Intra-company trading and transfer pricing arrangement
- Implications of international sourcing

1.3 Define selection and award criteria that can be commonly applied when sourcing requirements from external suppliers

You will understand:

- Typical selection criteria such as; quality assurance, environmental and sustainability, technical capabilities, systems capabilities, labour standards, financial capabilities and credit rating agencies
- The importance of supplier financial stability and due diligence checks

- Ratio analysis to make conclusions on profitability, liquidity, gearing and investment
- The limitations of ratio analysis

1.4 Define award criteria that can be commonly applied when sourcing requirements from external suppliers

You will understand:
- Typical award criteria such as; price, total life-cycle costs, technical merit, added value solutions, systems and resources
- Balancing commercial and technical award criteria

Introduction

Sourcing is a key element of procurement and so should be carried out responsibly and in accordance with the organisation's ethical conduct.

This chapter will explain the sourcing process and the related responsibilities that procurement professionals should demonstrate, as well as identifying the different options to consider when sourcing products and services.

Different sourcing strategies require different approaches and so this chapter will discuss the types of strategies along with the desired approaches.

One of the main aims of procurement is to award and manage contracts to the most suitable supplier in order to achieve the best value for money. Suitability can be judged on many factors, from price to corporate social responsibility to ethical accountability. This chapter will cover the process for awarding and managing the contract to ensure correct legal and ethical conduct.

1.1 Identify the sourcing process in relation to procurement

Sourcing is a key part of the procurement cycle. It involves establishing, evaluating and engaging with suppliers to achieve the best value for money when purchasing goods or services.

Sourcing covers many aspects including supplier analysis, make or buy decisions, the consideration of outsourcing and evaluating associated risks.

Definitions of sourcing and outsourcing

Types and aims of sourcing

Sourcing is the part of procurement strategy, where procurement professionals aim to find suitable organisations to become the suppliers of products and services.

Sourcing is the 'location, acquisition and management of all the vital inputs required for an organisation to operate. This includes raw materials, component parts, products, labour in all its forms, location and services.[1]

Sourcing can be tactical or strategic. Table 1.1 shows the differences between tactical and operational and strategic sourcing.

Tactical/operational sourcing	Strategic sourcing
Low-level decision-making	Top-level decision-making
High-profit, low-risk items	High-profit, high-risk items
Short-term projects	Long-term projects
Transactional relationships	Collaborative relationships

Table 1.1 Tactical and operational versus strategic sourcing

Tactical/ operational sourcing
Low level sourcing for low risk or routine items

Strategic sourcing
High level sourcing for core products or services

> *Check*
> What are the two types of sourcing?

Sourcing aims to achieve the best value for money by taking into account several factors. Table 1.2 shows what factors typically represent value to the procurement organisation when sourcing.

Aspect	What represents value for money
Price	Although important, price is rarely considered on its own when ensuring value for money
Delivery	Lead time should be acceptable and freight/transport costs fair
Quality	Goods should always be fit for purpose and meet the required specification
Ethics	Suppliers should follow ethical codes of practice and ensure workers are treated fairly
Sustainability	Suppliers should be sustainable in their existence, as well as promoting environmental sustainability
Availability	Products sourced need to be available – a competitive price becomes irrelevant if there is no availability

Table 1.2 Aspects that represent value for money

Lead time
The amount of time from placing the order to the goods/services being delivered

Fit for purpose
Being good enough to do the job it was designed for

Specification
A detailed description of the product or service required

Ethical codes of practice
A document outlining an organisation's accepted behaviours and principles of working

Sustainability
The ability to meet the needs of the present without compromising the needs of the future

New buy
A brand new requirement – the first time the product/service has been sourced

Modified re-buy
A product/service that has been sourced before but requires a slight change prior to sourcing again

The sourcing process

Novack and Simco's 11-stage sourcing process

In 1991, Novack and Simco[2] set out an 11-stage sourcing process.

1 Identify needs
2 Define user requirements
3 Decide whether to make or buy
4 Identify purchase type (new buy, modified re-buy, straight re-buy)
5 Carry out market analysis
6 Identify potential suppliers

Straight re-buy
Exactly the same
product/service as
sourced previously

7 Pre-screen suppliers and create a shortlist

8 Evaluate shortlisted suppliers

9 Supplier selection

10 Final product or service delivered

11 Evaluate supplier performance

Apply
Identify an example of a new buy, a modified re-buy and a
straight re-buy that relates to an organisation with which you
are familiar.

The CIPS procurement cycle

Many theories have been developed since Novack and Simco's original work,
including the CIPS Procurement Cycle. This is a comprehensive diagram that
identifies each stage relating to the procurement process. Figure 1.1 shows the
CIPS Procurement Cycle.

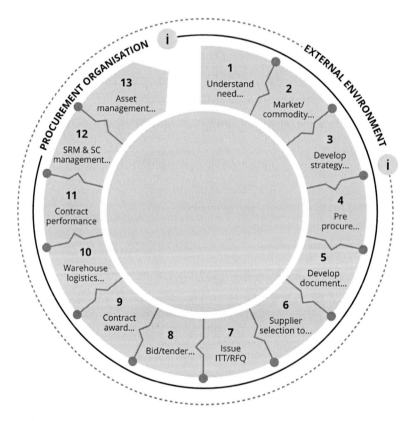

*Figure 1.1 The CIPS Procurement Cycle (Source: www.cips.org/en-gb/knowledge/
procurement-cycle/. Copyright CIPS 2014. All rights reserved.)*

In-house
Within an
organisation

What is outsourcing?

Outsourcing means contracting an external supplier to manage and run a function
that was previously handled **in-house**.

Outsourcing may be the preferred option for a procurement organisation for a
variety of reasons. These reasons may include the following.

- Financial: to allow costs (overheads) to be kept as effective as possible and enable the organisation to obtain value for money

- Technological: to reduce the need to continually invest in new machinery and work instead with suppliers that already have knowledge and resource in specialist areas

- Resource: to avoid the need to recruit additional staff or invest in training

- Skillset: to enable an organisation to benefit from an outsourced supplier's skills

- Improved focus: to enable an organisation to focus on its **core activities**

- Reduce risk: to move the requirements for managing services to another organisation.

Core activities
Activities that are key to an organisation's success

> *Remember*
> Outsourcing may bring cost benefits and reduced risk for the procurement organisation.

Not all functions or processes within an organisation can be outsourced. Core activities will normally remain in-house. This will be explored later in this section.

> *Check*
> Which activities or functions should not be outsourced?

Make or buy decisions

The concept of make or buy decisions is Stage 3 of Novack and Simco's 11-stage sourcing process and can be found within the Market Commodity and Options area (2) of the CIPS Procurement Cycle (see figure 1.1). The make or buy decision is whether to manufacture a product or provide a service in-house, or to source it from an external supplier. It requires thinking about the following factors.

- The product or service. If the product or service is core to the organisation, the decision should be to keep control in-house, i.e. to make rather than buy.

- The organisation's current position. If the organisation currently has capacity to make the item or provide the service without it negatively affecting other key business elements, make is likely to be the right decision. However, if the product or service requires individuals to be trained in order to make or deliver the product or service, or if the organisation needs to invest in additional **assets**, it may be more cost effective to buy.

Assets
Items of value owned by an organisation, which can be used to meet debts

- The current market situation. If buying the product or service would create **economies of scale** with an existing supplier or in part of the **logistics** operation within the supply chain, this could result in a cost saving. If, however, market prices for the raw materials are favourable and the organisation already buys a quantity of them, this could be an argument for making the product or delivering the service.

Economies of scale
Saving costs by increasing the levels of production

Logistics
The movement of something from one place to another

- The amount of competition. This is about the power of the buying organisation compared with the power of the supplying organisation. If there are few or no alternative suppliers, the buying organisation will not be in a strong position to negotiate a favourable price so would benefit from making the item. On the other hand, if there are several suppliers in the marketplace (lots of competition) the buying organisation will have the power and be well placed to negotiate a lower price. In this instance, buying may be the preferred option.

Understanding the levels of competition may help inform the make or buy decision. Porter's Five Forces, as seen in figure 1.2, show how competition can be examined within a marketplace.

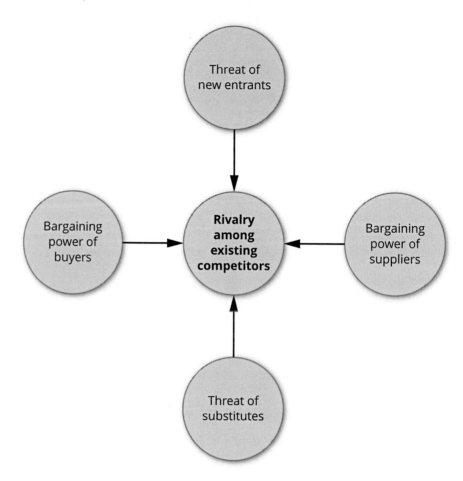

Figure 1.2 Porter's Five Forces (Source: Porter, M.E. (1980), Competitive Strategy: Techniques for Analysing Industries & Competitors. The Free Press, NY)

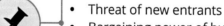

Remember
Porter's Five Forces:

- Threat of new entrants
- Bargaining power of buyers
- Threat of substitutes
- Bargaining power of suppliers
- Rivalry among existing competitors

Table 1.3 outlines the benefits of the make and buy decisions, and what factors are taken into account when deciding the best option for an organisation.

Make decision	Buy decision
Strategy of the organisation is to be self-sufficient	Specialised knowledge available
Enhanced control over processes	Technological advancements available
Improved quality control	Small volumes are not cost effective for 'make'

Make decision	Buy decision
Workforce remains stable	Cheaper to buy in than manufacture/deliver
Continuity of supply	'Make' organisation does not have the machinery required
No suitable 'buy' suppliers	Economies of scale available
Economies of scale available	No capacity in-house
Reduced risk	Less inventory
Easier to amend volumes/specifications	Reduced overheads

Table 1.3 Deciding to make or to buy

Procurement professionals must carefully analyse the advantages and disadvantages of whether to make or buy and consult **stakeholders** before making any final decision.

Stakeholder
Anyone with an interest in or who is impacted by decisions made by an organisation

Case study

Make or buy?

Christophe's Cards is a small family-owned organisation in a scenic European village. Christophe, the owner, prides himself on his core activity: making and supplying hand-made cards for all occasions, which include seasonal images of the local area.

Christophe has recently won a large order for a well-known retailer and has to produce 5000 cards to be delivered in six months' time. This is a considerably higher output level than the business is used to but a great opportunity for brand awareness.

Nadege, the head buyer, suggests to Christophe that they consider outsourcing the card manufacturing in order to meet the large order on time.

Christophe is reluctant to share his trade secrets with another company but Nadege tries very hard to persuade him, explaining the benefits, such as saving costs and reducing inventory levels at their factory.

Christophe can see the benefit and likes the idea of having a lower value of stock, but he thinks that there are other ways he can resolve that problem.

Christophe knows, based on seasonal trends, that after this order is completed, there will be a time where the workers have very little to do and he may have to consider reducing his workforce for a couple of months. This concerns Christophe so he decides to speak to the retailer.

"If we were to arrange a blanket order for the total number of cards with a call-off schedule, would that be acceptable? That way you do not have to hold all the cards in stock and you can be assured that I will deliver the quantities you want when you want them."

The retailer is happy with the idea, as long as Christophe agrees to keep a safety stock available in case sales increase more than they expect.

Christophe knows his loyal employees will work overtime to generate the safety stock and with this agreement he can both keep his inventory low by scheduling deliveries and ensure his employees have continuous work for the coming months.

Strategic and tactical sourcing costs and benefits of outsourcing

Check
What is the difference between strategic and tactical sourcing?

There are costs associated with all forms of sourcing, including the following.

- Procurement professional's salary
- Resources, such as computers and telephones
- Training
- Development of policies and procedures
- Time

In order to establish the amount of cost that should be attributed to a product or service need that has been identified, it is necessary to understand the category that the need falls into. By using the Kraljic matrix, procurement professionals can identify where a product or service sits in relation to the impact it has on the organisation's profit and the level of supply risk it poses to the organisation.

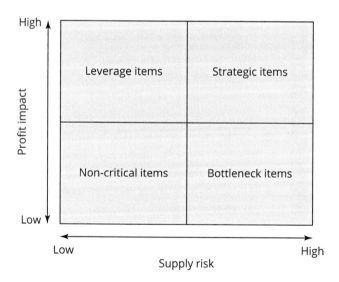

Figure 1.3 Kraljic matrix (Source: adapted from Kraljic, P. (1983), "Purchasing Must Become Supply Management", Harvard Business Review, September 1983)

Table 1.4 gives more detail about each of the four categories.

Category	Description	Procurement style	Relationship
Non-critical	Low profit impact, low supply risk	Tactical	Arms-length
Leverage	High profit impact, low supply risk	Tactical	Transactional
Strategic	High profit impact, high supply risk	Strategic	Collaborative
Bottleneck	Low profit impact, high supply risk	Tactical	Closer tactical

Table 1.4 Kraljic matrix explained

It is important to remember that, in practice, there will be circumstances for most organisations where they might also collaborate with top-end leverage and bottleneck suppliers. Certainly, relationships with those suppliers (which could be the highest risk and highest value contracts) could be considered to be closer than simply transactional and tactical.

Bottleneck
A specific stage in a process which slows down the flow of production and limits the overall output rate

> *Remember*
> The four categories of products or services according to Kraljic are the following.
>
> - Non-critical
> - Leverage
> - Strategic
> - Bottleneck

After categorising the product or service according to Kraljic's matrix, the organisation can make a decision about whether the need requires a tactical or a strategic approach.

It would not make good business sense to allocate high costs to sourcing an item that has been categorised as non-critical. This is because there are many suppliers in the marketplace and the item only has a low profit impact. So, increasing costs sourcing such an item would result in poor value for money.

Items that are strategic, that have a high profit impact and a high supply risk, where there may be little or no supplier competition, and where securing supply is critical, more costs may be required towards souring them.

The importance of a strategic item to the organisation demands that procurement professionals spend time and resources to ensure that the right supplier is awarded the contract and that supply is continuous. How suppliers are chosen for such categories of products and services will be explained later in this section.

> *Apply*
> In a factory that manufactures high-quality leather shoes, the head buyer has to decide, by discussing with the owner, which of the products requires most of their attention when sourcing.
>
> The products to be discussed are:
>
> - Leather
> - Glue
> - Packaging
> - Stationery
>
> Explain which of the products should be sourced using a strategic approach and justify the reasons why.

The costs associated with outsourcing are significantly different from the costs when production is carried out in-house.

When outsourcing, the chosen supplier has to carry out the sourcing activities to ensure that the contracted service or product is delivered. However, the buying organisation still has to manage the contract to a certain extent, as well as measure the performance. Table 1.5 shows the costs and key benefits of outsourcing.

Costs	Key benefits
Procurement involvement to establish whether outsourcing is a practical option.	Increased expertise – outsourced functions are often contracted to specialists who provide the buying organisation with knowledge, development or technical abilities that it does not have.
Procurement involvement in evaluating, selecting and awarding the contract to suppliers.	Core activity focus – outsourcing enables the buying organisation to focus on what it is good at, its core activities and where it can maximise profit.
Management of outsourced contract, i.e. performance levels and quality.	Potential reduction in risk – the risk and responsibilities are shared between the buying organisation and the outsourced supplier. By using the expertise of the outsourced supplier, better decisions can be made. However, it is important to note that the risk of completing the task is now with the supplier and this loss of control could increase the risk to the buying organisation.
Some organisations choose to employ outsourced contract managers to oversee the performance and remove the responsibility from procurement. This involves additional cost, so the outsourcing decision has to offer good value for money and clear benefits to the organisation if this strategy is to be successful.	Lower operating costs – because the outsourced suppliers are responsible for supplying some of the organisation's functions, the operational overheads are reduced, i.e. the amount of labour required could be lower, overtime is not required and less energy is consumed. Outsourcing generally moves fixed costs (and some variable costs too) to variable costs, i.e. the buyer will only pay for what they want to use.

Table 1.5 Costs and key benefits of outsourcing

Check
What are the key benefits of outsourcing?

Outsourcing non-core and core work or services

Outsourcing core work or services

As explained so far, core work or services are those that are integral to an organisation. Core activities are critical to the organisation and relate closely to its strategies and objectives. Outsourcing core activities is not recommended as it poses too much of a risk to the organisation.

> *Remember*
> Outsourcing core functions is usually not recommended.

Procurement professionals can use an outsourcing decision matrix to help evaluate which functions within their organisation could be considered for outsourcing. The matrix, shown in figure 1.4, measures the strategic importance of the function, activity or product against its contribution towards operational performance. The result suggests whether the function should be outsourced or should remain in-house.

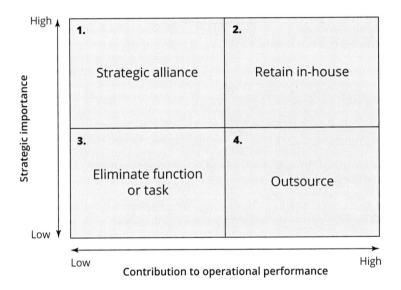

Figure 1.4 Outsource matrix based on Barnes (2008)[3]

Table 1.6 explains the four outcomes when using the outsourcing decision matrix.

Outcome	Explanation
Eliminate	These functions contribute little to the organisation's strategy so their value should be questioned and they may be eliminated.
Form a strategic alliance	Although some functions are strategically important, they contribute very little to the operational performance. These functions can be trusted to a strategic partner, but the buying organisation must keep an element of control.

Outcome	Explanation
Retain	Functions that are highly strategic and highly important to the operational performance should not be outsourced. These are core to the organisation and should remain in-house.
Outsource	Functions that are operationally important but not key to strategy can be outsourced with minimal risk.

Table 1.6 Outsourcing decision matrix outcomes

Apply
For an organisation with which you are familiar, create an outsource decision matrix and assign one function to each quadrant. Justify your reasoning for the position of each function.

Outsourcing non-core work or services

Outsourcing can be considered for any non-core work or services within a business. The following functions are frequently outsourced.

- IT support
- Catering
- Cleaning
- Marketing
- Social media
- Human resources
- Accountancy and payroll

When the decision to outsource turns out to be ineffective for an organisation or if, after a period of time, the situation or strategy changes, a business can opt to **insource** the function. Insourcing the function means that it is bought back in-house and the organisation's own personnel conduct the activity and take over control.

Insourcing can only occur when an activity or function has previously been outsourced.

Insource
To bring a function of activity back in-house after previously being outsourced

Check
When can insourcing occur?

Outsource or retain
Delima is a sole trader who owns a small business where she designs and manufactures bespoke garments for wealthy clients.

Although the business is only a year old, it has steadily gained momentum. Delima is finding it increasingly difficult to keep up with the workload as well as promoting her brand to acquire new clients. She has never missed a deadline for delivering a garment but is aware that if she does not seek some help the business may suffer.

Case study »

Delima does not want to employ anyone to work within her business and is not sure how to resolve the issue.

During a conversation with Amaal, a trusted client, Delima mentions that she is finding it difficult to manage the functions. Amaal asks if she has considered outsourcing some of her work.

Delima tells Amaal that she does not want anyone else to make the garments as this is key to the success of her organisation.

Amaal nods in agreement, stating that this is a good decision, but asks about the possibility of outsourcing the marketing to an expert.

Delima had never considered handing over control of the non-core functions but was very interested to understand more.

Amaal explained that she had a contact who ran a marketing company specialising in social media campaigns. Delima had wanted to have a presence on social media for some months but had not found the time.

This seemed like a good solution. The next day Delima contacted the marketing company to discuss the opportunity of outsourcing her advertising, branding and social media activities.

Delima knew she had the skillset to manage the function. It was simply time that was proving to be a barrier so should the outsourcing contract not be effective, insourcing was an option.

Supplier pre-qualification or criteria for supplier appraisal

Whether a procurement professional is considering a supplier for a standard sourcing or for an outsourcing solution, they must still carry out **supplier pre-qualification** and **supplier appraisal**.

Compiling a list of potential suppliers

Before pre-qualification, the procurement professional should find suppliers that appear to be able to meet the defined need. A variety of techniques are used to prepare a list of potential suppliers, including the following.

- Previous knowledge
- Recommendations
- Internet research
- Market publications
- Trade shows
- Networking

In some sectors (such as within the European Union or UK public sector), it is a legal requirement to advertise the contract opportunity on a suitable website.

Supplier pre-qualification
An early process within procurement to find out if potential suppliers meet the buying organisation's criteria on capability, capacity and financial stability

Supplier appraisal
A process of evaluating a supplier's ability to carry out a contract in terms of quality, delivery, price and other contributing factors

Pre-qualification questionnaire (PQQ)
A document sent to potential suppliers to assess their suitability against the buyer's minimum standards of performance – generally based on experience, capacity, financial standing and insurances

Pre-qualification questionnaire

Some organisations have a standard **pre-qualification questionnaire (PQQ)** that is sent to potential suppliers. Other organisations create specific criteria depending on the need that has been identified.

The pre-qualification questionnaire seeks to answer the following questions.

1. Is the supplier financially stable?

2. Does the supplier have the relevant and required experience and accreditations to carry out the contract?

3. Does the supplier have the capacity, control and commitment to manage the contract?

4. Does the supplier follow ethical and sustainable practices?

Carter's 10 Cs supplier/contractor evaluation model

The pre-qualification questionnaire aims to cover Carter's 10 Cs of supplier pre-qualification, which is a theory used to choose suitable suppliers. Carter's 10 Cs are as follows.

1. Competency: does the supplier have the required skills to be able to deliver the contract?

2. Capacity: does the supplier have the available space, resources and knowledge to be able to deliver the contract?

3. Commitment: is the supplier committed to the relationship and delivering the contract?

4. Control: does the supplier have quality and process checks in place to manage the contract?

5. Cash: is the supplier in a stable financial position? Do the accounts appear sustainable?

6. Cost: what is the total cost of the contract if awarded to this supplier? Is it ethical, environmentally friendly and does it have a good reputation?

7. Consistency: will the supplier be able to deliver consistent products or services that meet the required specification?

8. Culture: does the supplier fit with the buying organisation? Are the technological systems compatible, are the organisations in agreement culturally, and do the CSR and quality and cost policies align?

9. Clean: does the supplier act in an environmentally friendly way? Is this one of the requirements of the buying organisation and does the supplier have the required standards and accreditations?

10. Communication: can the supplier communicate effectively and without distortion in a time bound manner?

Check
Explain how Carter's 10 Cs model may be used to choose potential suppliers.

When the procurement professional receives the PQQs back, they can quickly and effectively see which suppliers meet the organisation's criteria and create a shortlist of successful suppliers to continue in the sourcing process. This might be undertaken by scoring the suppliers based on their responses to the questions within the PQQs.

Appraisal of suppliers

The buying organisation then evaluates the short-listed suppliers in more detail against more specific criteria. It can request copies of organisational policies, go on site visits and request samples of products or services for consideration.

Although the process of appraising suppliers before sending **invitations to tender (ITT)** or **requests for quotations (RFQ)** is often time consuming, the time is well spent.

During this stage of the procurement cycle, the buying organisation will remove any suppliers from the list that would not add value, as this helps to reduce the risk to which the organisation is exposed.

The following are some of the many risks that could affect organisations that do not conduct the pre-qualification or appraisal process.

- Poor quality

- Failed delivery

- Breach of contract

- Ethical concerns

- Environmental damage

- Stakeholder dissatisfaction

- Financial concerns

- Reputational damage

The appraisal process should not end when a supplier is awarded a contract. Although the supplier chosen should represent the best option to obtain value for money, this may not always be the case.

Market or environmental conditions may change and this could affect how the supplier's business is conducted. The changing conditions could be internal (micro) or external (macro). Figure 1.5 shows examples of the micro and macro environmental factors which could affect a supplier's organisation.

Invitation to tender (ITT)
A formal invitation sent to suppliers inviting them to make an offer to supply goods or services

Request for quotation (RFQ)
An invitation to suppliers to ask them to give a quotation to supply goods or services

Breach of contract
A situation where one party fails to deliver against the agreement made

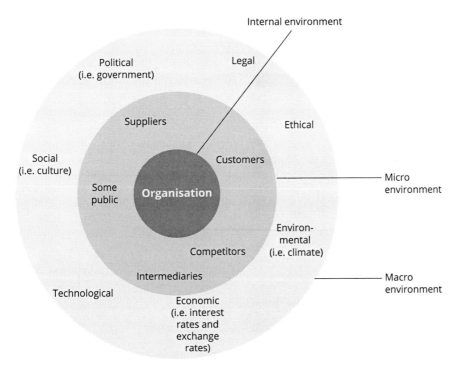

Figure 1.5 Environmental factors

Remember
Macro environments can be remembered with the acronym STEEPLE.

Procurement professionals should consistently monitor supplier performance against pre-determined objectives such as **key performance indicators (KPIs)** or **service level agreements (SLAs)**. This helps identify any changes in performance and address any areas of concern.

Check
What internal and external factors could have an effect on a supplier's performance?

Apply
Explain two possible risks if suppliers are not pre-qualified and appraised.

Key performance indicators (KPIs)
A measurable value that generates feedback on performance

Service level agreements (SLA)
An agreement to deliver and maintain an accepted and expected level of service

Qualitative
Measured in terms of quality

Quantitative
Measured in terms of numbers or quantity

Vendor or supplier performance management

The performance of suppliers is integral to the success of the organisation that they supply, and so requires ongoing management. As explained, supplier management can be monitored by implementing KPIs and SLAs in the contract.

KPIs can be **qualitative** or **quantitative**.

In order for KPIs to be effective and generate measurable data they should be SMART.

Specific   **R**elevant

Measurable   **T**ime bound

Achievable

KPIs and SLAs are agreed at the negotiation stage of the contract and documented in the agreement. Suppliers are obliged to keep to the KPIs and SLAs, and contracts can be terminated if this does not happen.

Remember
KPIs and SLAs form part of a contract.

Procurement professionals should regularly review the results from KPIs and SLAs and hold regular meetings with suppliers to discuss the results and address any areas of concern.

Check
What does SMART stand for?

Apply
Write a KPI and an SLA that relate to an organisation with which you are familiar.

Risks in outsourcing

1.1 **L01**

As discussed earlier, if outsourcing is conducted and managed correctly it can bring many benefits to an organisation. However, there are several risks associated with outsourcing, which can be detrimental to an organisation if not considered and addressed.

Table 1.7 outlines the risks and possible outcomes associated with outsourcing.

Risk	Possible outcome
Loss of control	Outsourcing gives control of the function to an external supplier, which removes responsibility from the buying organisation. Although this can be a positive factor, it is also a risk. Lack of control can lead to changes in the supply chain that the buyer is not made aware of.
Supplier reliance	Outsourcing relies on the external supplier to deliver the function. Buying organisations risk becoming too reliant on the supplier and, if any problems occur with the relationship, they may find themselves exposed to risk by not having the skills required to complete the function.
Confidentiality	Suppliers that win outsourced contracts may be given a lot of confidential information by the buying organisation. Without a **non-disclosure agreement (NDA)**, the buying organisation risks its information being used or shared within the industry.
Quality	When functions are completed in-house, quality can be tracked throughout the process. Outsourcing means that there is less transparency of how the function is carried out and quality could be lower.
Intellectual property	Outsourced suppliers could use or attempt to steal information that is crucial to the buying organisation, i.e. copy designs or make **prototypes** against a **patented** idea. A non-disclosure agreement should ensure this does not happen.
Reputation	A bad choice of outsourced supplier can lead to negativity from stakeholders and contribute towards an organisation gaining a poor reputation.
Loss of expertise	When outsourcing, any skillset related to that function is at risk of being lost. If employees that previously carried out that function are made redundant or relocated within the organisation, their skills will be lost over time and they will not keep up with industry changes. If the function is ever insourced, the organisation may no longer have the expertise.
Inflexibility	Outsourced contracts are usually long-term, with SLAs, volumes, etc., arranged in advance. The risk is inflexibility – if the buying organisation needs to make an urgent change this may not be possible.
Cultural differences	Outsourced suppliers may be from a different organisational culture or from a different country. The differences in culture can pose a risk due to differing working hours, standards, language barriers, etc.

Table 1.7 The risks of outsourcing

Non-disclosure agreement (NDA)
An agreement between two or more parties to agree not to disclose any information in relation to a project or contract

Intellectual property
An idea or creative work, which can be treated as an asset

Prototype
An early sample of a first attempt at making a product

Patent
A way of protecting intellectual property, excluding other parties from using, marketing or making products that relate to it

> *Check*
> What risks are associated with outsourcing?

The market development and growth of outsourcing

Low cost countries
Countries that have a slow-growing economy and where rates of pay are significantly lower than in countries with more affluent economies

Outsourcing has become a popular strategy for organisations. By outsourcing non-core activities, markets are developing in **low cost countries**, which are helping to build their economies. There are mutual benefits of developed countries engaging with developing countries.

Benefits linked to market development through the growth of outsourcing include the following.

- Cost saving to the developed country
- Ability to further grow organisations due to non-core functions being outsourced
- Increased employment in developing countries
- Ethical and sustainable behaviour promoted in developing countries

When a procurement professional chooses to outsource a function from their organisation, it can allow the company to develop in areas where previously there was no time or resource available. Organisations can explore markets and consider their strategy to develop and grow.

> *Check*
> Explain the key benefits of outsourcing.

Regulations affecting employees' terms of employment

TUPE
Legislation to protect employees when outsourced contracts are moved between suppliers

Although outsourcing can help procurement professionals achieve cost savings and value for money, it must not be forgotten that the employees that already provide the function may be affected.

In most countries there are regulations in place to ensure that employees are not treated unfairly.

When a function or activity is outsourced, it might not remain with the same supplier indefinitely. Like all procurement activity, the value offered by the current supplier is constantly measured. At the point of contract renewal, if another supplier can offer a more favourable deal, the buyer is likely to change supplier. In the UK, for example, this is when the **TUPE** regulation is relevant.

TUPE stands for Transfer of Undertakings (Protection of Employment) and is part of employment law. TUPE is used during organisational mergers, acquisitions and outsourcing arrangements.

This legislation was created to protect employees and to ensure that any individuals working to provide a service keep their jobs when the supplier is changed. Ultimately the outsourced supplier has to manage the contract with the staff that are already carrying out the function.

The individuals involved in providing the service are reassured that their terms of employment will remain unchanged, they will not receive a lower rate of pay and working hours will remain the same for an agreed period of time.

The two main advantages of the TUPE regulation are as follows.

- Continuity of supply for the buying organisation
- Continuity of employment for the workers

1.1 LO1

Case study

Outsourcing of catering

Raj owns a large factory that manufactures and distributes after-market spares for vehicles. The country was in a period of recession for almost a year and Raj was concerned that he had not made a profit in over six months.

Raj held a meeting with his head buyer, Nikita, to discuss how they could reduce costs.

Nikita proposed the idea of outsourcing a non-core function. Raj was not familiar with this concept so Nikita explained:

"If we outsource a non-core function it may save us money on staff, training, insurance and many other overheads."

Raj was intrigued. "But what an earth could we outsource? Our product range is so varied that no supplier will want to make a few bits of this and a few bits of that."

Nikita explained that it would make good business sense to consider outsourcing the catering function as this had a low strategic value but high operational importance.

She suggested that a specialist company could probably provide a better menu at a lower price and might even prepare the food offsite so that Raj could make some money by selling his kitchen equipment.

Raj smiled, then looked concerned, "What about my catering staff? They have been with me for years and I do not want them to lose their jobs – they have bills to pay and families to support."

Nikita told Raj about the TUPE regulation and that his workers would still have jobs, their pay would be no lower and their conditions the same – maybe even better.

The pair agreed that outsourcing catering certainly looked like an option and Nikita was tasked with pre-qualifying some suppliers and assessing the advantages and disadvantages of the idea.

International Labour Organization (ILO) A United Nations organisation uniting governments, employers and workers with the common goal of improving labour standards for all

Apply
Explain how the catering staff in the 'Outsourcing of catering' case study may be affected if the function they work for is outsourced.

The **International Labour Organization (ILO)** is a key organisation in ensuring that global workers are protected and that regulations relating to acceptable

working conditions are maintained. The ILO promotes fair working conditions, acceptable rates of pay and social protection for workers across the world.

Other organisations, such as Fair Trade, work globally to try to enforce regulations against discrimination and give workers and producers better prices for their goods.

> *Apply*
> What regulatory bodies and legislation exist in your country to protect workers?

1.2 Differentiate between approaches to the sourcing of requirements from suppliers

Sourcing can take many different approaches, which are related to the following factors.

- Category of product or service
- Quantity of product or service
- Supplier relationship
- Supply and demand
- Skill of procurement professional
- Culture of organisation

Sourcing arrangements can be single, dual or multiple, and each have their own advantages and disadvantages and are suited to specific situations.

Single, dual and multiple sourcing arrangements

Single sourcing
Sourcing from one sole supplier

Monopoly
A situation where one supplier has the entire market share and there is no competition

Single sourcing is where one supplier is contracted by the buying organisation to supply all the needs for an item. The single sourcing approach is used in the following circumstances.

- There is a **monopoly** supplier (the buyer has no choice)
- Economies of scale can be achieved
- Order quantities are very small
- One supplier offers outstanding value for money against the competition

The buyer may decide to single source even where there are several suppliers.

> ❝ *Single sourcing enables logistical cost reductions as a result of scaled-down supplier base.*[4] ❞

Dual sourcing is where two suppliers are responsible for supplying all the needs for an item to the buying organisation. Dual sourcing is used in the following circumstances.

- There is a risk of one supplier not being able to supply
- A product or service is critical to an organisation

Dual sourcing
Sourcing from two suppliers

Multiple sourcing is where many suppliers are responsible for supplying all the needs for an item to an organisation. Multiple sourcing is used in the following circumstances.

Multiple sourcing
Sourcing from many suppliers

- Supplier competition is vast
- The supplier relationship is not critical
- Constant supply is critical

> *Remember*
> There are three types of sourcing.
> - Single
> - Dual
> - Multiple

Each approach is linked to a chosen procurement strategy for the item or service it relates to.

Supplier relationships

The supplier relationships vary considerably depending on the sourcing approach.

- There must be partnerships or strong collaborative relationships within single sourcing approaches as the buying organisation is completely reliant on this one supplier to fulfil its needs.
- With dual sourcing the relationship still needs to be strong and should be collaborative in the form of a strategic alliance.
- When adopting a multiple sourcing strategy, the relationships are not critical as there are many supply options so the style is likely to be more transactional.

Figure 1.6 shows how the approaches to sourcing relate to the style of relationship between the procurement professional and the supplier.

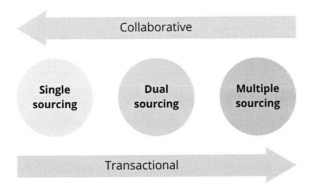

Figure 1.6 Sourcing approaches and relationships

Table 1.8 outlines the advantages and disadvantages of single, dual and multiple sourcing arrangements.

Sourcing type	Advantages	Disadvantages
Single	Maximum leverage can be extracted by giving the whole volume to one supplier Strong relationship Strong commitment Good communication New product development Innovation Confidentiality High trust Economies of scale Cost effective	Risk of failure to supply Price may inflate if there is no competition and the buyer is forced to go with a monopoly supplier Restricted options Over-reliance on supplier
Dual/multiple	Easy to drive down cost Switching between suppliers is easier Wide knowledge and expertise Low risk of failure to supply	Transactional relationship Lack of supplier commitment Lack of economies of scale No supplier loyalty

Table 1.8 Advantages and disadvantages of sourcing styles

Check
What style of relationship is linked to each style of sourcing?

The use of tendering: open, restricted and negotiated approaches to tendering

Within procurement, when professionals want to create a new contract they have to decide whether to send out an ITT or an RFQ to potential suppliers.

The tendering process

The ITT tends to be a more formal process and is used for a wide range of requirements. In most countries, the **public sector** handles the vast majority of its high value contracting needs by using invitations to tender.

Public sector
A sector of the economy that provides services to the people and is funded through taxes

Figure 1.7 shows the generic tendering process.

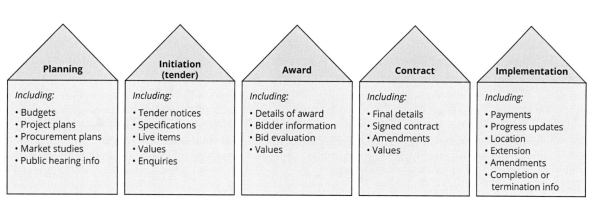

Figure 1.7 Tender process (Source: adapted from Mara Mendes, okfn.de/blog/2016/07/ from-publication-to-award/, CC BY 3.0 DE)

Tender documents contain lots of information for potential suppliers including the following.

- Company information

- Specifications

- Contract requirements including the terms and conditions

- Deadline for submission. The deadline stated in the tender documents is very important. If a supplier fails to meet the deadline and submits its bid after the stated date, its offer will not be considered.

> *Remember*
> Bids submitted after the deadline will not be considered by the buying organisation.

Approaches to tendering

There are several approaches to tendering, most typically the following.

- Open
- Restricted
- Negotiated

> *Check*
> What are the three types of tender approach that a procurement professional can use?

Open tendering

Open tendering is most commonly used globally. It is used when the buyer expects there to be relatively limited interest and so fewer bids to evaluate. The opportunity available to suppliers is advertised widely allowing any supplier that wishes to submit a bid. In some situations, suppliers may first express an interest and then bidders will be able to obtain an ITT.

When the procurement professional has received all the bids by the deadline, they evaluate the bids usually against predetermined evaluation criteria, and the one that offers the best value for money will be offered the contract.

Open tendering
The opportunity is widely advertised allowing any supplier to make a bid

Restricted tendering

Restricted tendering
A two stage tendering process

The procurement professional advertises the opportunity for interested suppliers to respond with an expression of interest. Suppliers that have expressed interest are then required to complete a pre-qualification questionnaire (PQQ) to establish if they meet the required criteria of the buying organisation.

The suppliers that successfully meet the criteria set by the procurement professional will then receive the invitation to tender and be invited to submit their bid as an offer to the buying organisation. The difference between this and the open tender is that **restricted tendering** is a two-stage process. Restricted tendering is used when the buyer expects there to be a high interest from bidders. Restricted tendering enables the buyer to create a shortlist of suitable bidders that will progress to a more detailed evaluation.

Negotiated tendering

Negotiated tendering
When only a single or a few suppliers are approached based on a previous relationship or track record

A negotiated approach to tendering generally has the same initial process as the restricted style. The procurement professional advertises the opportunity to contract with the buying organisation and invites expressions of interest.

The difference is that negotiated tendering may only involve a single supplier or might include a number of suppliers where the requirement is more complex. This supplier may be chosen due to a previous relationship with the buyer; due to its specialist skill, being a sole supplier or a precise specification; or because it involves amending or expanding on an existing contract.

While **negotiated tendering** can reduce the cost and duration of tendering and allow the supplier to get involved in the design stages of a product, it can be difficult to reach an agreement that is considered fair by both parties due to the lack of competition. Negotiated tending also risks the buyer becoming complacent and reusing the same supplier, rather than seeking better terms elsewhere.

Remember
Negotiated tendering is often used where there is only one bidder or where the buyer's requirement is complex.

Apply
Explain the differences between open, restricted and negotiated tendering approaches.

Direct negotiations with suppliers

Sourcing involves negotiating with suppliers, regardless of the type of sourcing arrangement used.

Negotiation involves communication between a procurement professional and a supplier to try to get the best value solution for the supply of goods or services.

Outcomes of negotiation

Negotiation has five possible outcomes.

1. The buyer wins and the supplier loses.
2. The supplier wins and the buyer loses.

3. The buyer wins and the supplier wins.

4. The buyer loses and the supplier loses.

5. Neither the buyer nor the supplier wins (a compromise).

Theoretically the best outcome is called **win-win**. This is where both parties collaborate to reach a satisfactory outcome. However, depending on the style of relationship, which may be linked to the sourcing approach (see figure 1.6), outcomes can vary. The win-win outcome would be appropriate in collaborative relationships, where it is appropriate for the buyer to spend time with the supplier.

Win-win
The best solution to a negotiation; where both parties are satisfied

Figure 1.8 shows how differing negotiating styles can result in different outcomes.

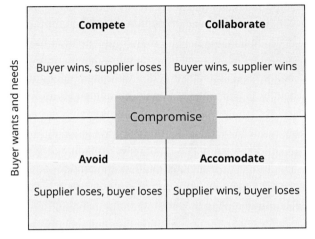

Figure 1.8 Negotiating styles

Styles of negotiation can change, depending on both the type of relationship and the desired outcome.

- **A competitive style** of negotiation is based on being assertive and achieving results, even if this disadvantages the other party and the long-term relationship.

- A **collaborative style** is an honest and open style where the negotiator is focused on finding a mutually beneficial outcome and fair solutions to any issues that may be presented. This focuses on long-term goals.

- An **avoiding style** is one full of apprehension and often the negotiator does not pursue their requirements. Relationships do not prosper and the outcomes rarely benefit either party.

- **Accommodating styles** are when the negotiator does not want to upset or offend the other party and so they often concede their requirements to ensure harmony.

- A **compromising style** is one where the negotiator is happy to meet in the middle on concessions rather than pushing for a win or backing down. Compromising focuses on developing relationships and finding acceptable outcomes for both parties.

The negotiating process

When negotiating with suppliers, preparation is essential and is the first stage in the negotiation process. The negotiation process is outlined in table 1.9.

Stage	What is involved
1 Preparation	Consider the following questions.
	Where should the negotiation take place?
	What is the ideal outcome?
	What is the relationship style?
	What issues may be raised?
	What concessions can be made?
	Is there a back-up plan?
2 Information exchange	Buyer listens to what the supplier has to say
	Buyer presents its information and requirements
3 Bargaining	Exchange takes place
	Concessions are made
	Alternatives are suggested
	Terms are negotiated
4 Closing	Agreement is reached
	Contractual documentation is created
	Contract is signed
	Contract is mobilised

Table 1.9 The stages of negotiation

Remember
There are four stages of negotiation.

- Preparation
- Information exchange
- Bargaining
- Closing

If negotiation takes place with a single sourced supplier, the outcome must be win-win. Both parties value the relationship and need it to be beneficial as it is likely to be a long-term agreement.

Multiple or dual sourcing negotiations do not have to have a win-win outcome as the relationship is less important and other options are available.

Check
What styles can a negotiator use?

Intra-company trading
Business conducted within a company, i.e. between two departments or locations

Intra-company trading and transfer pricing arrangement

Intra-company trading

Intra-company trading is business that is conducted between two or more companies that are owned by the same entity. This means that the transactions all occur internally within the business.

Intra-company trading may take place between two departments on the same site or between two or more different divisions of a company in different countries across the globe.

Intra-company trading between colleagues working for the same organisation often occurs when departments each have their own budgets to keep to.

Procurement can be involved in intra-company trading by sourcing and securing supply and delivery of products which are then 'sold' to the departments. This kind of arrangement happens in some large organisations to try to ensure that departments do not order more products than they need as they have a responsibility to keep to their budgets. For example, items such as stationery or consumables are often managed in this way to avoid overuse or lack of control or care.

On a larger scale, organisations may take advantage of **centralised procurement** functions and conduct intra-company trading.

Figure 1.9 shows the difference between centralised and **devolved procurement** structures.

Centralised procurement
A structure where procurement for the whole organisation is carried out by a centralised function often from one central location

Devolved procurement
Devolved or decentralised procurement is a purchasing structure whereby individual locations are responsible for their buying activity

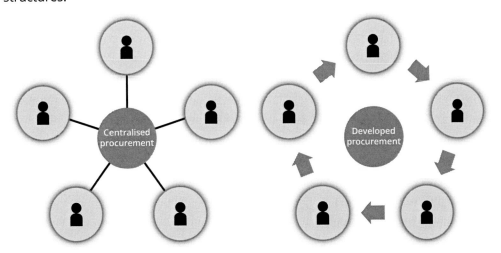

Figure 1.9 Centralised versus devolved procurement

If an organisation has sites across the globe that all manufacture the same or similar products, they will all have the same requirements for **raw materials** and **components**.

By using centralised procurement, the organisation can take advantage of economies of scale and source products for a lower cost than if each individual site were to manage its own requirements.

Figure 1.10 shows a typical economies of scale curve. This diagram shows that the larger the quantity produced, the lower the cost becomes. This is because fixed costs such as salaried staff or rent on premises remains the same, whatever the quantity.

Raw materials
The base material from which a product is made, e.g., steel

Components
A part that makes up a product

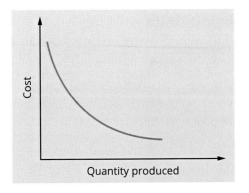

Figure 1.10 Economies of scale

Profit margin
The amount of profit made on a sale, i.e. profit expressed as a percentage of sales or revenues

Once the raw materials or components are sourced and in a central location, the associated departments can place orders for them, at which point an intra-company transaction takes place. The holding department will arrange to deliver the goods and invoice the other departments for the goods. The invoice will cover the cost of the goods and add a mark-up for the cost of storage, administration and delivery. It may also include a **profit margin**.

If the departments are separate businesses, each one will be trying to make the most money possible and as such, the act of intra-company trading can be profitable for both businesses.

Transfer pricing

Transfer prices are the amounts of money payable between divisions of the same organisation that have conducted business with each other. Common forms of transactions are supplying labour or trading products between divisions or departments.

Transfer pricing is audited closely to ensure that there is no dishonest activity occurring within an organisation, such as tax evasion.

Transfer pricing arrangements are a large part of international intra-company trading. The objective of transfer pricing arrangements is to reduce the burden of taxes payable on profits that are generated.

Inter-trading
Trading between companies that are owned by different entities

Transfer pricing arrangements feature heavily within global intra-company trading due to the variation in taxes. The aim of transfer pricing arrangements is for organisations to push the profits that they make into the global areas where tax rates are most favourable to them. For example, it is possible for companies that intra-trade to transfer goods from one country to another to avoid having to pay the tariffs on goods if they were exchanged through differently owned organisations, that is **inter-trading**.

The benefit of transfer pricing arrangements is that they have encouraged and promoted global trading within organisations, which has contributed towards economic growth in many areas.

There are strict rules and regulations for these types of arrangements to avoid companies trying to evade paying taxes and acting illegally.

The OECD (Organisation for Economic Co-operation and Development) produced a set of guidelines for organisations wishing to explore transfer pricing arrangements, which includes key aspects of the strategy and its legal implications as well as regulated international tax laws.

Remember
The OECD regulates international tax laws.

While organisations that benefit from transfer pricing arrangements pay lower amounts of tax on their profits and potentially remove that income from their home country's economy, it can be argued that they are a valuable part of another country's economy as they are paying further forms of corporate taxes.

Table 1.10 shows the advantages and disadvantages of transfer pricing arrangements.

Advantages	Disadvantages
Global tax bills can be reduced	Some countries' economies can be negatively affected
Simplifies internal accounting procedures	Careful and strict monitoring is required to avoid tax evasion
Entire organisation can have fixed pricing on products/services	Sourcing locally may be more cost effective
Divisions can be easily evaluated based on spend	Negative effect on local economy
No physical money needs to be transferred between divisions	Inter-organisational competition

Table 1.10 Advantages and disadvantages of transfer pricing arrangements

Apply
Explain why a global organisation may opt to use transfer pricing arrangements.

Implications of international sourcing

International sourcing is any sourcing where the supplier is from a different country to the buying organisation. International sourcing can be the following.

- Standard product sourcing

- Outsourcing

- **Offshoring**

There are a variety of implications associated with international sourcing. As with any procurement decision, the benefits and risks have to be evaluated to assess which option offers the organisation the best value for money.

Benefits of international sourcing

- Reduced costs: by taking advantage of low-cost labour and lower raw material prices, the price offered by an international supplier is often more competitive than one from a buyer's home country.

- Exposure to world class technology: some countries have more advanced technology than the procurement professional's country and as such, international sourcing helps an organisation stay up to date and ahead of the market competition in its own country.

- Availability of materials that may not be readily available in the home country: some products and services that a buying organisation needs to source may not be available in its own country, or may be in short supply or highly priced. Sourcing internationally where the products are readily available will be less costly and there will be enough supply to match the demand.

International sourcing
Sourcing goods or services from all over the world

Offshoring
The relocation of one part of a business, usually an operational function, to another country in an attempt to reduce cost

- Improved quality: if a product comes from another country, it may be more established and the quality may be higher than in a buyer's home country.

- Wider selection of suppliers available internationally: this helps procurement by giving the buying organisation the opportunity to obtain more quotations and helps it to remain competitive.

Risks of international sourcing

Even if the price offered by the international supplier appears to be a lot cheaper than that available in the home country, the decision should only be taken once the potential risks have been assessed. Is the money saved likely to be worth the risk? Strategies may then need to be put in place to mitigate the risks. The following are some examples of the risks.

- Extended lead times. For example, sourcing from outside a buying organisation's home country will increase the lead time of products being delivered. Purchase orders will need to be placed earlier and it will be important to understand the requirements of goods and services to avoid stockouts. If the product or service is strategic to the organisation, the risk associated with a failure of supply is much greater than that of a product that is routine.

  One way to reduce the cost from the supply chain while also mitigating the risk is to dual or multiple source (see section 1.2). Using this strategy, the procurement professional should be able to benefit from building a relationship with an international supplier while not risking supply issues as the usual supplier in the home country will still be contracted.

- Importation/exportation rules and regulations. There are stringent rules about the types of goods that can be imported and exported between countries, and what rates of duty should be paid.

- Currency exchange fluctuations. When sourcing from a developing economy, there is greater risk that a favourable price could become uncompetitive.

- Payment methods and guarantees. Paying international suppliers can sometimes be difficult. In today's technological age, payment may be made through electronic bank transfer or **letters of credit**. However, in developing countries this may not be an option and other methods of payment may have to be agreed. These methods take longer, which must be considered when deciding whether international sourcing is the best option.

- Cultural differences, language barriers and differing time zones. If there is a problem, international sourcing can make the situation harder. Differing time zones, language barriers and cultural differences mean conflicts can take longer to get resolved. For example, if a buyer discovers a problem with a delivery when they arrive at work, the buyer may be another eight hours before it can make contact with the supplier.

- Quality issues, different standards and ethical behaviour. Good and thorough due diligence is required with all suppliers but especially with international sourcing. Acceptable standards in one country may not match those in another. This may relate both to quality standards and also to ethical behaviour and expectations. Should an international supplier fail to conform to the ethical norms of the home country, an organisation's reputation could be damaged.

- Logistical problems. Details of transportation, **Incoterms®** and **transfer of ownership** should be included in a detailed contract between the parties to avoid any misunderstanding or confusion. By understanding when transfer of

Letter of credit
A document issued from one bank to another to act as a guarantee of payment against agreed terms and conditions, including the presentation of compliant documentation

Incoterms®
International commercial terms of sale that assign costs and responsibilities between the buyer and seller when delivering products

Transfer of ownership
The point where title to the goods passes from one party to another

ownership occurs, the procurement professional can ensure that in case of any problems, insurance is in place.

- Infringement of intellectual property rights. If the relationship with an international supplier is not developed and strategic, there may be no trust between the parties. Without trust, buyers could find themselves in a position where a supplier steals or copies their ideas and creates a competitive product of its own.

- Conflict is harder to resolve. Since the parties are in different countries, issues such as language barriers, time zones and the fact that the aggrieved parties cannot easily and quickly meet face to face may increase the time for conflict to be resolved.

Remember
Lead times are increased with international sourcing.

Check
What happens to prices as the country's economy develops?

Remember
Transfer of ownership is the point where title of goods passes from one party to the other.

≪ Case study

International sourcing initiative
In May 2018, Ministers Heather Humphreys (Minister for Business, Enterprise and Innovation), Pat Breen (Minister of State for Trade, Employment, Business, EU Digital Single Market and Data Protection) and Minister Patrick O'Donovan (Minister of State for Public Procurement, Open Government and eGovernment) undertook the annual Trade and Investment Mission to Dublin, Limerick and Sligo. This mission, part of a joint Enterprise Ireland and IDA Ireland 'Global Sourcing' initiative, had the important goal of promoting and creating business opportunities for Irish-owned companies with Ireland-based multi-nationals. The mission raised awareness of the innovative capabilities of Irish companies across a range of sectors, gave Ireland-based multi-nationals direct access to potential suppliers, and gave Irish companies the opportunity to meet with the procurement teams of Ireland-based multi-nationals.

Heather Humphreys commented that the mission would highlight existing relationships of many decades' standing, and also create new partnerships between multi-nationals and Irish companies through regionally-focused networking events in line with the Government's Action Plan for Jobs strategy. "We have great opportunities on our doorstep and we want to maximise these to help Irish companies scale and further reinforce their successful track records of servicing international buyers all over the globe."

IDA Ireland's Martin Shanahan agreed, "This Investment Mission provides multi-national companies with direct access to potential suppliers and promotes greater engagement between the two groups. Closer relationships through enhanced integration will bring huge benefits to local economies across the country and ultimately promote Ireland as a welcoming pro-business destination."

The two-day Trade and Investment Mission involved over 455 one-to-one meetings between 194 Enterprise Ireland clients and 111 IDA Ireland companies in Dublin, Limerick and Sligo.

(Source: adapted from www.businessworld.ie/news/Enterprise-Ireland-and-IDA-Ireland-launch-Global-Sourcing-initiative-570822.html)

Apply
Explain the advantages and disadvantages of international sourcing.

1.3 Define selection criteria that can be commonly applied when sourcing requirements from external suppliers

In order for procurement professionals to award contracts that give the best value, they must use strict selection criteria.

The criteria against which suppliers are evaluated will depend on the organisation and the need but most procurement professionals will follow a common set of elements, which will be explored in this section.

Conducting evaluation on pre-selected criteria is a valuable and essential part of the sourcing process. It attempts to remove any suppliers from the process that do not conform and that would present a risk to the buying organisation, whether that risk be through not being able to supply what is required or through unethical behaviour that could lead to reputational damage.

Typical selection criteria

To select suitable suppliers, the procurement professional can send PQQs to potential suppliers. The questionnaires contain requests for details on the potential supplier's policies and situations in the following areas.

- Quality assurance
- Environmental awareness and sustainability

- Technical capabilities
- Systems capabilities
- Labour standards
- Financial capabilities
- Credit rating scores

It is also important to make sure that potential suppliers have the resources to carry out the contract, by asking questions such as the following.

- Do you have capacity for the contract?
- Do you have the skilled labour to carry out the contract?
- Do you have the transport available to deliver the contract?
- Do you have internal staff available to accept and process purchase orders?
- Do you have strong communication skills?

A useful tool when defining awarding criteria is Carter's 10 Cs. By understanding if a potential supplier has Carter's 10 Cs, a procurement professional can gauge the readiness and suitability of a potential supplier.

Making sure that a potential supplier is resource-ready before awarding the contract can avoid any unpleasant surprises after implementation. Suppliers need to assure the procurement professional that they have the resources in place or provide a plan to show how they will achieve the required level of resources if they were to be awarded the contract.

> *Remember*
> Carter's 10 Cs: capacity, cash, clean, commitment, communication, competency, consistency, control, cost and culture

Quality assurance

In the specification that a supplier receives, there will be detailed descriptions of the quality required of the product or service to be supplied. There are two types of specification.

- A performance (or outcome-focused) specification states what the product or service should do but does not give instructions on how this has to be achieved. The supplier can meet the specification however they think is best.

- A conformance specification is more structured and details exactly how the product or service must be made. Examples of conformance specifications include recipes and chemical formulae.

> *Remember*
> The two types of specification are performance (or outcome-focused) and conformance.

When selecting external suppliers, the procurement professional should look at the way that they manage their quality processes. Many procurement professionals ask for suppliers to have the **ISO 9001** quality standard, which acts as reassurance that the organisation has procedures and policies in place to ensure a consistently high level of quality.

ISO 9001
An international standard for quality management

Continuous improvement
A concept based on constantly improving processes to eliminate waste

Total quality management (TQM)
A management approach linked to organisational culture and attitudes, which aims to gain complete customer satisfaction

Other ways of evaluating how quality is managed include understanding if the potential supplier is committed to:

- **Continuous improvement**/kaizen

- **Total quality management**

Continuous improvement is a based on a Japanese theory known as kaizen. Continuous improvement is about constantly looking for ways to improve processes within operations. It welcomes ideas from all individuals within the organisation with the objective of removing waste from the supply chain.

The process involves four stages.

1. Identify
2. Plan
3. Execute
4. Review

Figure 1.11 shows the continuous improvement process.

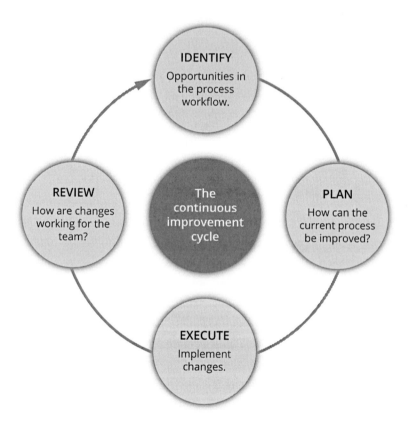

Figure 1.11 Continuous improvement (Source: Planview LeanKit, www.leankit.com/learn/kanban/continuous-improvement/)

Check
What are the four stages in the continuous improvement process?

Waste can be anything that does not add value during a process. Ohno defined seven key wastes that should be eliminated from the supply chain.

Figure 1.12 shows the seven wastes.

Figure 1.12 Ohno's seven wastes

Procurement professionals may also look for suppliers that promote total quality management (TQM).

This is a management approach that works towards long-term strategic success through complete customer and **consumer** satisfaction. TQM is based on the culture and attitude of the organisation and requires everyone to believe in the process.

TQM includes continuous improvement.

Figure 1.13 shows the TQM process.

Consumer
The end user of a product or service

Figure 1.13 Total quality management (Source: adapted from www.slideshare.net/poonamchaudhary1/total-quality-management-in-healthcare-organisations)

Potential suppliers that can demonstrate they have robust policies in place in relation to quality will be able to satisfy a procurement professional's views and standards on quality.

Environmental awareness and sustainability

Procurement professionals wish to work with suppliers that are environmentally aware and have sustainability policies. In order to evaluate these criteria, they may request copies of the supplier's **corporate social responsibility (CSR)** policies.

Many organisations write their own CSR policy, which is published on their website and is available on request. There is no legal requirement to produce or have a CSR policy but it does represent good practice within industry.

Corporate social responsibility (CSR)
The responsibility of an organisation to act favourably towards the environment, contribute to the community and behave ethically

A procurement professional will seek to choose suppliers that show the following behaviours.

- Contribute positively to the environment

- Do not pollute the atmosphere

- Replace any natural resources that they use within their supply chain

- Giving something back to the community where they are located

Samples
Examples of the product that is required

The importance of CSR

Berkshire Hills Bancorp, Inc. announced that Gary Levante had been appointed Vice President, Corporate Social Responsibility (CSR) Officer, a newly created position within the Berkshire Bank Foundation.

In this role, Levante will work to expand the Foundation's community engagement efforts to implement an all-encompassing CSR strategy. In doing so, Levante will lead Berkshire's efforts to integrate corporate social responsibility into all of the company's and Foundation's activities, supporting key objectives, such as strengthening communities and engaging employees. Levante will oversee the development of CSR goals, policies and programmes, with a strong focus on establishing a framework of standards and tools for advancing social responsibility.

"Giving back to our communities and focusing on how we impact the world around us are important components of Berkshire's culture and future," stated Lori Gazzillo, Berkshire Bank Foundation's Senior Vice President and Director. "Gary's deep understanding of Berkshire's core values, as well as his experience, knowledge and professional networks in the community, will be invaluable as we formalize and enhance our CSR strategies and programmes," she concluded.

Levante added, "I'm excited and honored to be able to evolve Berkshire's CSR efforts. The company has a culture of engagement and a commitment to advance our socially responsible practices, which is a win-win for our communities, customers, employees, and shareholders. I look forward to playing a key role in advancing and communicating our CSR accomplishments."

(Source: adapted from ir.berkshirebank.com/file/Index?KeyFile=394373978)

Case study

Technical and systems capabilities

A potential supplier must have the technical capabilities to manage the contract. Technical capabilities are the most important area, and without them, supporting criteria, such as quality assurance and CSR policies become irrelevant.

To assess a supplier's technical capabilities, the procurement professional should request **samples** to ensure that they meet the specifications.

The machinery owned or leased by the supplier must be technically capable of producing the volumes and batch sizes required for carrying out the functions needed. This should also be assessed as part of the criteria.

There must also be compatibility between the buying organisation's systems and those of the supplier. This should be checked as part of the selection process. If the systems are incompatible, there may be extra costs to resolve any issues. It is essential to consider the capabilities and limitations of the potential supplier's systems before considering them for any contracts as any incompatibility could result in delays or inability to supply. The additional costs may be a deal breaker.

Labour standards

The working conditions of a supplier's employees form part of the selection criteria. Ethical behaviour is very important and procurement professionals typically contract with suppliers that promote this.

- Buyers will check potential suppliers to ensure they are free from **modern slavery**. Potential suppliers and their associated supply chain must not be involved in or have any links to modern slavery. Where the buying organisation has any concerns that this exists, the contract will not be awarded to the potential supplier.

- Buyers will check that potential suppliers work in accordance with the standards and policies set by the International Labour Organization (ILO). Suppliers should be able to show that they are working in accordance with the ILO regulations and standards to make sure that employees are treated fairly, have good working conditions and receive fair pay.

Modern slavery
Individuals being forced to work for little or no pay, or humans who are trafficked to work in foreign countries

Financial capabilities and credit rating scores

An essential element of the selection criteria is the check on a potential supplier's financial stability. This will advise the procurement professional whether the supplier has the funds to run its day-to-day business, and therefore whether it will be able to fulfil the buying organisation's orders. A supplier in a poor financial position may not always have the cash to buy raw materials, for example, and this may cause a delay in deliveries. At worst, if the supplier were to cease trading, the contract would not be fulfilled.

To discover whether suppliers are financially stable, a **credit check** may be carried out through a third party. The agencies collate and analyse data on organisations to produce a report on their monetary affairs. The agencies also present the results in the form of a credit score or rating, which gives an insight into the supplier's financial stability and whether it poses a risk to the organisation.

Credit check
A process to evaluate an organisation to determine its financial stability

> *Apply*
> Select three selection criteria and explain their importance in the sourcing process.

The importance of supplier financial stability and due diligence checks

Due diligence checks on suppliers will include a review of their financial stability. A supplier that is not financially stable may pose several risks to the buying organisation. By conducting credit checks and evaluating suppliers against Carter's 10 Cs, due diligence will be carried out.

Due diligence
Appraising a supplier to ensure that it is a suitable match for an organisation

> *Remember*
> Financial checks form part of due diligence.

Cash flow
The money moved
in and out of an
organisation

Delay or failure to supply

As explained, when a supplier has financial issues there may be a delay in delivering products or services to the customer, or even a failure to supply.

A lack of financial stability often results from poor **cash flow**. This may mean that the supplier is unable to purchase raw materials and components required to produce products and fulfil customers' orders.

Within a supply chain, if one link fails, the effect is felt throughout the chain, both up and down. If a manufacturer cannot supply the buying organisation with the products needed, the buying organisation will be unable to serve its own customers and ultimately the consumer may be disadvantaged.

Kim's Biscuits

Kim's Biscuits is a small but successful organisation that bakes and distributes luxury biscuits. Kim, the owner, is an excellent baker but not a skilled buyer.

Kim wanted to reduce the organisation's costs. She calculated that the largest direct cost in her biscuits was the high-quality chocolate coating.

Kim did some research and found another supplier of the luxury chocolate, which appeared to be of the same quality but was 25% cheaper. She requested a sample and the specification. Since she could hardly taste the difference, she was sure her biscuits would be of the same high quality and her customers would not be disadvantaged. She decided to place future orders with the cheaper supplier and advised her current supplier that she was not going to renew the contract when it expired in two months' time.

Kim then advised the cheaper supplier that she would be placing orders with them soon and sent a copy of her terms and conditions of business. The supplier responded stating that they needed payment after seven days, not 60 days as per Kim's terms. Kim did not reply to the communication.

Two months later, Kim received her first delivery of luxury chocolate. It was exactly as she expected and the biscuits still passed quality control.

A week later, the day the second delivery was due, no chocolate arrived. Kim rang the supplier. They told her that she had not paid their invoice. Kim explained that she would pay the following week but this was unacceptable to the supplier. They advised Kim that unless she paid for her chocolate, they could not afford to supply her with any more. Equally, Kim could not pay the supplier until she had been paid by her customers.

Case study »

Kim found herself in a very difficult situation and quickly understood that she should have undertaken financial due diligence on the supplier. The new supplier might have required seven-day payment in order to maintain its cash flow to be able to purchase the raw ingredients required to fulfil the chocolate orders.

Reluctantly and slightly embarrassed, Kim rang her old supplier and explained her mistake, hoping they would be able to supply her again.

Inability to invest

If a supplier does not appear to be financially stable, they may not have the funds to invest in up-to-date technology or equipment necessary to fulfil contracts.

Poorly performing organisations may also have difficulty securing loans from banks and other financial institutions to enable them to invest in new equipment. They may also find it difficult to lease equipment or machinery if they are unable to make regular payments to the leasing company.

Supplier dependency on the buying organisation

Due diligence helps the procurement professional to understand how many customers the supplier has and how important the buying organisation's contract would be to the supplier. While it is important that any buying business is appreciated by the supplier, becoming over-reliant on one contract is not good practice financially.

By understanding the financial position of a potential supplier, the procurement professional also gains an idea of what style of negotiation to use. If a supplier is in a strong financial position, they may not be as keen to make concessions within the negotiation as a supplier that would benefit from more business.

Ratio analysis to make conclusions on profitability, liquidity, gearing and investment

As part of the financial due diligence process, ratio analysis may be used to give an overview of an organisation's profitability, liquidity, gearing, and investment. From this, the financial health of an organisation may be determined.

Financial ratio analysis has the following two main objectives.

1. To track company performance in order to track trends and raise awareness of any potential concerns.

2. To compare the supplier's performance against those of other organisations in order to gain competitive advantage.

Ratios can be used together with a credit score from a credit rating agency to get a full financial picture of a potential supplier.

The information required to calculate ratios comes from the key financial documentation that organisations produce and share with their stakeholders.

Lease
A contract between two parties – the lessee and lessor – where one party agrees to pay a sum of money for the use of an asset such as a car or a machine

Profitability
The organisation's revenues minus its total costs

Liquidity
A solvency measure to determine whether an organisation is able to meet its liabilities (short-term debts) when they come due from net current assets

Gearing
A measure of how the business is being funded, based on its ratio of debt to equity

These may be shared within or at the end of their financial year and include the following documents.

- Statement of comprehensive income (sometimes referred to as a profit and loss statement): a summary of income earned and expenditure incurred over a period of time.
- Cash flow forecast: a document showing the sources of cash coming into an organisation and the ways in which the cash is spent.
- Statement of financial position (sometimes called a balance sheet): a statement of assets and liabilities on a particular day, usually the last day of the organisation's financial year.

Profitability ratios

The various financial statements contain lots of detail about the organisation. Figures can be extracted and used to calculate ratios.

Profitability ratios measure the extent to which an organisation has traded profitably over a period of time. The ratios linked to profitability are shown in table 1.11.

Shareholder
An individual or organisation that legally owns part (a share) of a business

Equity
The amount of shareholders' funds and retained earnings is the difference between the value of the assets and the value of liabilities

Ratio	Purpose
Gross profit margin $= \dfrac{\text{gross profit}}{\text{sales revenue}} \times 100$	Demonstrate an organisation's ability to convert sales made into profits. Profitability ratios also help to determine the organisation's ability to manage its cost base.
Net profit margin $= \dfrac{\text{net profit}}{\text{sales revenue}} \times 100$	
EBITDA Earnings Before Interest, Taxes, Depreciation, and Amortization	
Return on assets	Demonstrate an organisation's ability to generate money for its **shareholders**.
Return on **equity**	
Return on capital	

Table 1.11 Profitability ratios

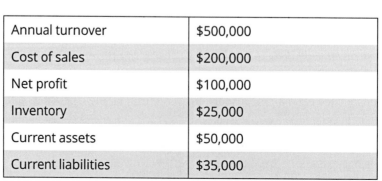

Apply
Using figures from the table below, calculate the gross profit margin of the organisation.

Annual turnover	$500,000
Cost of sales	$200,000
Net profit	$100,000
Inventory	$25,000
Current assets	$50,000
Current liabilities	$35,000

Liquidity ratios

Liquidity ratios calculate if an organisation has sufficient assets to meet its liabilities.

Table 1.12 identifies the ratios related to the liquidity of an organisation.

Ratio	Description
Current ratio $$\frac{\text{Total current assets}}{\text{current liabilities}}$$	The ability to pay short-term liabilities with current assets. This is a useful measure of a business' ability to pay its debts, but it may be misleading if the current assets consist mainly of inventory.
Acid test ratio or quick ratio (sometimes called liquid capital ratio) $$\frac{\text{Total current assets – stock (inventory)}}{\text{current liabilities}}$$	The ability to meet current liabilities with current assets. This is a more accurate measure of a business' liquidity, as it removes inventory from the calculation for some businesses inventory may be difficult to turn into cash quickly.

Table 1.12 Liquidity ratios

> *Apply*
> Using the figures from the table in the previous *apply* activity, calculate the quick and current ratios.

Gearing ratio

Gearing is a measurement of how much of an organisation's long-term funding is represented by long-term debt or loans, in relation to the equity in the business.

High gearing means that there is a lot of long-term debt within the company, which may present a risk in the long-term.

Low gearing suggests that the organisation is relying on equity capital and should therefore have less difficulty coping during tough economic times.

Table 1.13 shows the ratio related to the gearing of an organisation.

Ratio	Description
Gearing ratio $$\frac{\text{Long-term debt + short-term debt + bank overdrafts}}{\text{shareholders' equity}}$$ Or it is sometimes simply: $$\frac{\text{Long-term debt}}{\text{shareholders' equity}}$$	The proportion of an organisation's borrowing against its equity.

Table 1.13 Gearing ratio

Check
Explain what is meant by low gearing and high gearing.

Return on investment (ROI) ratio

Investment ratios are used to evaluate the financial strength and sustainability of an organisation. They are often used when stakeholders are looking to invest in the organisation.

Table 1.14 shows the ratio related to the investment of an organisation.

Ratio	Description
ROI ratio $\dfrac{\text{Net income}}{\text{Total assets}}$	How effectively an organisation uses its assets to generate sales.

Table 1.14 Investment ratio

The results of the ratios are explained in table 1.15.

Ratio	Ideal result
Operating margin	Market-dependent
Gross profit margin	Over 20%
Net profit margin	Over 15%
Return on assets	Over 5%
Return on equity	Over 15%
Return on capital	Higher than percentage rate of borrowing
Current ratio	Over 1
Acid test ratio	1:1
Gearing ratio	Under 50%
ROI ratio	As high as possible

Table 1.15 Ratio results

Check
What is the ideal ratio result for an acid test ratio?

Remember
Ratio analysis can give information on profitability, liquidity, gearing and investment.

The limitations of ratio analysis

1.3 L01

Ratio analyses can provide a useful understanding of a business' financial situation, particularly if they are used to benchmark against the industry standard, aggregate economy or organisational performance.

However, ratio analysis has limitations and so decisions should not be made using ratios alone.

The following are some of the limitations.

- The data used is historic and may not give a current or accurate result. An organisation could have recently increased its assets or liabilities significantly and the ratios may not reflect this change.

- The current rates of inflation are not taken into account. As the ratios are taken from a specific point in time, the calculations may not use the current rates of inflation.

- Ratios do not show the reasons for trends, e.g., seasonal variances, so could give an inaccurate result. For example, organisations may have to hold higher levels of inventory during periods of national or global celebration and a quick ratio calculated using data from this time period may show a poor result, which may not reflect the wider picture over a longer period of time.

- Operational changes are not always considered when comparing performance. If an organisation has recently invested in an asset or been involved with a merger, the ratios may appear unfavourable. However, if an organisation has just had a sale to reduce inventory levels, the ratios may appear more positive than they usually are.

- The economic situation may not be taken into account. If a whole industry is suffering during a period of slowdown, for example, the ratio may give a less favourable impression than is realistic.

- Not all organisations operate the same strategy, so comparisons may not be appropriate. What is important to one organisation may not be to another. If an organisation is reporting on ratios, the weighting used may vary from one business to another.

- The information from ratios is purely numerical and needs supporting with other data. An organisation could present excellent results in the form of ratios, yet could be performing unethically.

- They are not very effective as a short-term tool as they give a view at a point in time, rather than considering all financial and economic factors.

- Accountancy methods may vary. Some financial experts present data in different ways, which can lead to varied interpretations of the same facts. This could result in two buyers coming to a different conclusion.

- If some ratios are good and some are bad, what does that actually mean? For example, if the current ratio gives a favourable result but the gearing ratio is not positive, it makes it more difficult for the procurement professional to make a definitive decision.

As with any form of analysis within procurement, the buyer needs to consider the results alongside other information gathered and not in isolation.

Check

What are the limitations of financial ratios?

Apply

Describe the advantages and disadvantages of using financial ratios to make conclusions on an organisation's financial stability.

1.4 Define award criteria that can be commonly applied when sourcing requirements from external suppliers

When a list of suitable suppliers has been selected, procurement professionals can send out the ITT or RFQ, as explained earlier.

Once they have received the bids or quotations, they should analyse the offers to establish which supplier offers the best value for money.

Typical award criteria

Price

Price is one of the most basic criteria on which a company will base its decision about which supplier to award a contract to, but the skill of procurement is to evaluate the total offer from the supplier and take into account all of the following.

* Total life-cycle costs
* Technical merit
* Added value
* Systems and resources

Price should always be considered and compared against the competition. When comparing prices from bids or quotations it is important to carry out a fair analysis. This involves checking the following aspects.

* The exchange rate.
* Batch quantities quoted for.
* Is carriage included?
* Are taxes included?
* Are there any conditions on payment terms, e.g., after 7 days + 10%?
* Pricing mechanism used: fixed-cost, cost-plus.

If the price is not carefully examined, a supplier that does not offer the best overall value may be awarded a contract.

> *Check*
> What should be reviewed when analysing prices on quotations?

Case study

Budget yachts

A global organisation manufactures yachts at entry level pricing. It recruited a new head of procurement, Tarik. Tarik had worked in procurement for some years as an expeditor, then as a junior buyer, so this role was a significant promotion and increase in responsibility.

Tarik's first task after his induction period was to review the quotations for sales that the CEO had received in response to an RFQ she had sent out. She was going away on a business trip so asked Tarik to decide which supplier he thought was best suited to be awarded the contract and they would discuss it on the CEO's return.

Tarik analysed the quotations and remembered what a previous manager had once told him about ensuring that all factors are considered, not just price.

Tarik soon reduced the number of suitable quotations to two. He had looked at quality policies, references, financial reports, CSR policies and capacities.

The two he had left met all the selection criteria but had very different prices on their quotes.

Tarik made his final decision and opted to put forward the supplier that quoted a lower price for the contract.

Pleased with his work, he sent an e-mail to the CEO and said he looked forward to discussing his findings on her return.

The following week, Tarik explained his decision in a meeting with the CEO.

Initially she looked pleased with the work, but then highlighted an error in Tarik's research.

The chosen supplier had quoted a price for 'each' product but the other supplier's price was for 'packs of five'. When the calculations were done, the price from the second supplier was considerably cheaper per unit.

Tarik felt embarrassed – he had failed to consider that prices are not always displayed in the same format.

The total life-cycle costs should be assessed when looking at the price, including the following aspects.

- Price of product
- Transport/delivery
- Packaging

EXW
Ex works – goods are required to be collected by the buying organisation from the suppliers' premises

DDP
Delivery duty paid – goods are delivered to the buying organisation's location of choice with all associated costs included and paid for by the supplier

- Insurance
- Cost of installation

Some suppliers may include all of these in their quotations but procurement professionals should not assume this and should always check what is included. This will avoid unwanted surprises when invoices are received.

When sourcing from overseas, Incoterms® need to be considered as part of the criteria for deciding which supplier the contract should be awarded to.

The Incoterms® proposed by the supplier can significantly affect the total cost of acquisition. For example, if one supplier gives a quotation and states that the price is **EXW** and another supplier states that its price is **DDP**, this needs to be explored. The buyer would need to establish how much extra the buying organisation would have to pay to have the products collected, transported, delivered and insured in order to make a fair comparison. (Incoterms® are covered in more detail in chapter 3.)

> *Apply*
> Explain, with reasons, whether EXW or DDP would be expected to be the cheapest Incoterm®.

Life-cycle costs
The total cost involved in items of inventory, including purchasing price, inward delivery, receipt and handling, storage, packing and preparation, dispatch costs, insurance and overheads

Total cost of ownership
A structured approach to calculating the full costs associated with buying and using an asset or acquisition over its entire life cycle

Total life-cycle costs

As well as evaluating which option offers the best value in terms of the total cost of acquisition, the procurement professional needs to consider the **total life-cycle costs**.

Total life-cycle costs are also known as the **total cost of ownership** and will relate to a specific asset.

Table 1.16 explains the costs associated with total life-cycle costing/total cost of ownership.

Cost	Description
Acquisition	Costs associated with acquiring an asset such as sourcing, transport, insurances and installation.
Tooling	Costs associated with any specific moulds, cutting accessories or fixings that have to be purchased with the asset.
Insurance	Costs associated with insuring the asset against damage, theft or downtime.
Operating	Costs associated with running the asset, e.g., electricity or water consumption.
Maintenance	Costs associated with keeping the asset in good condition – is there a maintenance package included or is this an additional expense?
Training	Costs associated with training the operators of the asset, and health and safety requirements.

Cost	Description
Storage	Costs associated with storing the asset – how much space does it take up and is it a constant requirement or an infrequent need?
Disposal	Costs associated with removing the asset from site when it is no longer viable to keep. Is specialist equipment or expertise required to remove the asset? Can it be sold or, does it have to go in landfill or be recycled?

Table 1.16 Total cost of ownership (TCO) explained

Consumables
A commodity that is used up quickly or requires replacing frequently

> *Remember*
> TCO includes all the costs associated with owning an asset, from acquisition to disposal.

When deciding which supplier to award a contract to, a procurement professional should carefully consider the total life-cycle costs. This is to evaluate how much owning the product or asset will cost the organisation throughout its useful life. For example, a product may have a low acquisition price but require regular maintenance and **consumables**, such as changing **wearing parts** or deep cleaning. This could result in a higher total cost of ownership than a product that appears to be a higher price for initial purchase yet has low maintenance requirements and no requirement for additional consumables.

Wearing parts
Parts within equipment that have a limited life and require replacement regularly

> *Apply*
> Explain why total life-cycle costs should be evaluated before awarding a contract to a supplier.

Technical merit

Procurement professionals should evaluate the technical merit of suppliers before deciding which one a contract should be awarded to. Suppliers should be able to demonstrate that they would be a good **functional fit** with the buying organisation.

A supplier's systems should be compatible with the buying organisation's systems, e.g., if the procurement professional wishes to send over e-purchase orders for spares for an asset, the supplying organisation needs be able to accept and process these.

Functional fit
Be able to work with an organisation on the same technical level

It is very important to establish the technical merit of a supplier. If a supplier was awarded a contract based on many favourable factors but technical merit was excluded, this could have cost implications during the contract.

Case study

Coffee concerns
Mario is a buyer in a large factory. He was asked to source a new coffee machine for the workers. The current one had almost reached the end of its functional life after three years of heavy use.

Mario was experienced in sourcing and knew the procedure to carry out. He selected eight potential suppliers that met the organisational criteria and then sent them the RFQ.

All eight suppliers gave Mario a quotation, which he analysed in detail.

Several suppliers were eliminated due to the total life-cycle costs. Four of the eight suppliers did not offer any support or maintenance package, which was a concern to Mario as the coffee machine was an important part of the operational structure and workers very much looked forward to a hot drink during their breaks. If there was no support included in the contract, the risk of extended downtime was high and unacceptable.

The remaining four quotes were very similar.

Mario made his final decision based on the technical merit of Caring Coffee Ltd. This supplier had technology that linked in to the machine on site. It generated requisitions electronically for Mario to approve to keep the stock of coffee at an agreed level. This was very important to Mario as he did not have the time to constantly monitor the machine.

Caring Coffee Ltd also stated that all invoices would be sent electronically, and that the maintenance reports conducted periodically, as per the agreement, would be e-mailed to Mario within 24 hours, outlining any areas of concern.

The computer system that Caring Coffee Ltd operated was immediately compatible with Mario's in-house procurement system so IT upgrades were not required. The technical fit appeared to be perfect so, based on this, Mario recommended that Caring Coffee Ltd should be awarded the contract.

Added value solutions

Added value is not related to the price of a product or service but to other aspects of the offer that could generate a favourable solution.

Added value can be demonstrated by suppliers in many of the following forms.

- Innovation: suppliers are forward thinking and generate ideas for continuous improvement.
- On-time and in-full deliveries: suppliers consistently deliver as and when required and do not cause production delays.
- Strong supplier relationships: suppliers offer support, are flexible and are open to change.

- Sustainability: suppliers are financially strong and replace any natural resources they use.

- Good ethical practices: suppliers work to ethical standards and have a Code of Ethics that is regularly reviewed.

- CSR policies: suppliers have a CSR policy that is up to date, and work closely on improving their social impact and presence.

- Shorter lead times: suppliers hold stock and have improved internal processes to reduce the notice they require to fulfil purchase orders.

- Improved quality: quality standards have improved but price has remained constant.

- Support and training: Suppliers offer support to procurement when required and train buying organisations in new technology or relevant processes that could save time or money.

- Good reputation: suppliers with a good reputation add value to the supply chain which reflects positively on buying organisations.

> *Check*
> What factors could a supplier offer to generate added value for a contract?

None of the these factors costs the buying organisation any additional money but they do generate value within a contract. These factors make suppliers more desirable to work with.

By offering added value, suppliers may become more attractive to a procurement professional. For example, consider a company that has two suppliers that both charge the same hourly rate to provide telephone support to help resolve IT issues. One supplier offers support from 10:00 until 16:00 hours and the other offers support from 06:00 until 23:00 hours. The buying organisation has employees that work flexible hours so the supplier offering the extended hours for support would be seen to provide added value, compared to the one that is only available for six hours per day.

> *Apply*
> Describe an example relating to an organisation with which you are familiar, where a supplier adds value to a contract.

When reviewing quotations and bids from suppliers, procurement professionals should consider and compare any added value factors, and look at the benefits that they could create for the buying organisation.

Systems and resources

As explained earlier, ensuring that suppliers have the technical capabilities to carry out the contract and that their computer systems can easily integrate with the buying organisation's is very important (see section 1.3).

Balancing commercial and technical award criteria

When awarding a contract, the criteria used can be split into commercial and technical categories.

Technical criteria are concerned with whether the supplying organisation can physically produce and supply what is needed, in accordance with the RFQ or ITT, at an acceptable price. Technical criteria include the following.

- Specification
- Delivery
- Quality

Commercial criteria are concerned with the organisational fit – are the buying and the supplying organisation compatible to work together? Commercial criteria include the following.

- Cultural fit
- Ethical standards
- Sustainability

> *Remember*
> Awarding criteria can be technical or commercial.

It is important that both types of awarding criteria are balanced to enable a procurement professional to make an informed decision. One set of criteria should not be prioritised over another as this could generate a solution that is unacceptable in the long-term.

When evaluating quotations and bids from suppliers, procurement professionals often use tools to help them balance the commercial and technical award criteria.

Weighted scorecards and evaluation matrices can be used to balance the awarding criteria.

A weighted evaluation matrix is used to give more 'weight', i.e. importance, to certain elements of a quotation and to allow a fair evaluation for all suppliers.

Table 1.17 shows a weighted evaluation matrix and an example of a supplier's results when imported from a quotation or bid. Weighed point systems will be covered in more detail in chapter 2.

Criteria	Weight	Requirements score				
		A	B	C	D	E
Value	20%	80	45	40	15	35
Risk	20%	60	85	30	20	75
Difficulty	15%	55	80	50	15	25
Success	10%	30	60	55	65	30
Compliance	5%	35	50	60	50	50
Relationships	5%	80	70	50	85	80

Criteria	Weight	Requirements score				
		A	B	C	D	E
Stakeholder	15%	25	50	45	60	60
Urgency	10%	60	25	40	65	80
Weighted scores	100%	54.8	60.0	43.3	38.0	52.3

Table 1.17 A weighted evaluation matrix (Source: O'Loughlin, E. (n.d.) National College of Ireland, i.ytimg.com/vi/FefJ1paq750/hqdefault.jpg)

The best value offer from a potential supplier is the one that can offer the product or service for a fair total cost of acquisition together with added value, low total cost of ownership, high technical merit and high availability of resources.

Chapter Summary

This chapter has covered the following.

- The sourcing of products or services forms an integral role within any organisation. By understanding whether to make or buy or to outsource a need, procurement professionals can ensure that organisations are able to achieve the best value for money.

- When buying products or services, it is important to consider which style of sourcing to choose. Single sourcing has advantages but it also has risks so the process of evaluating whether single, dual or multiple sourcing works best is key.

- All suppliers need to be pre-qualified, appraised and evaluated against strict criteria. This enables procurement professionals to offer contracts to the most suitable suppliers and to obtain added value.

- The most suitable suppliers may be in a home country or may be international. International sourcing is often chosen due to the lower costs it offers, but money saved may be to the detriment of other important contributing factors. Again, as with all procurement decisions, the situation must be carefully evaluated before making a final decision.

- Within some organisations, intra-company trading occurs which has the advantage of allowing profits to be allocated more favourably. There are many rules and regulations on transfer pricing agreements that should not be overlooked when the procurement team is involved in this process.

Recommended reading

Sollish, F., Senmanik, F. (2011), *Strategic Global Sourcing Best Practices*, John Wiley & Sons

www.deloitte.co.uk (2013), *The Outsourcing Handbook: A guide to Outsourcing* [online]. Retrieved from: www.deloitte.co.uk/beinspired/publications.cfm [Accessed on: 23 January 2019]

Canez, L., Platts, D., Probert., D. (2001), *Make or Buy: A Practical Guide to Industrial Sourcing Decisions*, University of Cambridge Institute for Manufacturing

End of Chapter Assessment

EXPLAIN

1 Explain the benefits of evaluating the make or buy decision within sourcing.

DESCRIBE

2 Describe two financial ratios and give examples of how they should be used.

LIST

3 List and explain three risks associated with outsourcing.

DEFINE

4 Define what is meant by technical and commercial criteria.

References

1 Hinkelman, E. G. (2008, 8th edition), *Dictionary of International Trade*, World Trade Press, p. 578

2 Novack, R. A. and Simco, S. W. (1991), "The Industrial Procurement Process: A Supply Chain Perspective," *Journal of Business Logistics*, (12:1), 1991, pp. 145–167

3 Barnes, D. (2008), *Operations Management*. London: Thomson

4 Burke, G. J. (et al.) (2007), "Single versus multiple supplier sourcing strategies", *European Journal of Operational Research*, (182), pp. 95–112

CHAPTER 2

Understand the key processes that can be applied to the analysis of potential external suppliers

Learning outcome

By the end of this chapter, you will understand the processes that can be used to analyse potential external suppliers and how to carry them out effectively.

Chapter overview

2.1 Analyse commonly used sources of information on market data that can impact on the sourcing of requirements from external suppliers

You will understand:
- Compiling data on expenditure with suppliers
- Indices that measure economic data
- Secondary data on markets and suppliers
- Commodity pricing
- Analysing potential sales
- Financial reports and supplier financial stability
- The role of credit rating agencies

2.2 Identify the key processes used for obtaining quotations and tenders

You will understand:
- Advertising requirements
- Requests for information or quotations
- The operation of tendering
- Formalised arrangements for tendering
- Decision criteria for tendering

2.3 Identify the criteria that can be commonly applied to the assessment of quotations or tenders

You will understand:
- Assessment of suppliers' proposals
- The use of weighted points systems for assessment

- Recommending sources of supply
- Financial statements such as the profit and loss, balance sheet and cash flow statements
- Measures and ratios of profitability, liquidity, gearing and investment
- The limitations of ratio analysis
- Added value

2.4 **Analyse how electronic systems can be used to help the sourcing of requirements from external suppliers**
You will understand:
- E-requisitioning and purchase ordering systems
- E-catalogues on intranets and the Internet
- The use of e-auctions and reverse auctions
- E-tendering systems

Introduction

As explained in chapter 1, collating and evaluating information on potential external suppliers is an important part of sourcing. By thorough due diligence, unsuitable suppliers can be excluded from the process, leaving the best suited suppliers to continue in the process.

In this chapter you will learn about the types of processes that can be used and the associated analysis of them.

2.1 # Analyse commonly used sources of information on market data that can affect the sourcing of requirements from external suppliers

There is a huge amount of varied data available for procurement professionals to review in order to make informed decisions on which external suppliers they wish to work with. This section explains the types of information and market data that are available and the benefits of analysis.

Compiling data on expenditure with suppliers

Pareto principle
A theory that states that 80% of events are generated from 20% of the causes

A procurement professional should be aware of the total amount of spend they are responsible for and how it is broken down.

Most organisations have a similar breakdown of supplier spend, where 80% of the total spend is distributed between 20% of the suppliers. This percentage is a recognised theory within business and is known as the **Pareto principle**.

Check
In accordance with the Pareto principle, what is the percentage split of events against causes?

Figure 2.1 shows a Pareto curve and how it relates to the amount of spend suppliers are responsible for within an organisation. However, instead of the Pareto 80/20 split the figure splits the suppliers into three categories, 'A', 'B', and 'C'. This type of categorisation is known as **ABC analysis**.

ABC analysis
A categorisation process dividing the subject matter into three levels of value

In the figure, 'A' suppliers represent 20% of the total spend – these are the suppliers that are responsible for the highest level of spend. The procurement department considers 'A' suppliers to be the most important.

'B' suppliers are collectively responsible for a smaller percentage of spend and there are many more of them. The majority of suppliers fall into category 'C'. They are responsible for the smallest amount of spend.

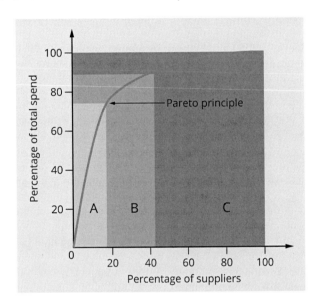

Figure 2.1 The pareto principle (Source: adapted from www.iotknowhow.com/2016/04/23/what-if-you-are-too-small-to-employ-a-procurement-professional/)

Remember
Suppliers can be categorised into A, B and C according to their levels of importance/spend to the buying organisation.

Apply
Explain which category of supplier you think needs to be managed most closely within the Pareto principle.

Understanding the value and importance of a supplier to an organisation helps to determine the style of management. Table 2.1 shows how the categorisation of suppliers can affect the style of relationship that is required.

Categorisation of supplier within ABC analysis	Style of relationship
A	Strategic
B	Closer tactical
C	Transactional

Table 2.1 ABC analysis and style of relationships

In accordance with the Kraljic matrix (see section 1.1), 'A' suppliers are likely to be contracted to supply the strategic products or services within an organisation.

When a procurement professional is considering changing a supplier of a product or service, it is critical to use the Pareto principle and ABC analysis to fully understand the importance of the supplier and the product or service that they supply. ABC analysis helps the procurement professional break down complex data into three segments, which are then easier to understand and manage.

For example, if a buyer aims to make a 10% saving on fasteners, they could use ABC analysis to work out which fasteners make up the majority of the spend. With this knowledge, the buyer can establish which supplier to engage with to try to get a reduction. The buyer will be more likely to save money by negotiating with a supplier of a large volume or high value, i.e. 'A' products, than by negotiating with lots of 'C' suppliers.

Using data on the expenditure with existing suppliers (on existing contracts) can affect sourcing because an existing supplier might also be a potential supplier for another contract.

Indices that measure economic data

When a procurement professional is reviewing supplier spend and performance, they have to have something **tangible** to measure it against. In order to fully understand the market and the **economy** before making a decision, buyers may review **indices** that measure economic data. Table 2.2 identifies the main indices and what they measure.

Index	Measurement
Stock markets (e.g., FTSE 100, SENSEX)	The value of public limited companies' stocks and shares
Gross Domestic Product (GDP)	The monetary value of the goods and services manufactured or supplied in a financial period.
Producer Price Index (PPI)	Average changes in prices that a producer receives in return for its goods or services.
Consumer Price Index (CPI)	A weighted measurement that evaluates the average cost of a 'basket' of goods bought by a consumer.
Commodity indices	The value of a particular commodity at a point in time, e.g., steel, oil, wheat.

Tangible
Something that you can see or touch

Economy
The state of a region, country or the world in relation to its production and consumption of goods and services

Indices
The plural of index – a statistical measure used within economics

Stock markets
A place where public limited companies' stocks and shares are traded (bought and sold)

FTSE 100
The United Kingdom's stock exchange

SENSEX
India's stock exchange

Index	Measurement
Small Business Lending Index (SBLI)	An indicator of small business lending trends.
CIPS Purchasing Managers' Index	A highly accurate set of facts about current industry conditions in manufacturing, construction and services.

Table 2.2 The main economic indices

By reviewing the economy using indices, procurement professionals can gain insight into how profitable a supplier may be and whether supply is plentiful. This helps to highlight any risks that the suppliers – and in turn the buying organisation – may be exposed to.

If indices show that prices of commodities are continually rising, the likelihood is that demand is exceeding supply. In such situations, the buying organisation faces the risk of paying inflated prices or not being able to source a supplier that has stock readily available.

For example, if a procurement professional wants to source a new supplier for an existing component that includes steel, they may refer to a commodity index to understand the current market situation. If steel is trading at a high value, it is likely that any new supplier will inflate its prices to reflect the increased prices. If this is the situation, it may not be a good time to change suppliers. This is because a new supplier may have to secure its stock of steel but the current supplier already has stock sourced at a lower price.

Supply and demand play a large part in the economy and significantly affect prices that are displayed in indices.

≪ Case study

Supply outstripping demand and causing profits to plummet

A new report by Rabobank suggests that the current low price of shrimp is unlikely to change soon. Shrimp prices plummeted in 2018 when supply exceeded demand for the first time since the outbreak of the devastating early mortality syndrome (EMS).

Despite EMS, it was only a matter of time before stocks rose - driven by the resulting high shrimp prices. Supply first started to exceed demand in 2017, exacerbated by a drop in demand from China, a major market, due to its weakening currency.

Harvests early in 2018 showed strong yields from India and Ecuador and improved production levels from Indonesia, Vietnam, and other regions. As a result, farmers are harvesting either at a loss or with a far lower profit margin than at any time in the last five years, due to rising costs of energy, feed and labour.

Farmers are expected to reduce production by reducing feeding and delaying harvesting, or by not restocking their ponds.

While a small short-term price recovery is likely, the trend is for lower prices as a result of improved supply, unless there is a further outbreak of the disease. Demand and price levels will therefore have a major effect on supply.

Overall profits will decline, with the farmers being the hardest hit and new farmers being discouraged from entering the industry.

(Source: adapted from www.seafoodsource.com/news/supply-trade/ rabobank-shrimp-price-crash-has-arrived-more-professionalization- to-come)

Having knowledge of the economy through reviewing indices and media reports helps procurement professionals to better understand their position when entering into a negotiation. A supplier who has surplus products will be more likely to concede on price than a supplier who is aware that it has a product or service that is in high demand.

For example, if a buyer enters a negotiation having researched the market and so knows that demand has significantly dropped, it will be better placed to agree a lower price with the supplier. Through reviewing indices and media reports, the buyer will be able to understand their position within the negotiation and determine who holds the greater bargaining power. Pre-evaluation of suppliers could include establishing if they hold inventory and to what value. If the inventory value is high and the demand is low, the buyer is well-placed to obtain a good price.

Alternatively, if the buyer knows that what it is trying to source has a very high demand and supply is scarce, it will be in a comparatively weak bargaining position.

If the procurement professional enters into negotiations without having done the research, there is a high risk that the supplier will take advantage, especially if the relationship is adversarial or arms-length. The price then proposed and agreed may not reflect the market.

Secondary data on markets and suppliers

Primary data
Data that comes directly from the source and constitutes new data for a specific purpose

Researching data on markets and suppliers helps procurement professionals in their pre-qualification work. Data can be collected in two forms: primary and secondary.

Primary data is new and is specifically collected directly from the relevant source by the individual or organisation that is going to use it. Primary data can be collected in the following ways.

- Direct communication: one-to-one communication with suppliers, i.e. conversations or e-mails.

- Networking: meeting professionals at events and exchanging information.

- Specifically-commissioned market research: focus groups, interviews, questionnaires, etc.

- Trade fairs and exhibitions: seeing products or services first hand at events.

The following information can be gained from these sources.

- Product availability
- Pricing strategies
- Trends and forecasts
- Contact details
- Company strategy
- Organisational pressures
- Personal opinions and views

The information from published research or indices is **secondary data**. This is information that has been gathered by another source and then presented or published. Secondary data is usually easily available and can be collected from the following places.

- Economic indices
- Supplier websites
- Financial journals
- Professional magazines
- Published surveys
- Professional bodies
- Third party comparison websites
- Published price lists
- Organisations promoting trade

Table 2.3 gives some examples of secondary data sources.

Secondary data source	Examples
Economic indices	• Money supply M2, Consumer Price Index (CPI) • Producer Price Index (PPI), Consumer Confidence Index (CCI) • Current Employment Statistics (CES)
Websites	Supplier websites, online databases and business listings.
Financial journals	Published documents containing information on market analysis and current trends.
Professional magazines	Publications such as *Supply Management* which give information on current procurement trends and concerns.
Published surveys	Information published by governments on **demographics** and social trends.

Secondary data
Data that already exists

Demographics
Data relating to trends within the population

Secondary data source	Examples
Professional bodies	Organisations such as CIPS, which provide regular information to members.
Third party comparison websites	Online tools that compare prices from similar industries.
Published price lists	Brochures, leaflets or online information containing prices for goods or services.
Organisations promoting trade	Embassies, trade associations or unions sharing global information.

Table 2.3 Secondary data

Both primary and secondary data can be distorted. Often primary data is distorted by, for example, researcher bias. Secondary data can be distorted by going through more channels before reaching the procurement professional.

Secondary data is easier and quicker to access (as it is already available) and it is often free to gather. However, it might not be entirely relevant for the purpose. Primary data, on the other hand, is very specific.

Remember
Both primary and secondary data can be distorted.

Both primary and secondary data are good sources of information for a procurement professional to use when they are exploring sourcing suppliers.

Primary and secondary data can complement each other but they can also conflict, so it is important that procurement professionals understand where their data has come from. Primary data gained from a direct conversation with a supplier may not be the same as the data seen in a professional magazine, for example. It is quite possible that quotations from individuals may have been taken out of context or are short extracts that may reduce the impact or weaken the message.

It is essential that the primary source is trustworthy. Secondary data can be used to validate primary data or challenge it. If the relationship with a supplier is collaborative, there would be no reason to suspect any primary data is incorrect, but if the relationship is weak or adversarial, there is a risk the supplier's data may be manipulated.

Using both types of data together acts as a form of safeguarding to establish data that is both accurate and current.

Apply
Describe three types of secondary data that would be useful to consider when analysing the suitability of suppliers.

Commodity pricing
The market average price charged for a product

Commodity pricing

For a procurement professional to get a positive result from a negotiation, they should be aware of **commodity pricing**.

Commodities traded on a stock exchange can be divided into four categories.

1. Energy
2. Agricultural
3. Metals
4. Livestock

> *Remember*
> Commodities can be divided into four different trading categories on the stock exchange.

Commodity prices are tracked individually for comparison on a daily, weekly, monthly and annual basis. All four categories of commodities are also monitored to establish any trends.

> *Apply*
> Choose a range of commodities that are traded on the stock exchange. Research how these commodities changed in price over the same twelve month period. Consider whether there are any trends in the price variation.

If a buyer understands trends and the current commodity pricing of raw materials that relate to a defined need, it is more likely to obtain a favourable outcome.

Procurement professionals who understand trends and commodity prices can seek to arrange contracts at times where prices are favourable. For example, where a trend shows that prices of a certain raw material always drop during April, a buyer would take advantage of this knowledge and lock into a **fixed-price contract** at that point.

A buyer that is not aware of the trends may try to negotiate a price during a pricing peak, and so may arrange a price for a period of time that is considerably higher than the market average. Lack of knowledge of commodity pricing would be seen as a weakness by suppliers and, depending on the style of relationship, the supplier could take advantage of the buyer.

Table 2.4 shows some examples of commodities that are traded on the stock exchange and related products that could be affected by price fluctuations.

Fixed-price contract
A contract where the price remains the same for the agreed period

Commodity	Category	Related products
Oil	Energy	Petrol, plastic
Natural gas	Energy	Propane, carbonated drinks
Wheat	Agricultural	Flour, bread
Cotton	Agricultural	Clothing, bedding
Cocoa	Agricultural	Chocolate
Steel	Metals	Cars, trains, machinery

Commodity	Category	Related products
Gold	Metals	Jewellery
Live cattle	Livestock	Beef, steak
Lean pigs	Livestock	Pork, bacon

Table 2.4 Commodities and related products

Commodity pricing can be affected by several of the following factors.

- Supply and demand: if supply is greater than demand, prices drop. If demand is greater than supply, prices increase.

- Currency fluctuation: when a supplier's currency is strong against the buyer's currency, the price to the buying organisation will be increased.

- Political situation: if there is political unrest, an election is imminent or a change of government personnel occurs, prices often fluctuate. Prices could go up or down, depending on the situation, the rules the politicians implement or any trade restrictions they apply.

- Conflict: if countries are engaged in conflict, it may become harder to import and export products and so prices will increase.

- Force majeure: if an event such as an earthquake or a volcanic eruption occurs, the supply of commodities could be restricted, and this would inflate prices.

- Severe or unseasonable weather conditions: these may affect the environment and so agricultural crops may not produce the expected yield or may exceed forecasts. Prices will then be affected. This relates to commodities such as wheat, barley, cotton, cocoa and tea.

- Prices of competitors: suppliers react to competition. If there is a lot of competition, prices will reduce. If there is limited or no competition, such as in a monopoly situation, prices will increase.

- Prices of substitutes: if the market has substitutes for a product or service, the product that is in competition with that substitute will be priced accordingly to try and gain **market share**.

- Speculation: if there are media reports that suggest, for example, that a product is going to be in short supply or become unavailable, the price will increase. Speculation can be started by suppliers to try and inflate prices.

Some individuals within industry, work on forecasting commodity pricing in order to **hedge** and attempt to invest and sell at the best times.

Most procurement organisations are in business to produce and sell goods or services. This means that they will hedge to take out or limit the impact of the risk of adverse fluctuations. This is compared with speculation in which organisations or individuals actively pursue risks to make gains when commodity prices move.

Experts attempt to forecast prices based on the following.

- Historical data

- Supply and demand

- The state of the economy

- Global events

Market share
The portion or percentage of a market owned or controlled by a supplier or product

Hedge
A form of risk management in investing used to reduce any potential losses

Figure 2.2 shows an example of a forecast based on historical data and trends. The figure has averaged out the pricing from January to December 2018 and created an average increase which has been replicated in 2019.

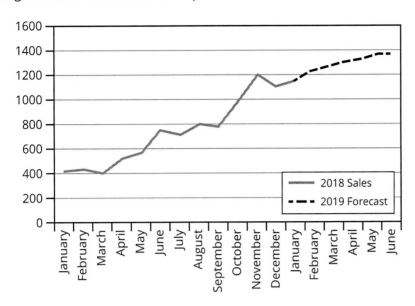

Figure 2.2 Sales forecast

Once these forecasts have been prepared, they are available for business' to view. These forecasts are used within a **futures exchange**, a financial marketplace where futures contracts are traded. Examples of futures exchanges are given in table 2.5.

Futures exchange
A marketplace where the seller of a commodity agrees to sell or buy a certain amount of the commodity to a buyer at a particular price on a specific date in the future

Futures exchange title	Full name
LME	London Metals Exchange
NASDAQ	National Association of Securities Dealers Automated Quotation
CME	Chicago Mercantile Exchange
ICE	Intercontinental Exchange

Table 2.5 Futures exchange examples

A Futures exchange is a centralised financial trading exchange where people can agree contracts for delivery at a period later in time and based on prices that are estimated.

By viewing futures data, procurement professionals can forecast the likely price of a commodity in the future, for example, whether it is likely to increase or decrease in price. They can make decisions accordingly to achieve the best value for money for their organisation.

Future fuel

Carl was a buyer for a large organisation that had over 50 trucks. Carl followed the news, subscribed to professional magazines and considered himself to be knowledgeable on market trends, the economy and commodity pricing. Coming up to the busiest part of the season, Carl decided it would make sense to consider locking into a futures contract for the supply of diesel required to run the vehicles.

Based on historical data, Carl was able to forecast a quantity that would be needed. He then spoke to several suppliers that viewed the futures exchange and asked them to give a quotation for the volume required.

Carl reviewed the prices he received. If he committed to buy the volume now, he believed he would save over 10% against spot buying throughout the busy season. It was a risk but based on the economic trends and the prices of oil over the last three years, Carl believed the risk was justified.

Apply

Explain how commodity pricing can affect how much goods and services cost a buying organisation.

Analysing potential sales

The procurement function reacts to any needs generated, forecasted or predicted. This often relates to sales of goods and services. By having a good understanding and receiving accurate information about potential sales, procurement professionals can make informed decisions on quantities, delivery schedules and ultimately price.

Analysing potential sales can mean the following.

- Working closely with internal teams so the procurement function can be proactive. For example, by working closely with the sales function to see what sales are coming up.

- Looking at trends to see if there are any cyclical patterns.

- Working with marketing teams to learn about any planned campaigns that might affect sale volumes.

To analyse potential sales, several tools and methods can be used.

- Porter's Five Forces

- Supply and demand

- Historical sales data analysis

- Trends

- Expert opinions

2.1 L02

Check
Recap your understanding of Porter's Five Forces – see section 1.1.

The amount of competition in the marketplace will have a large effect on potential sales. Markets can range from a position of **pure competition** to a state of a monopoly or **imperfect competition**. For example, if there is a lot of competition, there is likely to be fewer potential sales than in a market where there is only one supplier acting as provider.

Pure competition
A situation in the marketplace where there is plenty of competition

Remember
Competition can be pure or imperfect.

Imperfect competition
A situation in the marketplace where one supplier has complete control

Looking at supply and demand is an important part of analysing potential sales. It is possible to gain a fair idea of potential sales by understanding the state of the economy, and being able to assess whether products or services are meeting demand.

Consider Porter's Five Forces model. If a new supplier of a product entered the market at a time when demand was exceeding supply, that supplier would probably have a reasonable number of sales. It is likely that the current supplier base is unable to meet demand therefore sales are available to a new supplier.

ERP
Enterprise resource planning system, a multi-functional electronic system that combines work flows both in and out of the business from all functions

Reviewing historical data can help with analysing potential sales. If a product or service is seasonal, it is likely that history will repeat itself at the same time each year. For example, an organisation that sells sunglasses would be likely to see a rise in sales during the summer.

Historical data may be found in an organisation's archived records or may be stored electronically on systems, such as **ERP**. The sales director or finance director would be able to advise procurement professionals on trends from previous financial periods if the data was not readily available. Trends occur when something moves in a particular direction, such as fashion or lifestyles. Potential sales can be analysed in relation to trends as they pick up pace or slow down.

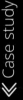

Case study

Sunglasses sales predicted to rise in June
One of the major challenges that Flavio faced in his role as a senior buyer was forecasting when the demand for sunglasses would rise. He needed to know this to establish when to buy in the components needed to make them.

In the past he had worked on the theory that summer in his country starts in June so that was the month that demand would start to increase. This year he decided to try a different approach. He pulled the sales figures from the computer system and plotted them on a graph. On another line on the graph he plotted the temperatures from information he had researched from previous years' weather reports.

This data showed Flavio that his customers started to buy sunglasses when the temperature reached about 18 degrees centigrade, which was not necessarily in line with when summer officially started.

Flavio then decided to try and find some information on the predicted weather for the coming year. With this information he could plot when the demand would start in relation to when the temperature was thought to rise above 18 degrees. The data showed Flavio which products sold most and at what temperature this happened. Based on that, he decided that a new product that had recently been signed off by quality control should be launched just before the peak in predicted sales.

Time would tell if Flavio's forecast was correct but this year he believed that his purchasing of components had some strategic relation to the sales figures.

Finally, experts can be asked to give their opinions on what will affect sales. Experts include economic experts, product experts who anticipate what consumers want or data analysts who produce and analyse demand forecasts. Experts may be individuals with vast experience within an organisation or may be external to the organisation, for example, consultants.

By combining all of the tools and methods, such as gaining and evaluating primary and secondary data, researching commodity prices and trends and using economic indices, a procurement professional should be able to obtain a good insight into, and be able to analyse, potential sales to construct a forecast of what needs will be generated.

Apply
Evaluate some historical data for a period of two to three years from an organisation with which you are familiar. Create a forecast for the next 12 months based on the trends the data shows.

Financial reports and supplier financial stability

In chapter 1, the importance of a supplier's financial stability was explored in the form of financial ratios (see section 1.3). By ensuring that a supplier is financially stable, a procurement professional can be more confident of the following.

- Prices are fair and favourable

- There is a guaranteed continuity of supply

- Risk is minimised

For potential suppliers, these checks should be conducted before awarding any contract. However, if a supplier is mid-way through a contract, there could be signs that indicate financial instability, including the following.

- Reduced levels of quality and performance

- High **staff churn**

- A change of bank

- Rumours

- Requested payment before the agreed due date

Another way of evaluating a supplier or potential supplier's financial stability is to review its formal **financial statements**. Financial reports or statements commonly contain three documents.

- Income statement/profit and loss account: this shows a company's trading performance in terms of revenue, profit, expenses and losses over a period of time (most typically a twelve month period).

- Balance sheet: this shows a company's equity, assets and liabilities at a particular point in time (usually at the year end date of the trading period stated in the profit and loss account/income statement).

- Cash flow statement: this shows the generation and utilisation of cash during the accounting period in question.

Financial reports are audited by professional accountancy bodies or government officials to give an independent evaluation of the financial statements. This ensures that they fairly and accurately reflect the financial position of the organisation, including its cash flow.

Through close inspection of financial reports, a procurement professional may analyse the current performance of the supplier, how much profit it has made, the value of any assets owned, its cash flow and its debts.

The documents associated with financial reports will be explained in section 2.3.

2.1 LO2

Staff churn
The turnover of employees in an organisation

Financial statements
A company's formal financial statements are their published year end accounts – in most countries it is a legal requirement for companies to publish these statements soon after their year end accounting date

---

Check
Which three documents are commonly featured within financial reports?

The role of credit rating agencies

Credit rating agencies assess the financial stability of an organisation. They use data provided by the following organisations or reports.

- Banks and other financial institutions

- Lenders

- Creditors

- Public information

- Financial reports

- Court judgments for debt

Use of credit scores

From the data, credit rating agencies are able to generate a score that reflects the level of risk an organisation poses when dealing with other businesses. Credit scores are made up of percentages created from different elements.

Weighted score
A score calculated by using a scoring system that emphasises the areas with the highest level of importance

Figure 2.3 shows how the different elements are segmented in order to create a **weighted score**.

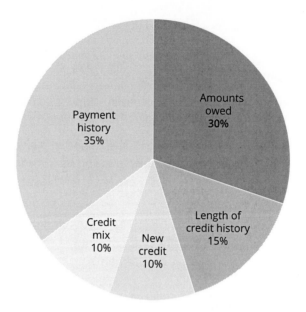

Figure 2.3 Credit score elements

Procurement professionals use credit scores to evaluate suppliers by reviewing the feedback from the credit rating agency. If the score is low, it would suggest that there is a high level of risk associated with the supplier and this should be investigated further before engaging with them. If the score is high, it would suggest the risk is lower and that the supplier is financially stable at the current time. This may mean that awarding them with a contract would come with lower levels of risk.

Table 2.6 explains the elements shown in figure 2.3.

Element	Description
Payment history	Has the organisation paid on time and in full in the past?
Amounts owed	What are the organisation's debts?
Length of credit history	What is the average time taken by the organisation to pay its debts?
New credit	Has the organisation been approved for any new credit recently?
Credit mix	Are there a variety of credit options, i.e. various lenders and terms?

Table 2.6 Credit score elements

Remember
Credit rating scores are weighted.

Procurement professionals usually request the credit scores of suppliers through the finance department as there is often a small cost to obtain a business' credit report.

From this, the procurement professional can establish the level of risk associated with the supplier. If the supplier has a high credit score, then the associated risk to the buying organisation is low and the procurement professional may continue with the process. Even if the supplier's credit score is low, it may be possible to mitigate the risk to the supplying organisation if the buyer still wants to enter into a contract with the supplier, rather than dismissing them from the process.

A supplier with a low score may be classified as higher risk for reasons that are not linked to poor credit.

- They may have recently set up as a new organisation.
- They may have no loans, including credit cards.
- They may have no high value assets (high value assets can suggest good financial stability and may be used to pay debts if needed).

In such situations the buyer may still wish to engage with the supplier but may add clauses or make changes to the documentation to reduce the level of risk to the buying organisation. Some examples include the following.

- The buying organisation may contract to pay the supplier in a shorter period of time than the standard terms and conditions, to help the supplier with set up costs, cash flow and to secure inventory.
- The buying organisation may accept products more regularly in smaller quantities, to help the supplier develop and to ensure that capacity is not exceeded.

Alternatively, a procurement professional may consider dual or multiple sourcing to ensure continuity of supply until a relationship has developed with the higher risk supplier and trust has been gained.

Cybercrime and credit checks

As industry continues to become more reliant on technology and the risks of **cyberattacks** increase, credit checks are evolving. New styles of credit checks evaluate the potential risk a supplier and its supplier chain has of being a victim of **cybercrime**.

The new style of credit check aims to generate a credit score associated with the level of protection and skills an organisation can demonstrate in relation to **cybersecurity**.

Cyberattack
A malicious act attempting to disrupt or steal information using computers

Cybercrime
Crime that involves computers or networks

Cybersecurity
The protection of computers and networks against cybercrime and cyberattacks

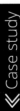 **Case study**

Tomorrow's credit ratings
Supply chains and individual suppliers can now be rated on their security and their vulnerability to cyberattacks, due to a recently-launched new service.

Everybody knows that a chain is only as strong as its weakest link: supply chains are no different. No matter how tech-savvy the organisations are at the top of the supply chain, all it takes is one susceptible company to put the entire chain at risk. The usual method is to send phishing e-mails and links to fraudulent websites to the company's employees.

According to BakerHostetler's 2017 Data Security Incident Response Report, as much as 43% of the cyber threats faced by organisations relate to phishing, hacking and malware. 32% of these incidents are caused by human error.

Basic human error and organisational failures in cybersecurity training are, however, only a small part of the problem. Organisations operating on a global platform will work with suppliers worldwide and these suppliers will potentially have very different rules regarding cybersecurity standards, in addition to IT systems which may be difficult to audit.

An Australian firm specialising in research and consultancy, Security in Depth, has launched a new service to tackle the problem and reduce the risk factors associated with the supply chain. The new service, Cyber Assurance Risk Rating (CARR), will rate organisations according to their cybersecurity and issue a 'credit score.' Using the score generated, organisations will be able to determine whether a new supplier poses a risk to their own corporate networks and security and will further be able to advise existing suppliers of security flaws that have the potential to affect current and future business relationships.

(Source: adapted from www.cbronline.com/news/cyber-credit-scores)

As with any information a procurement professional gathers about a supplier, credit rating scores should not be used in isolation. They only show some information, so in order to obtain a full and detailed account of a supplier's financial position, all aspects that are covered in this chapter should be considered.

Apply
Describe how using a credit score can minimise the risk to which an organisation is exposed.

Check
Explain how and why credit rating agencies obtain information about an organisation.

2.2 Identify the key processes used for obtaining quotations and tenders

When a procurement professional has conducted due diligence to evaluate and choose suitable suppliers, the next stage within the procurement cycle is to issue the request for quotation (RFQ) or invitation to tender (ITT). Although different in approach, both an RFQ and an ITT have the same aim: to establish which supplier can offer the goods or services for the best value for money.

There is no rule about when to use an RFQ and when to use an ITT. Table 2.7 indicates the common uses of each option. Both options ultimately lead to an offer being made.

2.2 L02

Request for quotation	Invitation to tender
Less formal	More formal
Generally used for less complex requirements	Generally used for more complex requirements
Less detailed than an ITT	More detailed than an RFQ
Low- to medium-value contracts	Medium- to high-value contracts

Table 2.7 RFQ v ITT: Similarities and differences

> *Check*
>
> Is an ITT or an RFQ described below?
>
> A buyer in the public sector puts an advert on its website asking for interested suppliers to express an interest.
>
> The suppliers that have expressed an interest are evaluated using a PQQ.
>
> The suppliers that meet the criteria then receive a detailed document, including a request to respond on how they would fulfil the defined need. The document has a clear deadline by which bids have to be submitted to the buying organisation.
>
> On receiving the responses, the buyer analyses and evaluates the offers and chooses the most suitable and cost effective supplier.
>
> When the supplier has accepted the contractual offer the unsuccessful suppliers are notified.

Advertising requirements

Advertising the opportunity to work with a buying organisation is likely to increase the number of suppliers expressing an interest. This will help to ensure that the best value is obtained. By limiting the supplier base, the opportunities for comparison are lower. However, if advertising generates more supplier interest, this in turn generates more work in terms of selection so more resources are required.

The way organisations advertise their requirements depends on several of the following factors.

- Value of contract (for example, a higher-value contract could justify a higher marketing budget)
- Strategic importance of contract
- Urgency of contract
- Resources available

Advertisements are typically placed in the following locations.

- Professional magazines
- Business journals
- Newspapers
- Supplier websites
- Specialist tender portals

Figure 2.4 shows an example of an advertisement inviting tenders.

Tenders needed!

Fly me to the moon has decided to tender the contracts covering interior and exterior advertising concessions at its four airports. The new contracts will start 1 January 2020.

In 2018, the advertising concessions delivered a turnover of 28m Euro.

The airports within *Fly me to the moon's* portfolio had a collective average of 73 million passengers in 2018. Passenger growth has averaged 4.3% from 2012 to 2018, and has further improved business opportunities for *Fly me to the moon's* partners. Investment in infrastructure is at the heart of the consortium's strategy, ensuring continued development in the future.

Inviting tenders will allow *Fly me to the moon* to determine the market value of internal and external advertising and inform the future positioning of the advertising concession.

Companies interested in participating in the tender are asked to download and return the expression of interest – pre-qualification document. Expressions of interest must be submitted by 12 Oct 2019.

Figure 2.4 A tender advertisement

Figure 2.4 is an example of a private sector advertisement. The public sector also uses this form of advertising but also has other tools and systems available. For example, a centralised, government-sponsored procurement portal or official databases. This allows organisations in the public sector to easily reach the market and promote the fact that they have contracts available on which to receive bids.

Public sector organisations advertise their requirements on their own dedicated public sector procurement websites as well as regional, national and continental portals. In England and Wales, for example, Contracts Finder gives suppliers the opportunity to search for information about contracts with the government and its agencies worth over £10,000. Similarly, Africa Gateway is a database of public tenders information for companies that are interested in African governments' tenders, projects and business opportunities.

Private sector organisations advertise their requirements less frequently. The private sector is not accountable in the same way as the public sector. Public sector organisations, which are funded by taxation, need to be seen to consider every option for supply and to invite as many suppliers as possible into the process. They are required by the regulations to advertise.

Private sector organisations usually advertise on their own websites, as there are no dedicated websites for private sector tenders. However, some dedicated public sector websites allow the private sector to upload their adverts to tender.

Whatever way the opportunity is advertised, the advert should include several important pieces of information. Table 2.8 outlines the important information that should always be included in advertisements for requirements from the procurement function.

Information	Details
Awarding body/company	Which organisation will be awarding and managing the contract?
Overview of awarding company/body	Brief description of the type of organisation, history, vision and mission.
Project description	Details of the requirements of the contract.
Experience/qualifications/ accreditations	Any specific requirements that are critical to the awarding of the contract.
Deadline	The date and time by which bids must be received.
Contact	Details of a contact for any queries.

Table 2.8 Advertising requirements

Check
Which sector is most likely to advertise its contractual requirements?

Apply
Write an advertisement for a tender opportunity for a commodity, product or service with which you are familiar.

Requests for information or quotations

Request for information (RFI)

A **request for information (RFI)** is a standard process used within procurement. It collects information from potential suppliers to help the buyer evaluate a potential supplier's suitability to work with the buying organisation.

RFIs are sent to many potential suppliers across the market to get as much data as possible. This helps the procurement professional to create a strategy on how to carry out the procurement, i.e. how and through what processes the outcome will be achieved. The RFI process is shown in figure 2.5.

Request for information (RFI)
A document used to gather information about suppliers and their capabilities prior to a formal procurement process

Buyer

Procurement professional seeks information from potential suppliers with the objective of creating a list of capable suppliers.

Supplier

Supplier submits response in the required format answering the questions and providing relevant information to highlight its suitability.

Buyer

Procurement professional receives the RFI response and evaluates the information to pre-qualify or reject the supplier.

Figure 2.5 RFI process

Potential suppliers do not have to respond to a buyer's request for information.

A request for information may be sent in the form of a letter or e-mail to a potential supplier, simply asking for details about them and their capabilities, or it may be a more formal document with a lot of questions.

A pre-qualification questionnaire (PQQ) is a form of RFI.

> *Check*
> What information is likely to be included in a PQQ?

RFIs typically gather the following information about potential suppliers.

- Financial position
- Capabilities
- Capacity
- Mission and vision
- Ethical and sustainability policies

The information gathered from RFIs is useful to procurement professionals as it generates the following data.

- Number of capable suppliers
- Number of suppliers with capacity
- Amount of supplier competition
- Amount of product/service competition
- Acceptable lead time
- Any market trends
- Any expected changes in the marketplace

And then there were two

Benjamin, an established procurement professional, had just started a new project to choose a suitable supplier to buy components for a child's scooter. The product had recently been signed off by the engineering department and quality team, and he now had the confirmation to begin sourcing.

Many components were already in this supply chain except one – the lightweight matt black wheels – was a new buy.

Benjamin had created a PQQ to send out to the selected suppliers as a form of RFI. He had already prepared the RFI, so it could be sent out as soon as the project was approved. The RFI contained information to assess which suppliers were able to produce and/or supply the wheel, which suppliers had the capacity to fulfil the contract and what the lead time would be.

Case study »

> Benjamin knew that once he had this information he would be in a position to understand how many capable suppliers there were, how many were in a position to produce or supply the wheels and how long it would take. He would also be able to determine the amount of competition in the marketplace, which would help him understand how he should approach negotiation.

From the information received in response to RFIs, the procurement function can create a suitable strategy for sourcing and begin to plan for the negotiation. If the information shows that there is a high level of competition in the marketplace, they can build a strategy for negotiation on the fact that the buyer has the power. If an agreement cannot be reached, the buying organisation can walk away and try to create a contract with another pre-evaluated supplier.

Request for quotation (RFQ)

It is important to note that an RFI/PQQ doesn't have to be used before issuing the RFQ. On lower value contracts, RFQs can be issued as the first step. However, ideally all suppliers should be pre-qualified, so RFQs can be sent to any suppliers that are left in the process after the responses from RFIs have been received and evaluated, that is, to the pre-qualified suppliers. It asks them to provide a cost for supplying the goods or services documented.

RFQs can contain the following information.

- Specifications
- Technical drawings
- Samples
- Quantities
- Delivery requirements
- Length of contract
- Terms and conditions
- Details of how the supplier's quotation will be evaluated

An RFQ attempts to assess which supplier can achieve the **Five Rights** of procurement for the buyer's defined need, in the most cost effective way. For example, an individual within an organisation identified a need for lighting in a side corridor. The need was defined by establishing the type of light bulb required and how many were needed to be sourced to replace the failed ones. When sourcing the replacement light bulbs, the procurement professional needed to ensure that the supplier could supply in the following way.

- The right light bulb in terms of specification and quality
- In the right quantity
- As soon as possible to reduce the risk (at the right time)
- To the right place
- At a fair price

Five Rights
The key objectives of procurement: the right quantity, the right quality, at the right time, delivered to the right place and at the right price

Figure 2.6 shows the five rights of procurement.

Figure 2.6 The Five Rights of procurement

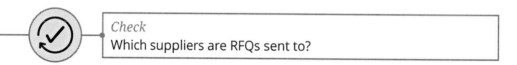

Check
Which suppliers are RFQs sent to?

The purposes of RFQs are outlined below.

- To align corporate strategy: RFQs form part of the procurement process which relates to organisational objectives and values.

- To ensure a fair and transparent process: RFQs ensure that all suppliers receive the same information and have the same chance to win the contract. An RFQ is issued to potential suppliers so they can all submit bids on the same basis. This means the buyer can carry out a consistent evaluation.

- To allow opportunities for many suppliers to bid: as a standard document, RFQs enable many suppliers to receive them and provide a quotation.

- To enable procurement professionals to evaluate the market and obtain the best value for money: by receiving responses to RFQs, procurement professionals can establish trends in the market, determine levels of competition and ensure they achieve the best deal.

If buyers use the same suppliers all the time for products or services, there is a risk that the suppliers may become complacent and the best value may not be achieved.

Procurement professionals can carry out regular benchmarking through comparing quotations received in response to RFQs. This can help them to understand the current market situation and to compare the prices that they are currently paying against what the competition could offer.

By conducting regular benchmarking and being open about it, long-term suppliers can be made aware that they should not be complacent and that their prices need to remain competitive to avoid the buying organisation moving the contract elsewhere.

Moving suppliers periodically (if possible and if acceptable within the organisational strategy) can promote innovation and help the buying organisation to develop in areas it is not strong in. Other suppliers may be able to bring new ideas, improve processes or re-engineer products to add further value to the organisation.

Table 2.9 outlines the differences between RFIs and RFQs.

Request for information	Request for quotations
Objective is to learn about suppliers	Objective is to obtain costs for comparison
Sent to large and varied supplier base	Can be sent to pre-qualified supplier base
Helps to develop strategies	Helps to achieve best value
Relatively informal process	Structured formal process
Generic	Specific

Table 2.9 RFI versus RFQ

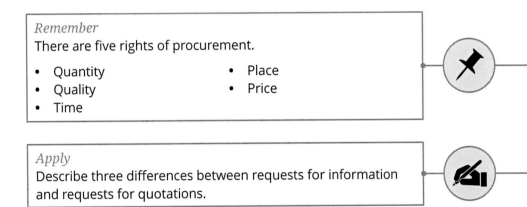

Remember
There are five rights of procurement.

- Quantity
- Quality
- Time
- Place
- Price

Apply
Describe three differences between requests for information and requests for quotations.

The operation of tendering

As explained in chapter 1, tendering is a more formal and regimented process than sending out requests for quotations. Tendering is used for goods, works and services. Generally, the higher value and more complex the contract, the more likely it is that tendering will be used. The following examples are services that are often put out to tender.

- IT contracts
- HR contracts
- Construction contracts
- Healthcare equipment contracts
- Cleaning contracts
- Maintenance contracts
- Catering contracts
- Office supplies contracts
- Security contracts
- Consultancy contracts

Figure 2.7 shows a flow chart of the tender process.

```
Develop tender
and evaluation
criteria
      │
      ▼
Send out RFI to ──────────────▶ Create a supplier
all potential                   shortlist from the bids
suppliers                              │
      │                                ▼
      ▼                         Carry out further
Create a pre-                   due diligence
qualified                              │
supplier list                          ▼
      │                         Select the best ◀ ─ ┐
      ▼                         value bid           │
Issue an invitation                    │           │
to tender to pre-                      ▼           │
qualified suppliers      Offer the contract ──▶ Supplier accepts ──▶ Award the
      │                         │    │          the contract          contract
      ▼                         │    └ ─ ┐
Hold a tender                   │        │
briefing cross-                 │        │
functional team meeting         │        ▼
      │                         └ ─ ─ ─ Supplier rejects
      ▼                                 the contract
Receive bids from
suppliers and evaluate
```

Figure 2.7 Tender process

When sending out an RFQ, procurement professionals are aware of their exact need. When sending out an ITT, procurement professionals are often more open to suggestions on how to carry out the contract in a way that constitutes the best value for their organisation.

> *Remember*
> Tendering is used for a wide range of requirements, most typically higher value and where requirements are more complex.

The type of tendering process used depends on several factors.

- Does the procurement function know its potential supplier base?

- Does the procurement function want to increase its potential supplier base?

- Does the procurement function know exactly how it wishes to achieve delivery of the contract?

- Does the procurement function assume that there will be limited interest in the tender?

The answers to these questions help to choose which type of approach is best. Table 2.10 shows OIEU specific approaches. Public sector organisations are bound by these but private sector organisations are not. The table shows how the answers to the questions above relate to the choice of approach for a public sector organisation.

Question	Answer	Approach
Does the procurement function expect there to be very high interest and therefore generate a high number of bids?	Yes	Restricted
	No	Open
Does the procurement function have stringent selection requirements that must be satisfied by bidders?	No	Open
	Yes	Restricted
Does the procurement function know exactly how it wishes to achieve delivery of the contract?	Yes	Open/restricted
	No	Negotiated
Does the procurement function assume that there will be limited interest in the tender?	Yes	Open
	No	Restricted (or negotiated if the requirements are very complex and there are few suppliers)

Table 2.10 Tender approaches

> *Remember*
> The restricted approach is used where the interest is expected to be higher and so the buyer needs a method of de-selecting unsuitable bidders and creating a shortlist of acceptable organisations.

> *Check*
> Which tendering approach would best be suited to a procurement function that did not know how it was going to deliver the solution to the business need?

Tendering can be a complex process and, although the procurement professional runs the project, there is often a need to involve other colleagues or team members from other departments. Both creating and evaluating the tender documentation may need input from the following departments.

- Finance
- Engineering
- Sales
- Logistics
- Operations

Cross-functional team
A team made up of people from different departments all working towards a common goal

By involving other departments, the procurement professional can better understand the services required and have help available to answer any technical queries that may arise. A team that involves people from different departments within an organisation is a **cross-functional team**. Figure 2.8 shows how a cross-functional team could be formed in order to work on a tender project within an organisation.

> *Remember*
> Cross-functional teams enhance knowledge to help achieve goals.

Procurement department	Research and design department	Finance department	Cross functional team

Figure 2.8 Cross-functional team

Some cross-functional teams also involve external stakeholders if their input would be valuable. For example, a cross-functional team in a food manufacturing company may include a sample panel of consumers to test, rate and give feedback on variations of recipes in order to establish which one would be best suited to the market and generate the most revenue.

Case study

Tender teamwork

Raul had just been chosen as the buyer to conduct a tender process for the cleaning contract for his company. He sent out RFIs to lots of suppliers that he had found from both primary and secondary sources, and from the responses he was able to create his pre-qualification list.

All the suppliers on the list received an invitation to tender with specifications and clear details of what the contract involved, as well as a clearly stated deadline for bid submissions.

While waiting to receive the bids, Raul liaised with his colleagues and created a cross-functional team who were briefed and happy to help him evaluate the bids.

Raul was able to assess the bids from a financial perspective and could see which supplier met the procurement criteria. Through his work he reduced the potential suppliers down to the best three options.

All of Raul's cross-functional team members had signed agreements to state that they would not share any information discussed during the tender briefing. The suppliers were aware that their tenders would be viewed by a cross-functional team. Raul took the data protection regulations (**GDPR**) very seriously.

The real benefit of his cross-functional team proved to be including the supplier of a piece of machinery that was on lease and used to clean the site. This supplier was able to inform Raul that some of the bidders, despite stating their competence, did not have the required training to use the machine.

Raul presented the results of the tender process to his procurement director in a business case, which outlined the reasons for his recommendation and the reason for excluding the others. The procurement director reviewed the case and commended Raul on his process management, decision-making and engaging with a cross-functional team.

GDPR
The European Union's General Data Protection Regulation

2.2 LO2

> *Apply*
> Explain how a cross-functional team could aid a procurement
> professional when analysing bids.

Formalised arrangements for tendering

In industry today, ethical and responsible behaviour is extremely important. Some processes are now considered unacceptable and, in some cases, legal action may be taken. For example, modern slavery is widely condemned, as is high levels of unnecessary pollution generated by organisations.

Acting fairly and transparently is a key part of ethical behaviour. In procurement, this is achieved by treating all suppliers equally, giving each of them the same opportunity when responding to tenders and making decisions based on pre-determined and published criteria.

It is important that there are no **conflicts of interest** and that no dishonest activity takes place when reviewing or awarding contracts.

Conflict of interest
Where an individual is unable to remain impartial due to a personal, professional or public interest

> *Remember*
> There should be no conflicts of interest in the tendering
> process.

To ensure the tendering process is carried out in an ethical, responsible and transparent way, organisations should have formalised arrangements in place, which reflect best practice. This allows suppliers and customers to see exactly how decisions are made during the bidding process. An example of a best-practice tender arrangement is outlined in table 2.11.

Process stage	Description
1 Preparation	Detailed and clear specifications are prepared, setting out exactly what is required of the supplier so that bids can be fairly evaluated.
2 Approach	The tendering approach is chosen and should be justified.
3 Timescales	Decisions are made on how long the process is going to take. Dates are set for the PQQs to be sent/received, the invitations to tender to be sent/received, the decision made and the suppliers advised.
4 Advertising	The opportunity to bid is advertised carefully, choosing locations in line with any regulations or legislation.
5 Documentation	The documentation to be sent out with the invitation to tender is collated.
6 Consistency	All suppliers receive exactly the same documentation which is sent out at the same time.
7 Submission	All bids are submitted and received by the buying organisation by the set deadline. Any that arrive after that date should not be included in the tender process. All bids that have arrived by the deadline are opened together.
8 Analysis	Careful and stringent analysis is carried out, in accordance with the criteria outlined at the preparation stage.

Post tender negotiation (PTN) Negotiation that occurs after the best value supplier has been chosen. This is to see if any further improvements can be made before the contract is awarded

Process stage	Description
9 Decision	A decision is made based on the criteria, which results in the most suitable supplier and best value bid being chosen.
10 Verification	Final supplier verification is carried out if required, i.e. requesting samples, prototypes or demonstrations.
11 Negotiation	Final arrangements are agreed and any fine-tuning carried out. Once the best bid has been chosen, **post tender negotiation (PTN)** can take place to see if there is any room for further improvement in the offer.
12 Contract preparation	The contractual documentation is drawn up in accordance with the bid and any amendments that have been agreed.
13 Contract awarded	The supplier is awarded the contract and both parties sign.
14 Notification	Any notification that needs to happen to comply with internal procedures or regulations should take place, such as advising which supplier has been awarded the contract.
15 Feedback	The unsuccessful suppliers are informed and feedback.
16 Debrief	There is an internal discussion of how the process ran that considers any improvements that could be made in the future.

Table 2.11 Formalised tender arrangements

Apply

Explain why each stage in a tender process should be formalised in its approach.

Decision criteria for tendering

The objective of a tender process is to establish which supplier can provide the contract and give the best value for money for the buying organisation. Decisions can be made in the following ways.

- Creating spreadsheets to compare data. Figure 2.9 shows a basic spreadsheet comparison.

- Using weighted points systems/scorecards (see section 2.3).

	A	B	C	D
1				
2		**Supplier A**	**Supplier B**	**Supplier C**
3	**Service price**	$2000.00	$2500.00	$1750.00
4	**Consumables price**	$500.00	$600.00	$800.00
5				
6	**Total price**	$2500.00	$3100.00	$2550.00

Figure 2.9 Comparing supplier bids in a spreadsheet

The results of some tender processes will be much easier to evaluate than others. In cases where one supplier is the obvious choice, the decision may be straightforward. This will not be the case when several suppliers appear to be equal.

The main objective for procurement professionals is to understand which of the potential suppliers can offer the most economically advantageous tender (MEAT).

If the decision is not an easy one, depending on the level of authority the procurement professional has, they may need to justify their decision to senior personnel. If a procurement professional does not have enough experience or is in a junior position, or if the decision of who to award the tender to is challenging, senior personnel may ask the project leader to present their recommendations for the chosen supplier. This can be done in several ways.

- Face-to-face conversations
- An e-mail
- By submitting a detailed report
- By presenting a **business case**

2.2 L02

MEAT
Most economically advantageous tender

Business case
A justification for a proposed project or undertaking on the basis of its expected benefits

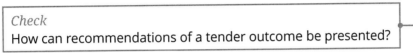

> *Check*
> How can recommendations of a tender outcome be presented?

Table 2.12 shows what should be included in a business case when trying to justify a proposed decision for the awarding of a contract.

Content	Description
Introduction	A general overview of the need that requires fulfilling.
Process undertaken	A description of which approach to tendering has been undertaken.
Options	Details of the options that were presented by suppliers.
Benefits available	Summary of what the chosen supplier could provide as a benefit to the organisation, e.g., save cost, enhance output, improve reputation.
Costs	Information related to how much the proposed supplier will charge the organisation to undertake the contract.
Risks	A summary of any risks related to (1) the proposed supplier and (2) not choosing that supplier.
Recommendation	Naming the supplier of choice and giving some details about them.

Table 2.12 Elements of a business case

Whether a procurement professional chooses to send out an RFQ or an ITT, the process should be efficient, effective and ethically responsible. Transparency is key, making sure that all suppliers and potential suppliers are treated the same. If a supplier believes that it has been unfairly removed from a tender process, the procurement professional should be able to explain their decision.

Case study

Transparency is key

Ying-Mae felt that she always followed the CIPS code of conduct and kept her processes fair while conducting tenders.

One day, Ying-Mae received an e-mail from a very unhappy supplier that had been notified the previous day that it had not been successful in being awarded a contract.

Ying-Mae responded to the e-mail complaint explaining that, with respect, the supplier was not found to offer the best value solution.

A chain of e-mails followed where Ying-Mae explained her process and decision-making criteria in detail. She was able to send the supplier some extracts of the process but had to ensure that no other supplier's details were disclosed due to GDPR regulations.

The data she was able to submit to the aggrieved supplier showed that it was not only the most expensive on price but that it did not meet the required criteria in relation to ethical conduct and sustainability.

On receiving the information that showed how fairly and professionally Ying-Mae had conducted the process, the supplier apologised and agreed that, in fact, it was not the most economically advantageous tender.

2.3 Identify the criteria that can be commonly applied to the assessment of quotations or tenders

As explained earlier, in order to achieve the MEAT outcome in the tender process, the assessment criteria have to be decided from the start.

The assessment criteria typically include the following.

- Price

- Total cost of ownership

- Total cost of acquisition

- Supplier compatibility

- Environmental activities

- Ethical conduct

- Sustainable practices

- Method of contract delivery

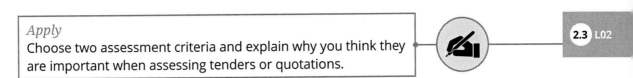

2.3 LO2

Apply

Choose two assessment criteria and explain why you think they are important when assessing tenders or quotations.

The purpose of assessment is to evaluate which supplier best meets the specification requirements in the tender documentation and to analyse the added value options, such as innovation opportunities.

Assessment of suppliers' proposals

The assessment process is usually declared to bidders at the start and will reflect the buying organisation's priorities, usually the needs of the stakeholders.

When assessing suppliers' proposals, the procurement professional must consider the following areas.

- The value of the product/service

- The positioning of it, e.g., strategic, routine

- Existing supplier relationships

- Economies of scale

- Risks of moving suppliers

If the value is minimal and the risk to the organisation is low, the procurement professional should not spend a significant amount of time assessing quotations. This applies to routine purchases such as stationery and consumables that are readily available and low value. The time spent assessing small value contracts could be better spent analysing more critical and high-risk proposals.

Similarly, a procurement professional needs to use their time effectively and prioritise assessing urgent and important proposals ahead of less value ones.

Figure 2.10 shows how the amount of time spent assessing proposals increases against the importance of the product or service to the organisation.

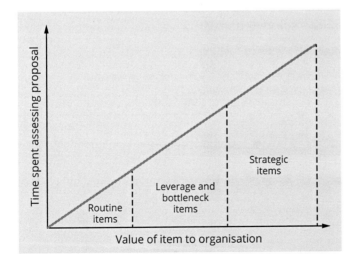

Figure 2.10 Time spent assessing proposals

The methods used to assess the bids must produce fair and transparent results.

Check
Which category of item requires the largest amount of time to be spent on assessing proposals?

The use of weighted points systems for assessment

The need to be fair and transparent throughout procurement also applies when deciding which supplier to award the contract to. A weighted points system is one method that can help to keep decision-making transparent.

A weighted points system is an evaluation procedure that enables fair comparison of set criteria. The weight of each criteria reflects its importance in the decision-making process and the total for all weights should equal 100.

Remember
The weight of each criteria reflects its importance in the decision-making process.

Check
What should the total for all weights add up to in a weighted points system?

Table 2.13 outlines the process of creating and conducting a weighted points system for assessment.

Step	Description of procedure
1	Define the criteria to be used in the assessment.
2	Decide on the weights of each of the criteria.
3	Determine a scoring system, e.g., 10/100 = poor, 20/100 = average, 50/100 = competent, 70/100 = good.
4	Allocate a score to each criteria in each supplier's proposal.
5	Calculate the total score for each supplier.
6	Rank the suppliers according to the highest score.

Table 2.13 The weighted points system procedure

Table 2.14 shows how weights can be attributed to individual criteria with the total amount adding up to 100.

Criteria	Weight
Price	30
Quality	25
Lead time	5
Method of execution	20

Criteria	Weight
Business Continuity capability	10
CSR contribution	10
Total	100

Table 2.14 Weight values

Once the weights have been determined and agreed, the next part of the process (see table 2.13, steps 4–5) is to calculate the scores for each supplier's proposals.

Figure 2.11 shows the following.

- The points allocated to each supplier against each criteria
- The calculation to create the weighted scores
- The weighted scores
- The total weighted scores

Criteria	Weight	Supplier A			Supplier B		
		Points	Weighted score calculation	Score/100	Points	Weighted score calculation	Score/100
Price	30	70	30% × 70	21	50	50% × 30	15
Quality	25	60	25% × 60	15	80	25% × 80	20
Lead time	5	20	5% × 20	10	20	5% × 20	1
Financial stability	20	40	20% × 40	8	30	20% × 30	6
Technical capability	10	30	10% × 30	3	30	10% × 30	3
Ethical conduct	10	40	10% × 40	4		10% × ~~40~~	~~0~~5
Total	**100**			**61**			~~56~~ **49** 45.5

Figure 2.11 Completed weighted point system

Apply
Create your own weighted points system to assess two or more supplier proposals for a contract within an organisation with which you are familiar.

Like most systems, the weighted pointed system has advantages and disadvantages. Table 2.15 outlines these.

Advantages	Disadvantages
Practical approach	Time consuming to create
Allows transparency	Reliant on numbers
Not easy to manipulate	May require software investment
Can involve cross-functional teams	Total objectivity is impossible
High stakeholder engagement	Training may be costly

Table 2.15 Advantages and disadvantages of weighted points systems

Recommending sources of supply

Using the weighted points system with suppliers' proposals gives the procurement professional a quantifiable method to use to recommend the source of supply. By presenting the results of the assessment in a business case, a spreadsheet format or in a SWOT analysis, stakeholders can see why the recommendation has been made.

The recommendation may be to enter into a single sourcing agreement or, if the findings suggest multiple sourcing arrangements are favourable, this could be the recommendation presented.

> *Remember*
> The recommended source of supply can be single, dual or multiple.

Case study

Decisions, decisions....
Charlotte, a buyer in a large manufacturing organisation, was asked to look at the resourcing of one of the company's largest volume components. The component was strategic to the organisation but the procurement director believed that, despite the long-term relationship with the current supplier, the total cost of acquisition was far higher than it should be.

Charlotte researched some potential suppliers, conducted pre-evaluation and then, when she had a shortlist, sent out the RFQ. The current supplier also received the RFQ as Charlotte knew that this would be a good benchmarking exercise.

The quotations all came back and Charlotte plotted the results of the pre-determined criteria on a weighted points system.

The current supplier came second in the process.

The supplier with the highest score was known to the organisation and Charlotte currently bought a few components from them. It was clear that this supplier really wanted to work with the organisation further and Charlotte suspected that they were taking advantage of economies of scale to generate an excellent price. The components on the RFQ were made of the same raw material as the other products sourced from this supplier.

Charlotte knew the risks of changing suppliers and fully understood the importance of being certain in her choice of moving a strategic item to a new supplier.

After thinking long and hard, Charlotte decided that for the next year, the contract should be a dual sourcing agreement so that the current supplier could ensure the buyer continued to receive high quality components,

2.3 L02

delivered on time and in full. At the same time, Charlotte could build up information on the new supplier's performance.

If the new supplier performed as well as it suggested it could, then the following year Charlotte would go back to single sourcing with this other supplier. Or on the other hand the current supplier might reduce its costs based on the fact it might lose the work.

Charlotte presented her findings to the procurement director in the form of a business case that explained the task, the options, the risks and the costs involved and finally her recommendation. The procurement director was very pleased with Charlotte's work and agreed that her recommendation was a sensible approach. He signed off the business case and authorised Charlotte to award the contracts.

Financial statements such as the profit and loss, balance sheet and cash flow statements

Check
Remind yourself about credit rating agencies and the use of credit scores by re-reading section 2.1.

Apart from reviewing credit scores, there are other ways to evaluate suppliers financially that can give a high level of detail.

Every organisation has to produce a set of accounts at the end of its financial year. Both public limited companies and private limited companies must file their annual accounts for others to view.

If procurement professionals or their associated organisations wish to carry out their own independent financial reviews on potential or existing suppliers, they can view the following documents.

- Profit and loss account/income statement

- Balance sheet

- Cash flow statement

Profit and loss account

A profit and loss account, often referred to as an income statement, is a document that summarises the **revenues**, costs and expenses that have been incurred within a financial period.

The main objective of organisations within the private sector is to generate a profit. If they are not able to do this, the business will not be able to continue.

Revenues
Income to an organisation

When a procurement professional reviews a profit and loss statement, they need to establish whether the supplier or potential supplier is generating a profit.

In a profit and loss account, there are many common entries. You will find descriptions of each entry labelled on figure 2.12, which is an example of a basic profit and loss statement.

The basic formula on which the outcome of a profit and loss account is created is the following.

Gross profit = total revenue – cost of sales

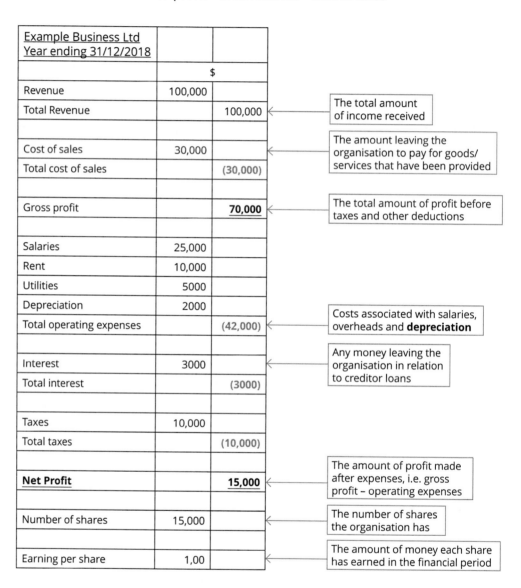

Example Business Ltd Year ending 31/12/2018			
		$	
Revenue	100,000		
Total Revenue		100,000	The total amount of income received
Cost of sales	30,000		The amount leaving the organisation to pay for goods/ services that have been provided
Total cost of sales		(30,000)	
Gross profit		**70,000**	The total amount of profit before taxes and other deductions
Salaries	25,000		
Rent	10,000		
Utilities	5000		
Depreciation	2000		
Total operating expenses		(42,000)	Costs associated with salaries, overheads and **depreciation**
Interest	3000		Any money leaving the organisation in relation to creditor loans
Total interest		(3000)	
Taxes	10,000		
Total taxes		(10,000)	
Net Profit		**15,000**	The amount of profit made after expenses, i.e. gross profit – operating expenses
Number of shares	15,000		The number of shares the organisation has
Earning per share	1,00		The amount of money each share has earned in the financial period

Figure 2.12 Profit and loss statement

Apply

Use the Internet to find a financial return or use a relevant document from an organisation with which you are familiar. Look for the common entries that are explained in figure 2.12.

Check

What are the common entries in a profit and loss account?

2.3 LO2

Remember
Gross profit = total revenue – cost of sales

Balance sheet

A statement of financial position or a balance sheet gives information on an organisation's financial position at a particular point in time. The purpose of a balance sheet is to shows assets, liabilities and **shareholder funds/equity**.

The formula for shareholder equity is as follows.

The total amount of assets − the amount of liabilities = the shareholder's equity

Shareholder equity
The owner/s of the organisation's residual claim once all debts have been paid

Apply
Create a list of assets and liabilities relating to an organisation with which you are familiar.

Figure 2.13 shows a balance sheet with some examples of assets and liabilities within an organisation.

Pretend Industries Limited
Balance Sheet
19/10/2018

Long-term debt

Assets		Liabilities & shareholders' equity	
Cash	5	Accounts payable	20
Accounts receivable	55	Credit card debt	5
Inventory	50	Bank operating credit	25
Pre-paid expenses	10	Accured expenses	10
		taxes payable	5
		Current portion of long-term debt	5
Current asset	120	Current liabilities	70
Vehicles	15	Bank debt	70
Equipment	50	Other long term notes payable	60
Land and bulidings	100		
Investment	5	Long term liabilities	130
Patents/goodwill	10		
Fixed assets	180	Total liabilities	200
		Equity from common shares	25
		Equity from preferred shares	25
		Retained earnings	50
		Total shareholders' equity	100
Total assets	300	**Total liabilities and shareholders' equity**	300

Interest payable

Taxes payable

Long-term debts (i.e. property, machinery, land)

Figure 2.13 Balance sheet (Source: adapted from www.bdc.ca/en/articles-tools/ entrepreneur-toolkit/templates-business-guides/glossary/pages/balance-sheet.aspx)

Remember
A balance sheet shows an organisation's financial position at a single point in time.

Cash flow statement

Cash flow statements contain details about the amount of money that came into and went out of an organisation during its accounting period. The aim of a cash flow statement is to assess how well an organisation is managing its cash in relation to paying its creditors and funding new investments, such as fixed assets.

Cash flow statements log cash coming in and leaving an organisation from three different activities. Table 2.16 outlines those activities.

Cash flow activity	Description
Operating activities	Cost of materials
	Sales of goods and services
	Payment of salaries
	Payment of taxes
Investing activities	Interest received
	Payment of loans
Financing activities	Payments to shareholders

Table 2.16 Cash flow activities

Remember
Cash flow statements show how cash has been generated and spent during an accounting period.

Check
What are the three types of cash flow activities?

A procurement professional uses a cash flow statement to determine whether a potential or existing supplier has enough cash coming in to be able to pay its expenses, as well as to assess the long-term strength of the organisation.

There are many ways for an organisation to decide which suppliers are most suitable to work and which suppliers should be awarded contracts. One method alone does not always give an accurate picture of what the supplying organisation can offer or the risks it may pose. When evaluating suppliers and awarding contracts, procurement professionals should use a variety of methods to ensure they gain a full view of the position of the supplier. These methods should include (but not be exclusive to) financial statements.

2.3 L02

Case study

Hanging in the balance

Pearl knew that it was important to evaluate suppliers to make sure that they were financially stable. She had always had difficulty understanding a cash flow statement but knew all about balance sheets.

During an annual review of one of her strategic suppliers, Diesel Deliverers Ltd, Pearl downloaded a copy of the organisation's balance sheet and studied the figures. As always, the supplier showed a high value of assets which satisfied Pearl that the business was financially in a good place.

Two months later Pearl received a telephone call from Diesel Deliverers apologising and explaining that it was not able to deliver the fuel that Pearl needed in order to keep her fleet of delivery vehicles running. Pearl was confused and asked why. She was told that the company did not have enough cash available to pay the refinery for the fuel. The supplier said that it would call back again the next day to update Pearl.

Pearl did not understand – she thought back to the balance sheet review and remembered that the supplier had a high value of assets.

She approached her procurement manager to advise him of the situation and explained that she did not see how this situation could have happened as she had conducted financial due diligence. The procurement manager asked Pearl how the cash flow statement looked when she did the review. Slightly embarrassed, Pearl had to admit that she did not understand that document and had only reviewed the balance sheet.

The procurement manager explained that the cash flow statement is critical and should always be reviewed as part of the process. The cash flow statement would have highlighted the fact that Diesel Deliverers did not have enough cash coming in to pay its short-term creditors.

Pearl learned a valuable lesson – that one financial document does not present the whole picture of how an organisation is performing.

Measures and ratios of profitability, liquidity, gearing and investment

Another way in which procurement professionals can evaluate their suppliers and potential suppliers as part of the sourcing process is to use ratios. Ratios can show financial information about how profitable a supplier is, how **liquid** a supplier is, how the organisation is **geared** and what level of investment a business is committed to.

Liquid
Having enough money to pay for short- to medium-term liabilities or debts

Gearing
A measure of how the business is being funded, based on its ratio of debt to equity

Financial ratios are divided into three categories.

* Profitability ratios
* Liquidity and gearing ratios
* Investment ratios

Profitability ratios measure the extent to which an organisation has traded positively and generated a profit.

It is important to understand whether a potential supplier is making a profit for several reasons.

* If an organisation is generating a profit, this shows that all of its costs have been covered.
* Shareholders desire a return on their investment and if an organisation is making a profit, they will get one.
* If an organisation makes a profit, it can return money to the business to protect its longevity.
* Without profit, a supplier may not be able to trade in the long-term.
* A lack of profit could result in a lower-quality product being supplied.

Ratios that relate to profitability include the following.

* Gross profit margin
* Operating profit
* Net profit

Table 2.17 shows the calculations associated with the ratios listed above.

Ratio	Calculation	Desired outcome
Gross profit margin	$\dfrac{\text{Revenue} - \text{cost of goods sold}}{\text{Revenue}} \times 100$	The higher the percentage, the stronger the organisation.
Operating profit	$\dfrac{\text{Operating income}}{\text{Revenue}} \times 100$	The higher the percentage, the stronger the organisation.
Net profit	$\dfrac{\text{Net profit}}{\text{Revenue}} \times 100$	The higher the percentage, the stronger the organisation.

Table 2.17 Gross profit margin, operating profit and net profit calculations

A profitable organisation is one that is liquid. An organisation that is liquid has enough money to pay its debts in the short to medium term.

Liquidity ratios include the following.

* Current ratio
* Quick ratio

Table 2.18 shows how to calculate these ratios.

Ratio	Calculation	Desired outcome
Current ratio	$\dfrac{\text{Current assets}}{\text{Current liabilities}}$	More than 1
Quick ratio	$\dfrac{\text{Current assets} - \text{stock}}{\text{Current liabilities}}$	Less than 1

Table 2.18 Current ratio and quick ratio calculation

If a current ratio produces a result greater than 1, this is a positive result. This shows that an organisation's assets have a higher financial value than its liabilities.

If an organisation generates a result less than 1 from a quick ratio, this is a good result. This shows that the value of the organisation's liabilities is lower than the value of its current assets minus its stock.

Another way to evaluate a supplier's financial situation is to review the gearing of the organisation. Gearing is the proportion of the organisation's funding that is covered by long-term debts or loans.

If a supplier is referred to as highly geared, this suggests that it has a high level of long-term debt secured against capital items. If a supplier is referred to as low-geared, it suggests that little or no long-term debt is secured against capital items.

The ratio formula for calculating the gearing of an organisation is as follows.

$$\frac{\text{Non-current liabilities}}{\text{Total equity + non-current liabilities}} \times 100$$

A percentage result below 50% suggests an organisation is lower geared and a percentage result above 50% suggests an organisation is highly geared.

> *Remember*
> High gearing equals high risk.

Investment is a measure of how attractive an organisation is to a potential investor and how likely the investor is to get a return on the money they put into the business.

Investment
A measure of the attractiveness of an organisation to a potential investor

A potential investor to an organisation may consider the results of the dividend per share ratio to assess whether they would receive a good return on their investment.

The dividend per share ratio calculation is shown below:

$$\frac{\text{Ordinary dividend for the year}}{\text{Number of ordinary shares in issue}}$$

> *Check*
> What are the three categories of financial ratios?

The limitations of ratio analysis

Ratio analysis should be used only as part of the supplier due diligence process with regard to sourcing, as it gives a general overview.

While ratio analysis is a good way to gain financial information about an organisation, the results of such analysis should not be used in isolation. The ratios show financial results during one period of time and it is important to realise that situations can change.

The limitations of using ratio analysis in isolation are listed in table 2.19 below.

Limitation	Reason
Figures are historic	The figures used are from previous data, so they do not give an up-to-date and accurate conclusion.
Inflation/interest rates/ exchange rates	If the economy has strengthened or weakened, the results from the ratios may be incorrect.
Operational changes	If an organisation has changed its products, strategy or structure, the ratio results could give an incorrect picture of the current situation.
Variation	Ratios have many variances and different accounting personnel use different ratios. The result may not be a true representation of the current state of play.

Table 2.19 Limitations of using ratio analysis

Added value

As discussed above, the results from financial analysis, such as profit and loss statements, balance sheets, cash flow and ratios, are a useful part of supplier evaluation prior to entering a contract. However, added value should also be considered.

Added value is separate from the financial analysis and covers many areas. These are listed in table 2.20.

Area of added value	How value is added
Good quality	A supplier with a high-quality product or service will add value by supplying something that lasts longer or functions better.
Short lead time	A supplier that can deliver faster will add value by reducing inventory and responding quickly to procurement needs.
CSR policy	A supplier that has a CSR policy will add value by giving back to the community.
Environmental responsibility	A supplier that is environmentally friendly will add value by reducing waste and creating little or no pollution, which favours the planet.
Sustainability	A supplier that is sustainable reduces the level of risk to the procurement organisation.
Strong communication	A supplier that communicates effectively adds value by sharing information in a time bound way.

Area of added value	How value is added
Positive relationship management	A supplier that has positive relationship management is likely to be open and trustworthy, suggesting a collaborative approach.
Good reputation	A supplier with a good reputation adds value by bringing positivity and strength to the procurement organisation.
Positive brand awareness	A supplier that has strong brand awareness may attract new consumers for the procurement organisation based on its success.

Table 2.20 Areas of added value

What adds value for one procurement organisation may not add value for another. Things that add value can be tangible or intangible, and short or long-term. As a procurement professional, it is therefore important to fully understand the procuring organisation's strategy and objectives to ensure that the added value being sought is relevant.

2.4 Analyse how electronic systems can be used to help the sourcing of requirements from external suppliers

As industry becomes more reliant on technology, procurement is moving more towards using electronic forms of sourcing.

Electronic sourcing can take the following forms.

- E-requisitioning
- E-catalogues
- E-auctions
- E-tenders

The use of electronic systems has many advantages and some disadvantages which are explained in table 2.21.

Advantages	Disadvantages
Speeds up the process	Less personal
Access to more suppliers	Communication can be misinterpreted

E-requisitioning
Sending a requisition via electronic methods

E-catalogues
Online catalogues

E-auctions
Auctions where the bidding takes place on the Internet

E-tendering
An electronic approach to tendering using e-mails or portals

Advantages	Disadvantages
Exposure to increased amounts of information	Reliant on technology – so there is a risk of failure
Fewer restrictions on working hours	Can promote a negative work/life balance
Easier to work globally	
Promotes environmentally friendly objectives such as paper-free	

Table 2.21 Advantages and disadvantages of electronic systems

E-requisitioning and purchase ordering systems

E-requisitioning is the use of electronic systems to raise and approve requisitions. This has taken over from paper methods in many organisations.

E-requisitioning has the following advantages.

- It is a faster process than using paper

- It has full traceability

- It saves time

Linked to e-requisitioning is the system of e-purchase orders. Some organisations have systems that are interlinked, such electronic MRP (material requirements planning) systems or electronic approval processes for e-requisitions. These make the process easier for the procurement function.

Systems such as electronic MRP reduce human intervention in processes and so reduce the likelihood of errors.

Figure 2.14 shows how an MRP system functions.

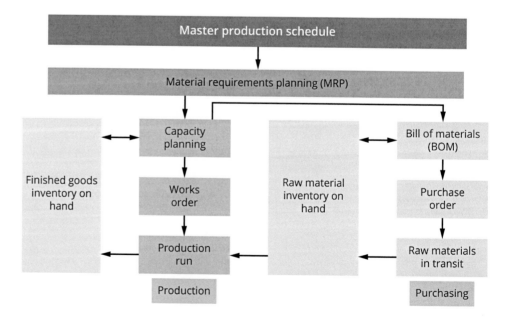

Figure 2.14 MRP System

Procurement may also use electronic systems for approval of requisitions before placing purchase orders. The process an e-requisition has to go through depends on the value of the requirement and the authority of the individual.

2.4 LO2

Figure 2.15 shows an e-approval process.

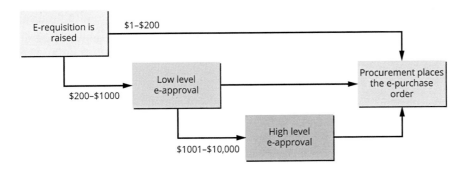

Figure 2.15 E-approval flow diagram

In the past, procurement was paper-based. More recently, electronic processes have become the accepted standard. Paper systems were much more time consuming, as well as being more susceptible to human error. The whole system of e-requisitioning through to e-purchase ordering speeds up the process, which means procurement professionals have more time to work on other activities, aside from the operational aspects of their role.

E-catalogues on intranets and the Internet

E-catalogues feature on both intranets and the Internet.

There are many benefits of e-catalogues for procurement. Table 2.22 identifies the advantages.

Advantage	Description
Accessible at the click of a button	No need to leave workstation to find a paper catalogue.
Various perspectives	Items can be viewed from different angles and seen in different colours, sizes or designs.
Live information	Inventory levels and new additions are up to date.
More detail	Lots of information available as there is no limit on printing space unlike in paper catalogues.

Table 2.22 Advantages of e-catalogues

Intranet
A private network within an organisation or group of organisations

Internet
A worldwide system of interconnected electronic networks

The use of e-auctions and reverse auctions

Online auctions are typically one of two formats.

1. Standard auction (e-auction)

2. **Reverse auction**

In organisational buying, the most common form of e-auction is a reverse auction.

Reverse auction
An auction where the bidding decreases over time to ensure the buyer gets the lowest price

E-auction

A standard e-auction is where a supplier offers goods for sale on the Internet and potential customers place bids against the items.

All bids are visible but the bidder's identity is kept private. This gives bidders the opportunity to increase their bid, if their original bid is beaten by a competitive party.

At the end of the auction the buyer that has put in the highest value bid wins the goods.

A well-known global online standard auction site is eBay.

Reverse auction

A reverse auction is where the buyer states its requirements or need and the suppliers respond. The suppliers submit their quotes against the buyer's need.

In this situation, bids are visible as per the standard auction but the difference is the bidding reduces as time goes on. This is because the buyer's aim is to push suppliers to bid as low as they can to provide the goods or services.

Reverse auctions are a popular method of buyers engaging suppliers but, as with most procurement practices, they have their pros and cons.

Table 2.23 outlines the advantages and disadvantages of a procurement function using reverse auctions.

Advantages	Disadvantages
Reduction in manual process which saves time	Possibility of technical issues which could disadvantage potential suppliers
No need for face-to-face negotiations	Impersonal
Enhanced savings for procurement due to suppliers constantly reducing bids	Supplier may end up bidding lower than is economically viable
Opportunity to interact with larger volumes of suppliers	Lack of relationship with suppliers
Opportunity for suppliers to gain information on their competition	Suppliers may lose competitive edge

Table 2.23 Advantages and disadvantages of reverse auctions

Reverse auctions for Indian Railways
Indian Railways plans to adopt a new electronic reverse auction process to save Rs 10,000 crore a year by increasing competition and reducing procurement expenditure, from 1 April, 2019.

The reverse auction process will only apply to high-value items. This encompasses items such as wagons, locomotives and coach parts, signalling and track equipment, and cement. The auction process will also cover works, services and production units, enabling suppliers to submit multiple bids and compete online (by offering the lowest acceptable bids).

2.4 LO2

The Railways procure about Rs 50,000 of goods annually, to better enable the production and maintainance of rolling stock, operate passenger and goods services, and provide other safety-related works. A further Rs 60,000 crore is spent on rail infrastructure expansion projects or upgrades, and Rs 10,000 is required for track supply materials.

Initially, supply tenders above Rs 10 crore will trigger the reverse auction process, as will works and services above Rs 50 crore, which equates to about 70% of the total Railways procurement budget. A senior Rail Ministry source advised that the process will begin 1 April, 2019.

Other department ministries, such as the Ministry of Power, already use the reverse auction process but it is the first initiative of its kind for the Railways.

Using an e-procurement system is expected to ensure that bids received by the Railways are more competitive. Additional benefits will be the removal of human error in the procurement process and the step taken toward paperless transactions. A further benefit relates to corruption: this should be reduced with the removal of the human element from the procurement process.

The Railways' reverse auction process will not involve any fees, will make the decision-making process transparent and will achieve substantial reductions in procurement expenditure. Improved competition is expected to bring about a 10% saving in cost and an overall annual saving of Rs 10,000 crore in the procurement of goods, services and works for the Railways.

(Source: adapted from www.freepressjournal.in/india/railways-opt-for-reverse-auction-bidding-to-save-rs-10000-crore-a-year/1233992)

Apply
Explain why an organisation may opt to use reverse auctions.

Remember
Online auctions can be standard or reverse.

E-tendering systems

E-tendering follows the same process as standard tendering, the only difference is that documentation and communication is conducted electronically.

Check
Remind yourself of the tender process by re-reading section 2.2.

The benefits of conducting e-tendering are described in table 2.24.

Benefit	Description
Process efficiencies	The information can be exchanged faster than standard tendering.
Consistency	All potential suppliers receive their documentation at the same time in exactly the same format.
Technological safeguarding	Computer systems can automatically reject bids if they are received after the deadline.
Free up time	The automation of processes means that procurement professionals have more time to concentrate on other issues.
Promotion of cross-functionality	By sharing data electronically, cross-functionality becomes easier.
Environmentally friendly	Less paper is used.
Screening of bids	Some computer systems can screen bids to remove any that do not conform to the criteria.
Storage	Bids can be stored electronically and can be easily accessible if they need to be reviewed or challenged.
Reduced risk	Suppliers can be assured that their bids will be received and issues such as delayed mail/couriers will not be a concern.
Assurance	Suppliers and buyers can receive automated delivery receipts to gain assurance that their ITT or bid has been received.
Auditing	Easier for auditors to evaluate processes due to all the information being in one central location.
Consistency of process	If one procurement professional leaves to work elsewhere, the processes used are stored to allow consistency for suppliers.
Transparency	Information sent out is the same for everyone, which promotes responsible and transparent procurement.

Table 2.24 Benefits of e-tendering

Electronic systems are common in procurement and automation is becoming more popular. There are many advantages of such technology, especially in cost avoidance and cost savings. However, within procurement, the relationship between suppliers and buyers is important and should not be forfeited in favour of the savings that technology can generate.

There should be a balance between the use of technology and interpersonal contact to ensure that suppliers feel valued and continue to offer the innovation and added value that procurement aims to achieve. For example, suppliers now accept that procurement professionals send RFQs, ITTs or purchase orders electronically. Some suppliers' and buyers' systems are even integrated to allow a streamlined process. Relationships, however, do not evolve and develop through a computer system. Technology aids processes and contributes to fewer errors, but a personalised business relationship remains integral to long-term and strategic relationships. It is important that procurement professionals and suppliers speak on the telephone and arrange face-to-face or video conference meetings. Through direct contact, suppliers may be more likely to share information, resolve difficulties and promote innovation.

> *Apply*
> Describe how using e-systems alone could be detrimental to a long-term supplier relationship.

Chapter Summary

This chapter has covered the following topics.

- Compiling suppliers' expenditure

- The use of indices and matrices that measure economic data

- Secondary data on markets and suppliers

- Financial reports including balance sheets, profit and loss statements and cash flow documents

- The role and results created by credit rating agencies

- Requests for information or quotations

- The operation and purpose of tendering

- Evaluation of offers

- Weighted points systems

- E-requisitioning, e-catalogues, e-tendering and e-purchase ordering systems

- E-auctions and reverse auctions

Recommended reading

Gordon, S. R. (2008), *Supplier Evaluation and Performance Excellence*, J. Ross Publishing

Mukherjee, K. (2017), *Supplier Selection*, Springer

Monckza, R. M., Handfield, R. B., Guinipero, L. M., and Patterson, J. L. (2009, 4th ed), *Purchasing and Supply Chain Management*, South-Western Cengage Learning, Mason, OH.

End of Chapter Assessment

DESCRIBE

1 Describe the purpose of a balance sheet, a profit and loss statement and a cash flow document.

DISCUSS

2 Discuss the benefits of using a reverse auction when trying to achieve the best price.

EXPLAIN

3 List and explain five elements that can be evaluated before making a decision on awarding a contract.

CHAPTER 3

Understand compliance issues when sourcing from suppliers

(Learning outcome)———• By the end of this chapter, you will understand the compliance issues that buyers may face when sourcing from within different sectors, and with suppliers on an international scale.

Chapter overview

3.1 **Compare the key legislative, regulatory and organisational requirements when sourcing in the not-for-profit, private and public sectors**
You will understand:
- The use of competitive tendering processes
- The impact of timescales on tendering processes
- Procedures for contract award
- Regulatory bodies that impact on the private sector
- Regulations that impact on product and safety standards

3.2 **Compare the key legislative, regulatory and organisational requirements when sourcing from international suppliers**
You will understand:
- Documentation relating to imports
- Import duties and tariffs
- Payment mechanisms
- The use of Incoterms®
- Customs control and clearance
- Currency regulations
- Applicable law

Introduction

An effective supply chain, where all items are expected to be delivered on time, in full, in the correct quantities, to the correct quality and at the right price, depends on a number of complex factors all successfully operating together. Poor sourcing decisions can lead to the selection of unsuitable suppliers, and this could cause complications receiving the desired end product. This might ultimately damage the procurement organisation's brand.

This chapter will outline the important considerations for sourcing within the not-for-profit, private and public sectors, and the various ways this activity is regulated. It will also discuss key requirements for sourcing from suppliers on an international scale and the mechanisms that enable this process to run as smoothly as possible.

3.1 Compare the key legislative, regulatory and organisational requirements when sourcing in the not-for-profit, private and public sectors

Competitive tendering within the public, private and not-for-profit sectors

In the past, it has been common for buyers or procurement professionals to directly choose companies that they wish to source from. With this approach, they do not request tenders from any other potential suppliers. They may have chosen to do this because they have a positive relationship or history with the supplier. Alternatively, the supplier may have been recommended to the buyer or could have been selected under more corrupt circumstances (for example, as a result of bribery or using a family member's company to supply goods or services).

It is important that procurement professionals take an approach that is fair and reasonable when working with current or potential suppliers. Always avoid discrimination, treat suppliers equally and respectfully and adopt a transparent approach to sourcing (in line with the **CIPS Code of Conduct**, 2018). This is especially important when it involves competitive tendering, where potential suppliers are invited to submit a bid for a package of work.

Though it is not mandatory to run competitive tenders in all sectors (described in detail later in this section), there a several strong reasons for carrying them out. However, under certain circumstances, running a competitive tender may be a disadvantage.

Table 3.1 outlines the advantages and disadvantages of competitive tendering.

Advantages	Disadvantages
Competition should be fair, so suppliers will be treated equally, receiving equal attention and opportunities to clarify queries.	Truly fair competition may prevent the quick selection of a preferred or current supplier, which could be restrictive when a procurement is required at short notice.

3.1 L03

Advantages	Disadvantages
Inviting suppliers to take part in a competitive tender may reduce the potential for the biased selection of a supplier. This means that the selected supplier may better meet the objective requirements of the tender.	Competition may drive the wrong behaviours in suppliers, encouraging them to make unachievably low bids to attract the buyer to select them. This results in additional costs later in the contract, or the supplier not being able to supply the goods (due to an unsustainably low profit margin).
It gives the stakeholders an opportunity to understand the capabilities of multiple suppliers.	It may take more time to carry out the validation and assessment of multiple tenders than it would for just one.
Time, money and resource could be saved by carrying out one competitive tender, rather than inviting suppliers to tender on separate occasions.	
Tendering encourages suppliers to be competitive to win the contract, which could result in a better deal for the buying organisation.	
There is a greater likelihood of finding a suitable supplier if several are invited to tender.	

Table 3.1 Advantages and disadvantages of competitive tendering

> *Remember*
> Always abide by the CIPS Code of Conduct when carrying out tenders, whether they are competitive or not.

Key regulations that affect the public, private and not-for-profit sectors

Regardless of whether an organisation is part of the public, private or not-for-profit sector, it is still subject to the laws of the country (or countries, in the case of larger, multi-national organisations) where it is based. Organisations that are found not to be abiding by the regulations within their domain may find that their reputation is damaged, as they have not demonstrated appropriate corporate social responsibility (CSR).

The following are some of the key areas of regulation that organisations must follow.

- Data protection
- Ethical practice
- Health, safety and environment and worker rights
- Marketplace competition
- Product safety standards

Data protection

Data protection regulations cover the movement, storage, ownership and distribution of personal data. This data can include names, addresses and other details that customers and companies may not want disclosed publicly, so companies must take adequate steps to protect this information. Organisations should also ensure that this data is deleted if there is no longer a reason for keeping it.

Ethical practice

Ethical practice includes regulations that govern and promote good practices and prohibit corrupt or unfair practices between organisations and their customers. Unethical practices could include bribery or corruption, as well as worse practices such as exploitation of slave labour and human trafficking (including the use of conflict materials). Though these practices do not fit the modern cultural ethos of many nations and organisations, they are still widely (and most often, illegally) carried out almost everywhere in the world. It is important that buyers watch out for these and ensure that their sourcing activities are not involved in any of them. Buyers must always ensure that the laws of their own nation are followed when working with suppliers in other nations (also following the host nation's where required).

Health, safety and environment and worker rights

Regulations that are designed to protect the health, safety and wellbeing of workers within organisations show a country's commitment to caring about its workforce. These regulations ensure that workers have the right to work without prejudice, suffer no injury in the process of carrying out their work and have a suitable balance of work and leisure time.

These regulations may vary greatly between nations, but buyers working on an international scale must understand any differences in attitudes towards worker rights and safety between their own country and the suppliers'. Any incidents relating to these could affect the timeliness of deliveries and may cause reputational damage.

Cartel
A group of organisations that work together to prevent competition, raise prices and gain control of a market

Marketplace competition

Marketplace competition regulations are designed to ensure fairness in business and trading, while promoting and facilitating competition within different markets to ensure that customers can find products at a good value. They prevent the deliberate limiting of supply, as well as the formation of **cartels**. Cartels work, through their independent actions, to fix the prices of commodities within their sector, and so prevent competitors from joining.

Product safety standards

Product safety standards are regulations that set minimum levels of safety or quality that a product should conform to before it can be sold within a country or region. This may vary between intended uses of product, and a good example of this is the metal lead. Lead used to be a key ingredient in many common paints, but was later discovered to be harmful to health, resulting in the reduction of its use in paints through regulation. However, the use in manufacturing for other purposes is still permitted and common (for example, in car batteries and weights).

In all industries, product safety is vital and in the UK, the UK Consumer Rights Act 2015 specifies that products must be 'fit for purpose' in order to protect the health

3.1 L03

of the user. In the past, the consumer was not always protected from potentially harmful products that were released on the market (though at times, this may be because the harm posed by the product was not known, such as lead paint and asbestos). If an end user is harmed by a product while using it in the way in which it was intended, this could result in the manufacturer being held liable, which in turn could lead to legal action and potential reputational damage. To avoid such situations, manufacturers are required to follow a number of strict product standards before certain products can be sold within the EU (European Union) and EEA (European Economic Area).

To give confidence to their customers, manufacturers may mark a product with a marking of 'CE' (meaning 'Conformité Européene' in French, or 'European Conformity' in English). This marking shows that the product meets the requirements of relevant European directives, is safe, fit for use and suitable for sale within the EU and EEA. At least 21 categories of product must be marked with a 'CE' mark before they can be sold within the EU and EEA, including toys, pressure equipment and medical devices.

In the UK, the **British Standards Institution (the BSI Group)** produces the technical standards that products must conform to. Historically, this body certified products with a 'kitemark', which, when marked on a product, signified that it complied with a particular standard of product quality or safety. This is now a world-recognised marking, and while it is not a requirement of other nations, it is recognised and valued by buyers worldwide, particularly for safety equipment, where poor quality equipment could lead to death.

British Standards Institution (BSI Group)
An institution that produces the technical standards that products must conform to in the UK

Apply
Go online and research the BSI Kitemark™ for products. Explain three benefits for consumers who encounter this mark on a particular product.

Case study

The BSI kitemark
Electronics manufacturer Ei Electronics is based in Ireland. It provides fire alarms to companies worldwide. As the company produces safety equipment, it is important for it to demonstrate the quality and reliability of its products. To achieve this, Ei Electronics has closely followed BSI standards, and is now approved to use the BSI kitemark on its products. The company believes that the kitemark, together with other BSI certifications, offers the following benefits.

- Allows Ei Electronics to demonstrate the quality and reliability of its products to customers.

- Shows that high standards of environmental management, health and safety management and quality control are present. This highlights the organisation's commitment to working with recognised best practice.

- Allows the company to have a competitive advantage over organisations manufacturing similar products.

(Source: adapted from Information from Multiple BSI certifications, The British Standards Institute, page.bsigroup.com/l/73472/2018-03-19/ bb49gw/73472/160006/Ei_Electronics_Case_study_web.pdf?_ ga=2.212136660.1936399120.1537734084-1651559481.1532972012)

Table 3.2 gives examples of some key pieces of legislation in the categories covered so far. Procurement professionals must be familiar with the basic intent of these legislations, especially if they cover their home country or a country that their suppliers operate in.

Regulation subject	Legislation name	Country/region
Data protection	Data Protection Act 2018	UK
	General Data Protection Regulation 2018	EU
Ethical practice	Bribery Act 2010	UK
	Unfair Contract Terms Act 1977	UK
	The Modern Slavery Act 2015	UK
Health, safety and environment and worker rights	Enterprise Act 2016	UK
	The Equality Act 2010	UK
	The Working Time Regulations 1998	UK
	Health and Safety at Work Act 1974	UK
	Environmental Protection Act 1990	UK
	Environment Act 2000	UK
	Environmental Damage (Prevention and Remediation) Regulations 2009	UK
Marketplace competition	Treaty of Rome (Section 7)	EU
	Competition Act 1998	UK
	Competition Act, No 89 of 1998	South Africa
	Competition and Consumer Act 2010	Australia
	The Sherman Antitrust Act	USA
	The Clayton Act	USA
	The Federal Trade Commission Act	USA
	Enterprise Act 2002	UK
Product standards	Consumer Rights Act 2015	UK
	The General Product Safety Regulations 2005	UK
	The General Product Safety Directive 2001/95/EC	EU
	Consumer Product Safety Act 2011	USA

Table 3.2 Key regulations that affect the public, private and not-for-profit sectors

3.1 L03

> *Remember*
> Similar regulations exist in many other countries and it is important that procurement professionals are familiar with those that apply to any sourcing they carry out.

> *Check*
> Give examples of legislation in the following areas.
>
> - Data protection
> - Ethical practice
> - Health, safety, environment and worker rights
> - Marketplace competition
> - Product standards

Public sector sourcing

Organisations within the public sector are generally owned by the government of the country in which they are based. They tend to provide a service and may include schools, local government authorities and health services, for example, the National Health Service in the UK. These organisations are all funded by the government, using money generated through taxation.

Key aims and challenges

As organisations within this sector depend on government funding to carry out their service, they operate on tight budgets and are under pressure to achieve best value for money. This means that whenever they carry out any procurement activities and whatever they buy, they must always look for a deal that is the best possible value for money while still looking to provide a service at a pre-agreed quality or service-level.

Purchases made in this sector may be audited by government to ensure that they have been carried out in line with regulations. Public sector purchases might also be subject to public scrutiny and so the application of equal treatment, fair competition and transparency are key. Procurement professionals must maintain a good audit trail to show the procedures they followed. Purchases or spending that is seen to be wasteful may be subject to criticism from the press and meet with public disapproval, which may have political implications for the party in power. Competitive tendering undertaken as part of this procurement should be ethical and transparent, with equal preference given to all.

≪ Case study

Unfair advantages
A report by the Auditor General on public procurements in Singapore highlighted that a number of companies have received unfair advantages when submitting bids for public sector procurement activities. These undermine the public sector principles of ethical and transparent competition. They include the following.

- The approved submission of a revised bid by one tenderer, but not others (despite fair treatment being a requirement of local law).

- The highest bidder in a competition being allowed to re-submit a revised bid, which then became the lowest, winning that bidder the contract.

- An organisation awarding a contract to a company that was operated by several members of staff also based at the awarding organisation.

(Source: adapted from The Straits Times (18 July 2013) Auditor General flags procurement lapses [online]. Retrieved from: www.straitstimes.com/singapore/auditor-general-flags-procurement-lapses [Accessed on: 05 February 2019]

Key regulations that apply to public sector sourcing

UK law affecting public sector sourcing

Public sector organisations are bound by the laws of the nation they operate within. These organisations must follow a number of the same laws and regulations that apply to businesses in the private sector, some of which were shown in table 3.2. Due to their nature, public sector organisations are also subject to the following additional regulations in the UK (many other nations also have additional regulations).

- The Freedom of Information Act 2000: this allows members of the public the right to request access to information held by a public sector organisation. These organisations must respond to the request within 21 days, but may choose not to release the information if it is determined not to be in the public interest, following application of the logic of the **public interest test**.

- UK Public Contract Regulations 2015: these regulations govern how public sector organisations should carry out procurement. They implement the EU 2014 Public Procurement Directives, which apply to all nations based within the EU and the EEA.

Public sector tendering within the EU and the EEA

Within the EU and the EEA, public sector procurement and sourcing is governed by the European Parliament through the 2014 Public Procurement Directives. Under *Directive 2014/24/EU*, public sector contracts above a certain value must be open to competition for tendering (there are some exemptions). For tenders that fall below any of the qualifying values specified by the EU, the same defined principles of fairness, proportionality and transparency should be followed, with competitive tenders carried out where appropriate. Under this directive, EU member states must have a procedure at the national level to define how this should be carried out. This is to ensure that the requirement for competition is enshrined across the EU's member states.

In England and Wales, the requirements of EU *Directive 2014/24/EU* have been implemented in The Public Contracts Regulations 2015.

One of the key requirements of the directive is that buyers must start their competition by advertising it as a **call for competition** in the *Official Journal of the European Union* (OJEU). This notice gives information about the process the competition will follow and outlines the buying authority's requirements, allowing suppliers to participate.

If the buyer is not ready to issue a call for competition, but would like to inform suppliers that there will be one in the future, the buyer may instead publish a

The public interest test
The test used by public sector organisations to determine whether or not information should be released to the public when it is requested. Information will not be released if it is not seen to be in the public interest

Call for competition
A notice released by a buying organisation through the Official Journal of the European Union (OJEU) to make potential suppliers aware that they may participate in a sourcing competition, in line with the organisation's requirements

prior information notice (PIN) in the OJEU. This notice allows buyers to share information about a future procurement activity, giving potential suppliers the opportunity to prepare for or forecast their involvement before the competition starts.

The UK Public Contract Regulations 2015 contain rules for the following key requirements for public sector sourcing.

- A number of procedures that specify the format of the tender, including how it is advertised, who is eligible to attend and the information provided by suppliers before joining the tender.

- A process that outlines the stages the buyer must follow when carrying out a tender, from as early as specifying requirements up until the award of a contract to the successful bidder.

- Timescales that allow tenderers a suitable amount of time to compile and submit a tender and showcase their capabilities.

- Contract award criteria that outline what the buyer should consider when appraising the viability of submitted tenders, ultimately helping it to choose the most suitable one.

Prior information notice
A notice released by a buying organisation through the OJEU to make potential suppliers aware of a sourcing competition that it intends to run in the future

Procedures available for public sector tendering under the EU 2014 Public Procurement Directives

As tenders must suit the specific needs of the buying organisation, a number of different options have cascaded down from the EU 2014 Public Procurement Directives and been implemented in the UK Public Contract Regulations 2015. These procedures range from tender processes open to all interested suppliers, to focusing on just one or a small number of specific partners by invitation only. This spectrum exists to cater for very different needs but all procedures are regulated to ensure consistency within public sector spending. These procedures are outlined in table 3.3.

Procedure	Description
Open procedure	Used for well-specified requirements with no pre-qualification of bidders. As it is open to all, many suppliers could potentially submit a bid and take part in the competition so it is important that the buyer is aware of this, as they may have a lot of bids to assess.
Restricted procedure	Used where the interest from the supply market is likely to be high. In this procedure, the buyer may want to assess the technical capability of the suppliers and carry out financial assessments. This allows the buyer to choose which of the suppliers that responded to the call for competition it would like to take part in the competition. The specification of requirements should already be so clearly defined that follow-on negotiations will not be required (and indeed, they are not permitted).
Competitive procedure with negotiation	Suppliers that respond to the call for competition are invited to join by invitation only. This procedure is used by the buyer to let potential bidders know that there may be negotiations following submissions of their bids. This supports getting the best possible outcome for the buyer.

Procedure	Description
Competitive dialogue	While otherwise the same as a restricted tender, this procedure allows the buyer to speak with the suppliers after selection but before evaluating bids. An outline solution is provided to bidders and the buyer's requirements are discussed during the dialogue phase. When the buyer has more clarity about how their requirements can be met a final specification is issued and final bids submitted (and evaluated).
Innovation partnership	In some situations, buyers may be looking for a supplier to provide a product that the organisation does not itself have the capability to produce and also that does not exist on the market. Where suppliers have the expertise and capability, the buying organisation may choose to form a partnership to take an idea through development and into production jointly, supported by the procurement process. Where required, this partnership may be established with more than one supplier.

Table 3.3 Procedures for tendering as set out in the EU 2014 Public Procurement Directives

Remember
Buyers should choose the appropriate process before inviting suppliers to tender and continue to follow this throughout, in line with the law.

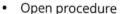

Check
Describe the benefits of using each of the following procedures from the EU 2014 Public Procurement Directives.

- Open procedure
- Restricted procedure
- Competitive procedure with negotiation
- Competitive dialogue
- Innovation partnership

Stages in the procurement process under the UK Public Contract Regulations 2015

The UK Public Contract Regulations 2015 outline key stages within the procurement process that must be followed in public sector procurement activities. These stages specify the requirements that the buyer should review at each point, and are summarised in figure 3.1. The specification stage is particularly important because any requirements listed here must be present and correct, as these will form the response submitted by the supplier at the selection stage. If a supplier is awarded a contract from a tender based on poorly defined requirements, there may be problems in the provision of the goods or services that it is contracted to provide.

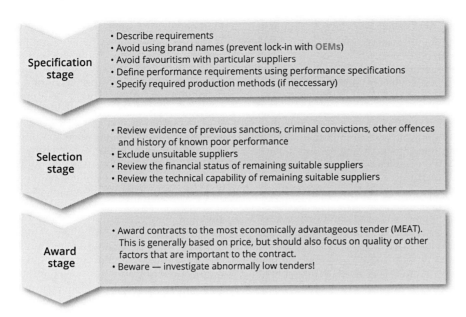

3.1 L03

Original equipment manufacturer (OEM)
The producer of own-branded parts or equipment which are sold to other manufacturers for production and retail

Figure 3.1 Stages of the UK Public Contract Regulations 2015 (Source: adapted from Crown Commercial Service, A brief guide to the 2014 EU Public Procurement Directives, October 2016)

Remember
Avoid including brand names in the specification as this may limit the sources of supply, reducing the number of suppliers that can supply the product and drive up their prices, making the competition less effective!

The impact of timescales on tendering processes in public sector procurement

When sourcing, the purchasing organisation will be planning its procurement activities in line with its schedule (production, sales, etc.). Naturally, this schedule will be built around specific deadlines that need to be met. Private and not-for-profit sector organisations are able to define their own sourcing processes, meaning it may be possible to carry out tendering activities that meet the deadlines, in order to save money and meet schedule demands.

In the public sector however, there are often a number of rules that define what timescales are appropriate when tendering, and these can vary from country to country. The UK Public Contract Regulations 2015 specify the minimum time periods within which the buyer must accept tender submissions. These are linked to the procedures for public sector procurement that have been discussed earlier in this section.

These timescales exist to allow all tenderers a fair and reasonable amount of time to prepare and submit their bids. Buyers must plan their tenders around these timescales to be compliant under EU and UK law. Buyers are able to reduce timescales if tenders are being received by electronic submission exclusively (in the interest of fairness to all tenderers), or if a prior information notice is released with the advertisement in the OJEU.

The timescales in the UK Public Contract Regulations 2015 are outlined in table 3.4.

Procedure	Submission activity	Minimum number of days per procedure		
		Time for standard tender submission	Time for electronic tender submission	Time if PIN is published
Open procedure	Receipt of tenders	35	30	15
Restricted procedure	Requests to participate	30	30	30
	Receipt of tenders	30	25	10
Competitive procedure with negotiation	Requests to participate	30	30	30
	Receipt of initial tenders	30	25	10
Competitive dialogue	Requests to participate	30	30	30
	Receipt of initial tenders and further tenders	No timescale specified	No timescale specified	No timescale specified
Innovation partnerships	Requests to participate	30	30	30
	Receipt of initial tenders	30	25	10

Table 3.4 Timescales in the UK Public Contract Regulations 2015 (Source: adapted from Crown Commercial Service, A brief guide to the 2014 EU Public Procurement Directives, October 2016)

Remember
Timescales are not suggestions in public sector sourcing. Organisations must be able to demonstrate that they have kept to them.

Contract awarding in public sector procurement

In public sector procurement, the buyer should try to get the best possible deal when making purchases. This is essential, and the buyer will be expected to prove that the decisions made are good value for money and are an appropriate use of public funding.

The processes outlined in the EU 2014 Public Procurement Directives are designed to support the buyer in choosing the most economically advantageous tender. However, buyers should be cautious when making their final selection, as the Directives state that abnormally low tenders should be investigated or discarded. This may be because the product or service on offer is of a poor quality, potentially requiring costly re-work, re-sourcing and reputational damage to the purchasing organisation.

Buyers must also discard the submissions of tenderers that have been found to be in breach of international social or environmental laws, as these do not fit the principles of trading within the EU and EEA.

> *Remember*
> Though price is a key driver in public sector procurement, the quality of purchased goods or services and the ethical practices followed (or not) in its production are also important. Failures or poor standards of quality or ethical practices may cause financial or reputational risk to the buying organisation.

> *Apply*
> Compare the stages of the public sector sourcing process outlined above with the sourcing processes of an organisation with which you are familiar.
>
> • Do the processes differ and if so, how?
> • Are there opportunities to improve the organisation's processes based on these provisions?
> • When considering a public sector organisation, are you confident that it properly follows this process?

Private sector sourcing

Key aims and challenges

In the private sector, organisations sit within any of the economic sectors shown in figure 3.2.

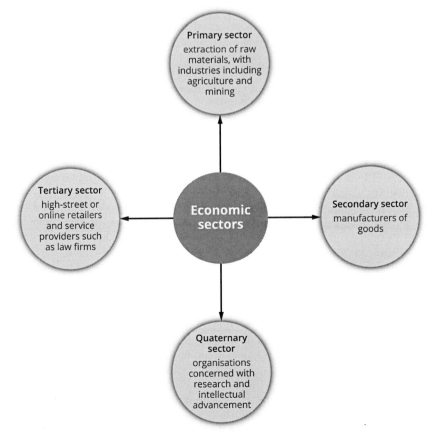

Figure 3.2 The four main economic sectors

The main purpose of private sector organisations is to make a profit from the product or service they sell. This profit enables them to grow and potentially make more profit, if this is the company's intention.

In order to achieve this, a buyer must get the lowest possible prices from its suppliers whilst still preserving quality, which can be a point of differentiation for them in the market. This will allow it either to undercut its own competition by selling its product or service at a lower price, or to increase its own profit margin if it already has a competitive position. In many cases, private sector organisations are in a competitive position with other organisations, so their efforts must focus on attracting customers.

Private sector organisations generally make their money from customers who buy their product or service. Investors may choose to fund a company by supplying it with capital to help it to grow (in the case of public limited companies, the investors may be shareholders). Investors take these funding risks in the hope that they will receive a favourable return on their investment. Investors generally favour organisations that are aiming to grow, as these are most likely to be profitable to them in the longer term.

Organisations within this sector thrive in environments where customers value their product. This means that reputational damage or negative media could lead to a loss of custom and, potentially, shareholders and other investors rapidly withdrawing their funding if they believe the company is at risk of losing money. A private sector organisation must ensure that it keeps its customers and stakeholders satisfied to enable continued funding to allow the organisation to grow and further increase its profit.

Unlike public sector organisations, those in the private sector are not bound by the same strict sourcing process outlined in the UK Public Contract Regulations 2015. However, they can still use this process if it benefits them, or they can use the best practice processes and advice of other organisations or the Chartered Institute of Procurement & Supply. Private sector organisations can be more flexible in their approach to tendering, giving them the opportunity to prioritise other needs within the five rights of procurement.

- The quality of a product
- The timescale the product can be delivered in
- The supplier's ability to deliver to the required location

If a buyer (or other stakeholder) determines that any of these factors are the most important during a purchase, it may be that the price offered by the supplier is only a secondary consideration. This could mean that if a competitive tender is run, the cheapest submitted tender may be rejected in favour of another that better meets the buying organisation's other requirements. This is especially important in situations where an organisation's reputation rests on the quality of its product, meaning it does not want the product to fail during use and be returned. In cases such as these, sourcing from a more expensive supplier may be more effective for long–term purchases, if it keeps customers satisfied.

Private sector organisations may also choose not to carry out a competitive tender (which may be as a result of the disadvantages of competitive tendering, outlined earlier in the chapter). Instead they may issue a contract to a supplier that is chosen outright, if this meets their business need. Whether tendering is competitive or not, the procurement professional should follow the processes specified by their organisation throughout the sourcing process.

Private sector organisations are still bound by the laws and regulations of the nation they operate in. A number of these regulations that apply to all businesses are listed in table 3.2.

3.1 L03

> *Apply*
> Critically discuss the advantages and disadvantages for a private sector company of using competitive sourcing. Write your ideas down.

Not-for-profit sector sourcing

Key aims and challenges

As the name suggests, organisations based in the not-for-profit sector are not looking to make a profit from their activities, but are instead looking to support causes that people consider to be important, based on their social and ethical values. This sector is mostly made up of **non-governmental organisations (NGOs)**, which may do any of the following.

- Fund caregiving activities and provide other support for people in need. Examples include the Red Cross (Switzerland), Oxfam (UK), Childhood Cancer Foundation South Africa, Foundation for International Development (Japan) and Marie Curie (UK).

- Highlight topical issues or causes and actively campaign to correct them, for example, human rights violations, flaws in government policy and environmental issues. These groups also often act as 'pressure' groups and push for action to be taken by authoritative bodies, such as governments. Examples include Society for Threatened Peoples International (Germany), Amnesty International, Greenpeace (Netherlands), Green Action Japan and World Wildlife Fund (WWF) (Switzerland)

- Represent or provide a service to subscribing members as a professional body or union. Examples include the Chartered Institute of Procurement & Supply, and the UK trade union, Unite.

Non-governmental organisation (NGO)
A nonprofit organisation that operates independently of any government

> *Check*
> What three types of activities do NGOs in the not-for-profit sector undertake? Give examples of organisations that carry out these activities.

In this sector, organisations are funded almost entirely by donations from fundraising activities (such as events, advertising, etc.,) by people who support these causes and wish to see them prosper.

Although these organisations may save money by being mainly operated by volunteers, the key challenge with running an organisation based on donations alone is that cash flow can fluctuate and may be difficult to predict. This means that during a procurement, buyers must make every effort to save money so that it can be most effectively put towards furthering the organisation's cause and provide for those it supports.

If a charity or NGO is perceived to be acting in a manner that does not align with the beliefs of its donors or its own objectives, this could cause long-term reputational damage. There may be a reduction in donations, which would constrain the organisation's ability to operate or cause it to stop completely. Strong leadership, consistent values and a clear goal are essential to ensuring that a not-for-profit organisation survives and thrives.

Perpetuating poverty

In 2005, the well-known charity Oxfam took part in the 'Make Poverty History' campaign with a view to fundraising by selling accessory arm bands. It was later revealed that these arm bands were being produced using 'slave labour' in 'sweatshops' in China. As this went against the organisation's aim of promoting 'fair and ethical trade', it attracted a lot of negative media attention, affecting many people's perception of the charity.

(Source: information from David Harrison, 'Ethical wristbands made using "slave labour", The Telegraph, 29 May 2005)

Case study

Problems such as the one in the case study can be prevented by the buyer carrying out proper due diligence during the tendering process, and by reporting any ethical concerns that it may have to a suitable authority.

As with organisations in the private sector, not-for-profit organisations have a lot of flexibility in how they source. This includes whether or not they choose to run a competitive tender or to source directly from a preferred supplier. Again, this decision will depend on which option suits the needs of the organisation and, ultimately, what best supports its aim of not wasting donation money while providing an efficient, effective campaign or service, using a team of (mostly) volunteers.

In larger not-for-profit organisations, there may be a dedicated team of procurement professionals, who are skilled in making this crucial sourcing decision. However, in smaller (often local) organisations, procurement specialists may not be available and so spending is carried out by people without procurement knowledge. This is not to say that they will not be effective (particularly if procurements are low value or for off-the-shelf commodities), but it is possible that money may be wasted through lack of knowledge of how to make a more effective purchase.

Remember

Keeping stakeholders satisfied by meeting their needs is important, regardless of which sector an organisation belongs to.

Though not-for-profit organisations do not have to follow the same strict sourcing process as those in the public sector (within the EU and EEA), they are still bound by the laws and regulations of the nation they operate in. Some of the regulations that apply to all businesses are listed in table 3.2. Whether tendering is competitive or not, the buyer should follow the processes specified by its organisation throughout the sourcing process.

Due to the nature of their work, not-for-profit organisations are also subject to additional regulations in various countries. Some of the applicable regulatory bodies are outlined in table 3.5.

3.1 L03

Regulatory body	Responsible for
Australian Charities and Not-for-profits Commission	Regulating the voluntary sector, including charities and other not-for-profit organisations in Australia.
Charity Commission for England and Wales	Registering and supporting the proper operation of charities within England and Wales.
International Revenue Service (USA)	The regulation of charities in the USA (among other responsibilities) under section 501(c)(3) of the Internal Revenue Code, which specifies the exemptions that allow charities and nonprofits to operate as such.

Table 3.5 Examples of different regulatory bodies for not-for-profit organisations

Apply

It is important to clearly understand the differences between public, private and not-for-profit sector sourcing.

Copy the table below and fill in answers to the questions for each of the sectors.

	Public sector	Private sector	Not-for-profit sector
Describe the character of organisations within this sector.			
Name two types of organisation that sit within this sector.			
What is their aim?			
Who must they satisfy?			
Who regulates them?			
What key regulations must they follow?			
How much freedom do they have over how they carry out sourcing?			
What challenges do they face?			

Trade bloc
An economic group, formed by different countries in a geographical zone, to create preferential trade conditions

Tariff
Rules regulating the type of goods, their volume (determined by quota) and their import duty when imported from specific countries. Tariffs may have a unique code, making them easy to identify and reference

Import duty
A payment made to allow the entry of goods into the destination country. The payment is made to the local customs agency of the receiving country

3.2 Compare the key legislative, regulatory and organisational requirements when sourcing from international suppliers

International trade has taken place for centuries. Over time, the risks that once slowed down cross-boundary business have been reduced, through the formation of international regulators, the development of globally used standards to support supply chains, improvements in transport and improvements in communications technology.

Trade blocs

As well as trade between nations, trading blocs or preferential trade areas are also common. **Trade blocs** are formed by a number of nation states, with the countries they represent receiving benefits for internal trading, including lesser restrictions on **tariffs** and duties such as **import duties**. These may take the following forms.

- Common market: a trade bloc where the member nations may choose to waive tariffs or duties for imports and exports between themselves, for example, CARICOM (Caribbean Community) or ASEAN (Association of Southeast Asian Nations).

- Free trade areas: a trade bloc where the member nations waive tariffs or duties for imports and exports between themselves, for example, the EU Customs Union (Europe).

Case study

ASEAN 'One Vision, One Identity, One Community'
The Association of Southeast Asian Nations (ASEAN) is a trade bloc. It was established in 1967 under the ASEAN Declaration in order to promote economic, social and cultural growth in its five (now ten) member states, in addition to maintaining peaceful relations within the region.

The organisation is committed to improving understanding of the problems that affect international trade and encourages collaboration between organisations and industries with a mutual need or compatible goal. This drive to forge a peaceful, international community is embedded in the group's charter and clearly outlines what is required of the organisations operating within member states.

(Source: adapted from Association of Southeast Asian Nations web page, About ASEAN)

The advantages and disadvantages of international trade are summarised in table 3.6.

3.2 L03

Advantages	Disadvantages
Prosperity from international trade may help nations form more collaborative and peaceful relationships.	Pressure on companies or markets in nations where a practice or product is accepted as a cultural norm, but is considered to be undesirable or incompatible by other cultures (horsemeat has been a very topical product for a number of years).
Some nations may form trade connections that grant them relief from import duties.	Companies may move their supply base to another country at short notice, abandoning factories and leaving full workforces unemployed.
A country that welcomes international trade opens its economy and market to stimulation, as a result of sales from exports and capital generated from duties imposed on imported goods.	Suppliers in emerging nations may not be able to invest the capital required to improve their manufacturing culture, making it difficult to be considered by buyers in established markets elsewhere in the world.
Consumers have greater access to products produced in other nations, giving them the opportunity to purchase cheaper alternatives, which could drive competition between retailers and manufacturers.	Poor political relations between governments may result in disruptions or barriers to trade.
Suppliers have greater access to customers who may have varying tastes (requiring a wider range of products to be produced) and more disposable income.	Changes in currency values can affect the amount the buyer pays for goods, costing it more (or potentially costing it less in more favourable circumstances).
Companies based in emerging economies (formerly known as 'developing countries') have an opportunity to adopt the high standards of successful companies from foreign nations, enabling them to better compete for contracts with complex technical specifications that demand higher standards of quality.	Differences in ethical standards that the buyer may not be able to accept in its supply chain, for example, the supplier may use slave labour or have workers work in unsafe conditions with insufficient protection, etc.
	Suppliers may operate from countries that have high levels of corruption (as ranked by the Transparency International *Corruption Perceptions Index 2017*), exposing the buyer to potentially unethical practices such as bribery and money laundering.

Table 3.6 Advantages and disadvantages of international trade

> **Remember**
> International trade can involve higher risk than domestic trade, but a good understanding of laws, cultural practices and trade documentation can help prepare for this.

The regulation of international trade

As international trade takes place across many different countries, each with different cultures and working practices, it was decided that a regulatory body was required to support cohesive trade. Since its formation in 1995, the World Trade Organization (WTO) has regulated the international trade of goods, services and intellectual property between member countries. It provides a forum for negotiating trade agreements and, importantly, mediates disputes between members, supporting them in resolving their grievances. This is outlined in the Dispute Settlement Understanding (DSU), which includes rules about the following.

- Procedures of review panels and their function: ensuring that a structured and consistent approach is taken to reviewing disputes.

- Conciliation and mediation: intervening in a dispute to reduce frustration between parties and work to find a resolution. This is non-judicial, but is also not legally binding, meaning that neither party is required to accept any decisions made by the mediator.

- Appellate reviews: reviewing appeals made against any decisions made.

- Time frames for decision-making: ensuring that the approach is consistent and time bound.

- Arbitration: a non-judicial method of resolving disputes, where a third-party adjudicator reviews the dispute and issues a legally binding decision, with which both parties must abide.[1]

The role of customs organisations

Quota
A quantity of something. In international trade, the quantity of a commodity being imported or exported

Over time, border controls between nations have become stricter to ensure that only approved goods are imported. While tariffs may limit the amount of a commodity that can be imported through quotas, there is still the potential for prohibited items to enter a country illegally. The local customs control agency will stop these items entering, preventing the product from reaching the end user, potentially preventing harm, as well as damage to the buyer or supplier's reputation.

Another key function of customs control agencies is ensuring that the quotas given in tariffs are not exceeded. They also make sure that all goods are properly accounted for when entering a country, along with checking that they arrive with all the correct documentation.

Each country has its own customs control agency. In the USA, the US Customs and Border Protection organisation is responsible for collecting payments owed through tariffs and submitting them to the Commerce Department. Equivalent organisations in other nations include the Central Board of Indirect Taxes and Customs in India, Korea Customs Service in South Korea and HM Revenue & Customs in the UK.

Remember
If a customs controller decides that imported or exported goods do not satisfy local tariff, duty or legal requirements, they will not let the goods be delivered to their destination.

Documentation relating to imports

As importing goods can be complicated, it is important that the process is closely managed with suitable documentation. These documents should cover all aspects of delivery and should enable the goods to easily pass from their point of origin to their destination. Documentation requirements will vary between countries so both the buyer and supplier should have a good understanding of the export and import requirements of any local or international laws that may apply. This includes staying up to date with these requirements as outdated documents will not be accepted at custom control points and could cause goods to be rejected or seized (with the purchasing organisation potentially bearing the cost for the release of the goods).

Origin
The economic nationality of goods in international trade (European Commission definition)

Documents and systems that allow the movement of goods within the EU

The European Single Market uses systems and documentation to enable free and traceable movement of goods within its borders. Some of the key systems and documents are outlined below.

- **T1 Document**: a document that must accompany goods while in transit through the EU until they reach their final destination (enabling traceability). While travelling under this document, the goods are not subject to duty charges, but will be when they reach their final destination (if duties exist).

- **Import/Export Licence**: this may be required to permit the import or export of a particular product.

- **Single Administrative Document**: this document is not required for goods arriving from within the EU, or those being transported outside of the EU. It is used instead to control the traceability of goods entering the EU or leaving it. It is predominantly used in the event of computer system failures where manual processing is required.

- **New Computerised Transit System**: this system is used to electronically track the movement of goods that are being transported within the EU. Users can electronically submit Union Transit (UT) and Transports Internationaux Routiers (TIR) declarations instead of paper declarations to facilitate easy movement of goods in transit. The procedure for TIR applies where goods are delivered to, transported from or pass through EU member states. This system allows greater traceability of movement.

- **Customs Declaration Service**: the UK system previously known as Customs Handling of Import and Export Freight (CHIEF). This versatile system allows users to submit electronic import and export requests. This is especially useful as it maintains an audit trail of previous requests and calculates tariff and duty requirements on a user's behalf.[2]

The origin of goods relating to imports within the EU and EEA

The European Single Market applies to all EU member states and facilitates the free internal movement of goods and people within its borders. It aims to better enable trade and foster good relations between nations.

Binding Origin Information (BOI)
A legally binding decision on the origin of goods provided by an EU member state

As discussed earlier, ensuring traceability is an essential part of importing and exporting goods, and where this cannot be demonstrated, it may cause supply to be disrupted. If the origin of goods is uncertain and the buyer wants legal certainty, it may apply for a **Binding Origin Information (BOI)** decision, provided by an EU member state. This decision is delivered in writing and can be used for goods of both preferential and non-preferential origin (see below). To arrange this, either the buyer or supplier may apply to the relevant authority within their home country in the EU, or to the relevant authority in the EU country where the item is being delivered. However, even where a BOI is in place, the supplier is still expected to provide some proof of origin for the goods.

Within the EU and EEA, two key types of 'origin' are used to describe goods transported into or through these areas.

- Non-preferential origin: goods that are subject to tariff quotas and other customs commercial regulations.

- Preferential origin: goods that are traded between countries that allow their entry with no duty charges or limitations applied through tariffs.

> *Remember*
> Language barriers may be a problem – ensure paperwork is in a common language and that it can all be understood by customs officials at points of exit and entry to prevent delays.

Documents that facilitate international imports and exports

Th documents required to facilitate the flow of international imports and exports are shown in figure 3.3.

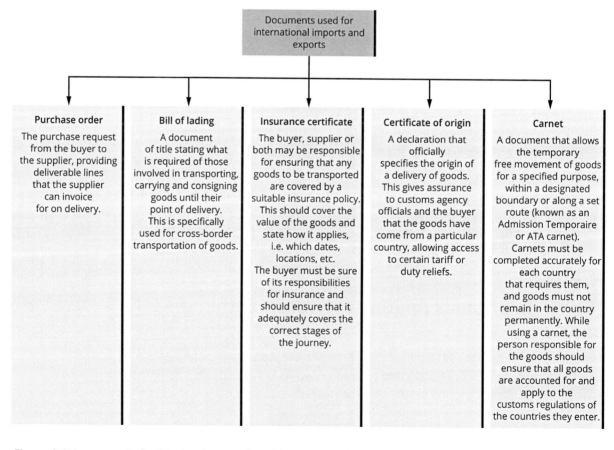

Figure 3.3 Documents facilitating international imports and exports

An example of a situation where a carnet may be required could be for the movement of instruments and sound equipment used by a band on an international tour, which must arrive at every destination on the tour, uninterrupted.

For vehicles, a *Carnet de Passage en Douanes* may be required to allow their temporary import and movement within certain countries such as Japan, India and Singapore. However, free movement is permitted in the majority of EU countries and the import of vehicles is not subject to import duties that may apply to other goods.

Though all of the documents in figure 3.3 are important, perhaps the most crucial document for a successful export and import is a clear written contract between the buyer and supplier. This should fully define the requirements of the product delivery, including any provisions to satisfy import requirements. Details of any Incoterms® that are in effect should be included here, covering a number of important details about insurance and risk (see in section 3.2).

It is important that buyers are aware of any documents the supplier needs to complete in order to export the goods, as these may require input from the buyer.

Whether a delivery is proceeding as planned or is facing problems, it is important that the buyer makes every effort to maintain good communication with the supplier. This is essential in preventing issues, or mitigating any that arise between the purchase order being placed and the final receipt of goods. Poor communication may lead to incorrect documentation, loss of control (from a scheduling perspective) and damage to the relationship between the supplier and buyer.

> *Check*
> Describe the purpose of each of the following documents in international trade.
>
> - Purchase order
> - Bill of lading
> - Insurance cover
> - Certificate of origin
> - Carnet

Import duties and tariffs

Sometimes, goods entering the destination country may be subject to import duties and tariffs. It is important that, before contracts are awarded, both buyers and suppliers have a good understanding of import duties and tariffs that may apply to purchases. This will guard against potential unexpected price increases or delays in delivery. When these requirements are known, it is important to factor them into pricing.

Import duty is a tax charge that may be applied where items are imported into a country from outside its borders. Import duty must be paid before goods will be permitted to enter the country and proceed to the final destination. Duty charges can be found in tariffs, which are rules set by a country that determine the quantities of goods that can be imported into that country's borders. Tariffs apply to the import of specific commodities from named countries.

Tariffs and duty charges are enforced by customs control agencies in each country, and they may limit categories or quantities of goods for a number of reasons, as shown in figure 3.4.

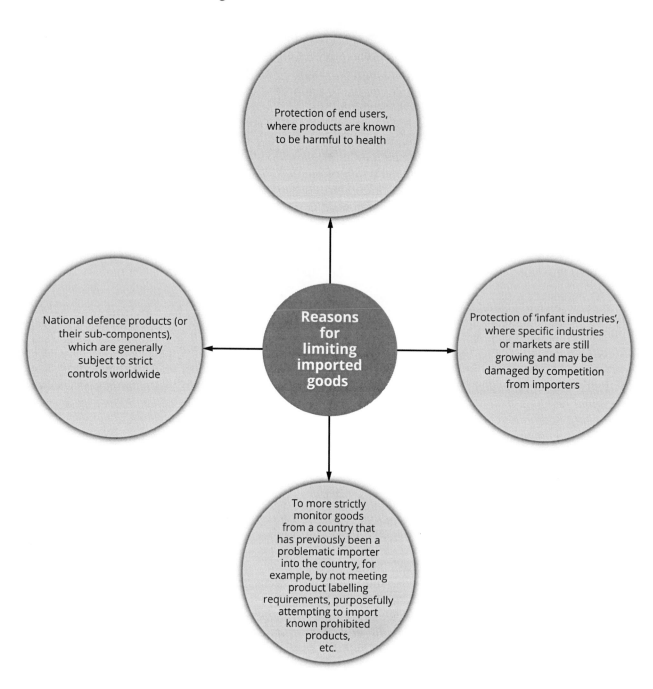

Figure 3.4 Reasons for limiting categories or quantities of goods imported into a country

Free movement of goods within the EU

For the benefit of its member states, the EU promotes the free movement of goods that originate within the European Single Market, which was established following the completion of the Single European Act (1986). The requirements from this originate in the Treaty on the Functioning of the European Union (Article 30), and these are cascaded down to each of the EU's member states. Each member state is required to ensure that its legislation and customs procedures support the requirements of this treaty to best enable the free movement of goods.

Legislation affecting the importing of goods into the UK

3.2 L03

In the UK, the requirements of Article 30 of the Treaty on the Functioning of the European Union are supported by the Integrated Tariff of the United Kingdom. This tariff sets out import duties and measures that affect imports and is made up of three volumes.

- Volume 1: duty relief schemes, details of key contacts and guidance on topics such as tariff quotas and excise duty.

- Volume 2: duty rates schedule and trade commodity codes.

- Volume 3: customs freight procedures guidance.

These volumes define how importing should be carried out in the UK and by whom, and what reliefs apply to certain commodities. The commodity codes are especially important in this document, as they state the quota of particular goods allowed to enter the UK, as well as stating where duty reliefs apply (goods for charities, low-value samples, etc.).

In the UK, these requirements are applied by HM Revenue and Customs, the customs agency responsible for import and export control. For items imported into the UK, this customs agency expects the organisation sending the goods to provide an *Ad valorem* estimate of the value of the goods for the following purposes.

- To calculate the duty owed to the local customs agency

- To calculate the import Value Added Tax (VAT)

- To support trade statistics (collected using the Intrastat system in the EU) in recognition of tariff requirements

Ad valorem
An estimated value of goods that are imported, based on the value of the goods plus a number of other factors (insurance, freight and other costs) that is calculated to give a total value

> *Remember*
> Countries within the European Union are required to implement European law into their own regulatory framework.

Duty and VAT reliefs in the UK

When commodities meet particular criteria in the Integrated Tariff of the United Kingdom, based on their use or movement within the EU, they may be subject to 'relief' of duty. This means the duty is not required or is reduced in value. The same may also apply to the payment of VAT in some situations. The following are examples of duty reliefs on goods being imported to the UK.

- Customs Warehousing Relief: where goods are stored duty-free and VAT-free at a 'defined location'. If these goods are later exported out of the EU, they are not subject to duty or VAT.

- Inward Processing Relief: where goods enter from outside the EU and are later exported from the EU.

- Outward Processing Relief: where goods are only temporarily exported to a country outside the EU (for repairs, for example).

- End-use Relief: where goods meet a specific purpose and can only be used within a set period of time (for example, fresh products, such as cheese or fish).

Duty may also be charged at different rates to different importers. This may be because the supplier's nation has good trade relations with the country it is delivering into, meaning that more favourable rates are applied.

Case study

Preferential duty rates

Duty reliefs and preferential rates are in place in many countries other than the UK. At the time of writing, the South African Customs & Excise Tariff shows different rates of duty that are available for general importers, and for those importing from specified regions such as the Southern Common Market (MERCOSUR) or the European Union (EU). An example of commodity duty rates from this tariff for onions and shallots is as follows.

Commodity identifier	Commodity name	Rate of duty (as a % of the value of the commodity being imported)				
		General	EU	EFTA	SADC	MERCOSUR
0703.10	Onions and shallots	15%	Free	15%	Free	Free

As you can see, preferential rates are offered to members of the EU, SADC (Southern African Development Community) and MERCOSUR, but suppliers located in the countries based in the EFTA (European Free Trade Association) or elsewhere are charged a duty of 15% for importing their goods.

(Source: information from The South African Revenue Service (2018) www.sars.gov.za/AllDocs/LegalDoclib/SCEA1964/LAPD-LPrim-Tariff-2012-04%20-%20Schedule%20No%201%20Part%201%20Chapters%20 1%20to%2099.pdf)

The use of Incoterms®

In supply chains, there can be risk at many stages of the sourcing process, and in international supply chains there may be a greater potential for risk. Language barriers, variations in customs processes and import/export standards, along with many other factors, can lead to items being rejected or held up in quarantine areas, potentially for a long time. This can heavily affect programme schedules. Buyers can take control over the level of delivery and transport risk by defining how this should be carried out within contracts and purchase orders.

The International Chamber of Commerce (ICC) publishes a list of commercial rules known as Incoterms®. In the past, these rules were used in international trade but have more recently grown in domestic use. Incoterms® are used to provide a recognised standard of trade understanding and terminology between buyers and suppliers. In most cases the rules cover trade via any means of transport, but they include special provisions for transport on water.

Importantly, Incoterms® are used to describe the point when a deliverable is no longer the responsibility of the supplying organisation, with the risk then transferring to the buyer.

One of the biggest advantages to using Incoterms® is that they can easily take the place of otherwise lengthy contractual clauses. They can be used to represent the following information when included in contracts.

3.2 L03

- The point at which the goods will be considered to have been 'delivered'.
- Which party is responsible for organising transportation and what form this takes.
- Which party pays to insure the goods and which party is responsible for arranging this.
- Which party is responsible for making duty and tariff arrangements and arranging passage through customs control agencies.

The Incoterms® 2010 edition has 11 rules as shown in table 3.7, along with an indication of which organisation bears the least risk with each.

Incoterms®	Rule name	Point at which obligation and risk transfers to buyer	Lowest risk
Rules for all modes of transport			
EXW	Ex Works	Named place	Supplier
FCA	Free Carrier	Named place	Supplier
CPT	Carriage Paid To	Named place of destination	–
CIP	Carriage And Insurance Paid To	Named place of destination	–
DAT	Delivered At Terminal	Named port	Buyer
DAP	Delivered At Place	Named destination place	Buyer
DDP	Delivered Duty Paid	Named destination place	Buyer
Rules for transport over water			
FAS	Free Alongside Ship	Named loading port	Supplier
FOB	Free On Board	Named loading port	Supplier
CFR	Cost and Freight	Named destination port	–
CIF	Cost, Insurance and Freight	Named destination port	–

Table 3.7 Incoterms® and their meanings (Source: adapted from information from International Chamber of Commerce, Incoterms® rules 2010 www.iccwbo.org/ resources-for-business/incoterms-rules/incoterms-rules-2010/)

« Case study

Rules for all modes of transport
Incoterms® are versatile, and procurement professionals should understand how they are applied and at what point the risk transfers from being the supplier's responsibility to the buyer's responsibility. It is important to consult the ICC for the most recent definitions, but the rules are explained in further detail here.

EXW – Ex Works
The goods are considered 'delivered' at the point of release from the supplier's premises or another named place. The supplier is not responsible for loading or

transporting the goods and does not have to arrange any export clearance – this must be arranged by the buyer. The risk is on the buyer from this point.

FCA – Free Carrier

The supplier is responsible for placing the goods in the hands of a carrier chosen by the buyer, at which point the buyer takes on the risk.

CPT – Carriage Paid To

The supplier is responsible for delivering the goods to a carrier or to an intermediate agreed place. From this point, the buyer is responsible for ensuring these goods reach their **named destination**.

CIP – Carriage and Insurance Paid to

The supplier is responsible for delivering the goods to a carrier or intermediate agreed place and should ensure that the goods have at least minimal insurance cover until this point. Again, the buyer is responsible for ensuring that the goods reach their named destination from here.

DAT – Delivered At Terminal

The supplier is responsible for delivering the goods to a named port or destination (such as an airport or warehouse), as well as unloading them at the terminal. From this point, risk passes to the buyer.

DAP – Delivered At Place

The supplier is responsible for delivering the goods to the buyer's premises, bearing all risk up until this point.

DDP – Delivery Duty Paid

The supplier is responsible for delivering the goods to the buyer's premises including arranging any customs clearances that apply, bearing all risk up until this point.

Rules for transport over water

FAS – Free Alongside Ship

The supplier is responsible for delivering goods to a point alongside a water vessel (such as a dock or quay) as determined by the buyer at a named port. Once delivered, all risk is transferred to the buyer until the goods are transported and delivered to their named destination.

FOB – Free On Board

The supplier is responsible for delivering the goods directly onto the vessel that will transport them to their named destination. As soon as the goods are on the vessel, the risk transfers to the buyer.

CFR – Cost and Freight

The supplier is responsible for delivering the goods directly onto the vessel that will transport them to their named destination and must also cover the cost of this.

Named destination
The final destination goods should be delivered to. This should be clearly defined from the start

The supplier bears all risk until the goods are delivered to the buyer at their named destination.

CIF – Cost, Insurance and Freight

The supplier is responsible for delivering the goods directly onto the vessel that will transport them to their named destination, covering the cost of both the transport and the insurance to cover this. Again, the supplier bears all risk until the goods are delivered to the buyer at their named destination.

(Source: adapted from information from International Chamber of Commerce, Incoterms® rules 2010 www.iccwbo.org/resources-for-business/incoterms-rules/incoterms-rules-2010)

3.2 L03

Remember

While Incoterms® are well known worldwide, it is still important to work closely with suppliers to ensure that both parties have interpreted them to mean the same thing.

Check

List the Incoterms® shown in this chapter and give the following details for each one.

- Which organisation bears the most risk
- The point at which responsibility for the goods transfers to the buyer
- Whether there are any additional requirements, e.g., export documentation

Apply

A buyer awards a contract to a supplier to provide a crate of glass bottles. The supplier delivers this crate to a marina, but the crate is dropped when it is being loaded onto a ship, damaging the goods inside. Which organisation is responsible for covering the cost of these damaged goods if each of the Incoterms® below are used in the contract?

- DDP
- FOB
- DAT

Payment mechanisms to enable supply

Maintaining a healthy cash flow is important when operating a business. This means that securing the most beneficial payment method can be essential to ensure business continuity, for both the buyer and the supplier. One of the greatest concerns in commerce is that the buyer may pay a supplier up-front but then not receive the goods they paid for. This could be due to reduced motivation for the supplier to deliver, or following fraudulent claims from the supplier. The same may apply in reverse, however, and the supplier may not be willing to begin manufacture until the buyer has paid up, enabling the supplier to secure the money it is owed and to cover initial costs for materials if required.

The payment mechanisms shown in figure 3.5 may be used to reduce payment and delivery risks in international trade.

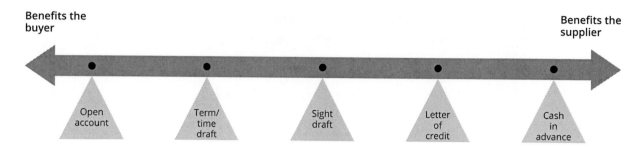

Figure 3.5 The payment mechanism spectrum of preference for supplier and buyer

Open account

Here the supplier delivers the goods before receiving payment and will expect to be paid on the agreed credit terms, usually within a specified number of days from the date of the supplier's invoice. A lot of domestic trade is done in this way. While this may be beneficial to the buyer (if they have the capacity to receive and store the goods this far in advance), it may not benefit the supplier as they risk not getting paid. While suppliers may work to these timescales to keep a competitive edge and satisfy the buyer, an open account needs to be carefully managed to prevent cash flow problems for the supplier. Agreeing payment terms before awarding the contract is important for both parties to establish when payment will take place.

Term/time draft

A guarantee of payment from the buyer's bank ensures the exporting supplier retains title of the goods until the importing buyer has receipted them. At this point, following confirmation that goods have been received and, following a short delay, the supplier will be paid. This delay is to give the buyer enough time to inspect the goods and ensure that it is satisfied before paying the supplier.

Sight draft

A guarantee of payment from the buyer's bank ensures the exporting supplier retains title of the goods until the importing buyer has receipted and paid for them. Though the supplier is not paid until this point, it is called a 'sight' draft because the buyer must pay for the goods as soon as they are received and there can be no delay.

Letter of credit

A guarantee given by the buyer's bank to the supplier, stating that the exporting supplier will be paid only when it meets the conditions set out in the letter generally when documentation requirements have been satisfied fully. This option supports the payment of the supplier, but is especially favourable to the buyer as they are not obliged to repay the bank until the terms of the letter of credit are met, with all required documents provided.

Cash in advance

The buyer pays the supplier for goods before they are received. This benefits the exporting supplier in terms of cash flow, but may have risks for the buyer. There is the potential that the buyer may not receive the delivery (due to loss in transit, the supplier never despatching it, etc.,) and at this point, the buyer may not be able to recover the money it has already paid as the supplier may not accept any responsibility for the loss. With these terms the buyer also carries the risk that the goods may not meet quality and other requirements.

Check
Describe the use of each of the following payment mechanisms in international trade.

- Letter of credit
- Sight draft
- Term/time draft
- Open account
- Cash in advance

Remember
While it may seem preferable to have a supplier deliver far in advance with no money paid up front, a supplier with cash flow problems may be vulnerable and could cease trading. This would not be a good situation for the buying organisation if it was dependent on the one supplier for the goods.

Apply
Put the following terms in order, ranging from most beneficial to the buyer, to most beneficial for the supplier.

- Letter of credit
- Sight draft
- Cash in advance
- Term/time draft
- Open account

The impact of currency on sourcing

The Foreign Exchange Market

Supply chains may be exposed to considerable financial risk at an international level, mainly due to the differences between nation states. In addition to managing all other aspects of the purchase, the buyer must also have a thorough understanding of the potential impact that differences in **currency** could have on its purchases. The value of currencies is determined by supply and demand on the Foreign Exchange Market (Forex). Supply and demand here is dictated by the actions of traders buying and selling huge amounts of currency worldwide daily.

In order to carry out business across borders, exchanges of currency must take place, where one currency is traded for another. However, these are not an equal exchange. For example, 1 euro (EUR) may be exchanged for 15.37 South African rand (ZAR) at the rates determined by the Forex Market. This would be expressed in terms of currency codes by foreign exchange currency converters as follows.

1 EUR = 15.37 ZAR

Currency
A monetary system used within a country, for example, the rand in South Africa (ZAR) or Australian dollars (AUD)

Or   1 ZAR = 0.065 EUR

This shows that the euro is the stronger currency, as a single unit of this can be used to purchase 15.37 South African rand.

If the perceived value of the euro was negatively affected (perhaps as a result of several of its key users being in conflict), its worth may decrease. Then 1 euro would be worth fewer South African rand, which could be expressed as follows.

1 EUR = 7 ZAR

However, if the economy within the EU was perceived to be positive, the euro's worth could increase, meaning that a buyer could purchase more South African rand for 1 euro as follows.

1 EUR = 32 ZAR

The main reason that currencies vary in worth in comparison to one another is that buyers buy large quantities of a particular currency, possibly because that country is prosperous and its currency is perceived to hold value. As a result, the perceived worth of the currency increases, leading to an increase in monetary value, which under the right circumstances can increase rapidly. When a country suffers an economic downturn, it may experience a reduction in currency value. This can be made worse when market traders react by selling their currency, attempting to mitigate their losses.

Case study

Global financial crisis 2008
As a result of banks over-lending, pushing property price increases and speculating on financial markets, many economies suffered sudden but lasting damage in 2008. After a long recession there has been some economic recovery, but some believe that there is still a long way to go before these economies are back to full strength.

The recession caused the value of the currencies used by these economies to plummet against other currencies, putting companies based in those economies in a weak position when planning and securing currency for international trade.

Apply
Consider an organisation with which you are familiar. Does the organisation source from foreign suppliers? If so, check the following.

- Are different currencies used by both parties?
- Which company's chosen currency has the most favourable exchange rate?
- Are suppliers paid before goods are received to secure a preferential rate?
- With the previous points in mind, if there was an increase in a supplier's currency tomorrow, what impact would this have on the organisation's purchases?

Currency management for supply chains

3.2 L03

Where possible, it is in the interest of the purchasing organisation to monitor the Forex market and analyse any trends or significant changes. This allows the buyer to know what effect the exchange of currency will have on prices proposed by suppliers (who may also be supplied by suppliers foreign to them, also affecting price). It may be possible to predict what currency rates will be like at the time of payment. If the organisation already purchases from foreign suppliers, or is planning to do so, this knowledge is especially important in strategically planning purchases.

The ideal situation for the buying organisation is to have a national currency that is strong against that of the supplier's nation. This puts it in the better position, as it may be able to exchange a smaller quantity of its own currency for a much greater quantity of currency from the supplier's country. This would give the buyer a greater purchasing power with more foreign capital to commit, if required.

A simple way to guard against price fluctuations is to specify that prices in all suppliers' tenders are given in the currency of the buying organisation's nation. With this in place, the buyer would not be affected by problematic currency market fluctuations, though the supplier would bear a lot of risk when accepting the contract.

Sourcing can involve delays, sometimes for several weeks or months. This may be risky for the buyer as there is the potential for the buyer's stronger currency to weaken against the supplier's currency value during that time. This could mean that their values are near-matching or even cross over, making the supplier's currency stronger. If this were to happen, the buying organisation would be in a weaker position and it would have to purchase more foreign currency to continue its purchase.

It is possible to mitigate the effect of currency fluctuations by simply paying the supplier up front when the order is placed. This secures a good currency rate as early as possible. However, this is not advisable as it may cause the supplier to lose focus on the delivery of the contract due to the incentive (payment) being issued too early.

A more common way to mitigate the potential impact of currency fluctuations is by carrying out **currency hedging**. Hedging is a proactive risk management technique where the buyer will use different techniques and products (available from commercial banks) to minimise exposure. For example, a forward contract can be used to fix a foreign exchange rate for the purchase or sale of a specific amount of currency on a specified future date. Currency options can also be used and provide more flexibility if amounts and dates are not precisely known, although a fee (the premium) is payable when using these instruments.

Currency hedging
A method of purchasing foreign currency ahead of an expected payment in order to prevent the financial loss caused by market fluctuations

Currency Regulations

When sourcing internationally, in addition to many other factors, the currency of the contract will be a key concern for all contracting parties. This must be agreed beforehand and is an important part of the contract. Where it is agreed that the currency will be that of the buyer's country issues relating to foreign exchange risk (for the buyer) will be avoided although there still might be challenges for the buyer in making payment to the supplier's country.

Essentially, currency considerations, from a regulatory perspective, focus on the following.

- Access to the currency
- Ability to make and receive payments
- General considerations

Access to the currency

Not all currencies are freely tradeable, which means that if a currency payment is due or a currency receivable received in settlement it might not be easy to convert the proceeds into another currency. Commonly traded currencies include the US Dollar (USD), the Euro (EUR), the Japanese Yen (JPY), British Pound (GBP) and the Swiss Franc (CHF). These currencies are straightforward to obtain (both buying and selling) and are tradable on foreign exchange markets. Some currencies, known as 'exotic', are traded less and so availability is more restricted, for example the Colombian Peso (COP). Some currencies are known as 'non-convertible' meaning there are government restrictions both on accessibility to the currency and its use. Often these restrictions mean the currency can only be used domestically, i.e. in country. As a general principle these restrictions are imposed by regulations created and implemented by the central bank which ultimately has responsibility for maintaining the value of its domestic currency.

Ability to make and receive payments

Historically, many countries had exchange controls in place which restricted accessibility to currency and limit its movement. Today these controls are less prevalent but still do exist. So, procurement professionals should check to ensure they will be able to access any currency and can make payments when invoices are due.

Not all payment related regulations are restrictive however. For example, the EU Payment Services Directive, which has been widely implemented across the EU, has been introduced to enhance security and increase competition in the payments industry. In the UK there is a Payment Systems Regulator, which is a subsidiary of the Financial Conduct Authority, with responsibility for oversight of the payments industry. Other regimes exist around the world.

General considerations

There has been a general global movement towards 'tightening up' in the area of payments as anti-money laundering and countering terrorism measures. This has made it much more difficult for individuals and businesses to make payments without providing supporting rationale, especially where the transaction is unusual based on, for example, the nature of the business. There are numerous best practice guidelines and policies, for example, issued by the Financial Action Task Force (FATF), the Wolfsberg Group (an association of thirteen global banks) and the International Monetary Fund. These are supported by legislation in many countries, for example the Proceeds of Crime Act in the UK and the Money Laundering Control Act in the US.

Chapter Summary

This chapter has covered the following topics.

- The three sectors that businesses operate within
- The requirements and considerations for success when operating and carrying out sourcing activities
- Potential barriers to the delivery of goods and services in international trade
- Documents used in international trade
- The impact of customs organisations and the tariffs and quotas they set
- The impact of currency on trade

Recommended reading

Incoterms® 2010 English Edition, The International Chamber of Commerce (ICC)

World Trade Organization, (1996), *Rules of conduct for the understanding on rules and procedures governing the settlement of disputes* [online]. Retrieved from: www.wto.org/english/tratop_e/dispu_e/rc_e.htm [Accessed on: 23 January 2019]

End of Chapter Assessment

1. What are the advantages of using competitive tendering when sourcing? **DESCRIBE**

2. Give examples of regulations and standards that affect product safety and explain their importance. **EXPLAIN**

3. What is corporate social responsibility and how can an organisations actions affect it? **DESCRIBE**

4. Why are timescales important in public sector sourcing? **IDENTIFY**

5. Why might a private sector organisation choose to select a single supplier, rather than initiate a competitive tender? **EXPLAIN**

6. Why is seeking value for money important in not-for-profit sector sourcing? **EXPLAIN**

7. What are the key risks in international sourcing? **LIST**

8. Give three examples of documents that are used to facilitate international imports and exports, and outline their purpose. **IDENTIFY**

9. What is the difference between a duty and a tariff? **IDENTIFY**

10. What information is summarised in an Incoterms® rule? **IDENTIFY**

11. Which two payment mechanisms are most preferential to a buying organisation in international trade? **EVALUATE**

12. Explain the use of hedging with regards to currency exchange and international payments for goods. **EXPLAIN**

References

1 World Trade Organization (n.d.), *Understanding on Rules and Procedures Governing the Settlement of Disputes* [online]. Retrieved from: www.wto.org/english/docs_e/legal_e/28-dsu_e.htm [Accessed on: 24 January 2019]

2 GOV.UK (n.d.), *Getting ready for the Customs Declaration Service* [online]. Retrieved from: www.gov.uk/government/news/getting-ready-for-the-customs-declaration-service [Accessed on: 24 January 2019]

CHAPTER 4
Understand ethical and responsible sourcing

Learning outcome

By the end of this chapter, you will understand more about the responsibilities of a procurement professional in terms of ethical and responsible sourcing.

Chapter overview

4.1 Describe the impact of international ethical standards on procurement and supply

You will understand:
- Bribery
- Corruption
- Fraud
- Human rights
- Modern slavery

4.2 Identify practices that support ethical procurement

You will understand:
- Application of the CIPS Code of Conduct
- Ethical codes of practice
- Pre-qualification and assessment criteria
- Due diligence on suppliers and risk assessment
- Supporting information on ethical practices in supplier quotations and tenders
- Contractual clauses
- Supplier monitoring
- KPIs

4.3 Compare the use of audits and other feedback mechanisms to evaluate ethical standards in the workplace

You will understand:
- Monitoring supplier performance
- Encouraging dialogue with suppliers on process improvements
- Recommending remedial actions where appropriate
- Identifying and addressing potential conflicts of interest

Contrast processes and practices that the organisation could adopt to meet the requirements of Corporate Social Responsibility (CSR)

You will understand:
- The triple bottom line – profit, people and planet
- Adopting sustainable practices, standards and specifications in the supply chain
- Considering the social impact of the organisation's behaviours
- Designing procurement processes to deliver social outcomes as well as, or as an alternative to, normal economic measures of value
- Expanding reporting frameworks to include ecological and social performance
- Defining organisational value for money to include social outcomes – use of local labour, participation of disadvantaged groups

Introduction

In this chapter, you will explore the importance of two key principles that underpin the way business should be conducted: ethical responsibility and sustainable practice. Supply chains are exposed to a number of unethical or corrupt practices in international business, and the buyer is responsible for defending the organisation against these practices. Where possible, the buyer should also focus on protecting the human rights of others and ensuring that suppliers support the ethics of the organisation.

Through the use of supplier due diligence, pre-assessment and auditing, buyers can monitor their suppliers in a number of ways. This is vital to protect the organisation from reputational risk, which is especially important in the modern, international business environment.

You will also gain a stronger appreciation of the fact that organisations create ripples in society with their operations and behaviours, and these can have both positive and negative effects on various scales. A buyer's role may involve supporting positive contributions to society or may mean mitigating the negative effects. Either way, it is important that for a buyer to understand how much of an influence an organisation can have.

A procurement professional may be presented with situations where they are offered a bribe or asked to tolerate other corrupt behaviours, but it is important to be resilient and not to accept or give in to unethical practice in any form.

Considerations of ethics may vary from culture to culture and person to person, and this may cause conflicts. You will learn more about standards that can be employed to diplomatically uphold ethical practice.

4.1 Describe the impact of international ethical standards on procurement and supply

4.1 LO4

The impact of corruption

« Case study

Transparency International

Transparency International is a not-for-profit organisation funded by donors (from private sector and government agencies). It is based in more than 100 countries and has a vision to get rid of **corruption** on a global scale. Corruption used to be hard to fight as challenging as it was considered to be a taboo, but Transparency International believes that the key to ending it is to highlight the impact it has on individual and community wellbeing, business and trade, and political relations worldwide. The organisation encourages increased transparency to reduce the number of dishonest practices, as these ultimately harm people's trust and perceptions of how law-abiding, legitimate and conscientious organisations or individuals actually are. In particular, Transparency International wants individuals to appreciate that corruption occurs in many aspects of society and business, and its practice could lead to the following.

- Loss of freedom to individuals
- Loss of money to individuals, organisations and countries
- Harm to the health of individuals, potentially leading to their death

Each year, Transparency International produces a valuable piece of research known as The Corruption Perceptions Index. In 2017, the Index highlighted the fact that countries where corruption had been found to be high in previous years were doing very little to reduce it. The research also found that corruption is perceived to be higher in places where members of the press are not well protected, and where there are few not-for-profit NGOs (non-governmental organisations) to campaign against corrupt practice and the practices that contribute to corruption.

The Corruption Perceptions Index is a ranked list of 180 countries and territories across the world and along a scale of 0–100, with a score of 0 meaning highly corrupt and 100 meaning that there is almost no corruption.

Corruption
Abuse or misuse of a person's entrusted position, power or authority for personal gain. In procurement, this could include a person with authority agreeing to give a specific supplier a contract before a fair competitive tender has been carried out (making it unfair)

The ranking is based on the perceived level of corruption in a region using data from a perception survey, taken by business people and experts, to gain a more accurate picture of the state of corruption. In addition to the Index, an interactive map is produced, visually displaying the extent of global corruption for the user.

(Source: information from www.transparency.org)

The research carried out by Transparency International is especially useful for procurement professionals to look at the country-level perception of corruption when planning to work with overseas suppliers. While it is clear that that not *all* individuals or organisations within a country will be corrupt, though the score may suggest it, the Corruption Perceptions Index may help procurement professionals prepare themselves for any corrupt circumstances that they may be presented with.

Where possible, procurement professionals should reduce the potential for becoming involved in corrupt circumstances by carrying out effective due diligence (discussed later in this chapter) before agreeing contracts with suppliers. Due diligence can use the research of Transparency International, as well as other sources, to advise whether or not a supplier or its employees have been convicted or suspected of being corrupt. A buyer can use this information to exclude potentially corrupt suppliers from any sourcing activities.

Cultural considerations with corruption

One of the biggest issues with all types of corruption is that some individuals may try to defend its use with the excuse of **cultural relativism**, where they try to apply their own laws, principals and beliefs to a situation. This means that corruption is treated and accepted differently across different cultures and that individuals may be accused of being 'wrong' for following their own values when challenging corruption. A common example of this cover-up would be **facilitation payments** (discussed later in this chapter) which are considered to be a cultural norm in some regions of the world (as well as a standard business practice), but are considered to be bribes by many nations and NGOs.

However, buyers need to be careful not to make assumptions based on certain cultural stereotypes that could suggest, for example, that people from a particular nation are all corrupt or offer bribes in every business transaction. A procurement professional can best prepare for these challenges by learning as much as possible about the other cultures they intend to do business with and seeking advice from others who have direct experience of this.

Anti-corruption legislation

Across the world, many countries have demonstrated their disapproval of corruption by passing legislation to make it a punishable offence. In the USA, The Foreign Corrupt Practices Act has been in place since 1977, mostly relating to practices of or with foreign officials. This act is not concerned about the amount of a material transfer in bribery (money, property, etc.,) but instead considers its intent, which is perceived to be the abuse of power or authority. This act also distinguishes 'graft' as a specific type of corruption, which is a politician's misuse of their authority for their own personal advancement. Interestingly, while there are provisions for facilitation payments in this act, these are not condemned if they are permitted in the host country's laws.

Cultural relativism
The idea that the way a person behaves, what they believe and what they consider to be normal are not universally applicable, but may be different from culture to culture

Facilitation payment
A type of bribe where a payment is made to enable something to take place or to speed up its progress. This corrupt practice may also be known as a 'grease payment'

While the UK Bribery Act 2010 also includes provisions for general bribery and the bribery of foreign public officials, it also provides further legislation for commercial organisations' responsibility to prevent bribery. The requirements on the organisations are cascaded down to their employees, meaning that anyone working for an organisation who is found to be carrying out bribery in the course of their work could be prosecuted. To ensure this does not happen, procurement professionals in the UK should make every effort to act in an ethical manner, preferably in line with codes of practice such as the CIPS **Code of Conduct**.

Corruption takes many forms. Two key types are discussed below.

- Bribery

- Fraud

Bribery

In its most basic form, bribery is the corrupt exchange of something of value (the bribe) by one party in order to enable a desirable outcome from another party. In procurement, this could be a bribe from a potential supplier to a buyer, or even the other way around. This differs from a normal transactional exchange as its intent is underhand and it defies ethical practice in order to reach the desired outcome. It may be kept secret or covered up to try to shield it from the criticism of others.

A bribe could be money, political favour, company shares or any number of other things, as long as it is of value to the recipient. Equally, the desired outcome could take a number of forms similar to the above, but this should be something that the bribing party desires, such as the awarding of a contract.

Sometimes, bribes may go by other names in an attempt to make them sound more official and ethically acceptable. A facilitation payment (or grease payment), for example, is a payment or incentive that may be given to a foreign or domestic government official. The payment is intended to encourage them to carry out a particular function, such as award a contract to the person/organisation making the payment, or to speed up a process so that they progress faster than rules permit. Whatever the payment is called, this still meets the definition of a bribe and would be considered as such in a court of law.

Research carried out across 41 countries by The Organisation for Economic Co-operation and Development (OECD)[1] shows that certain industries are more affected by foreign bribery than others, including the following.

- The defence industry

- The property development industry

- The mining industry

- The medical industry

Bribery is a serious concern in both national and international supply chains, mainly because cultural relativism means that in some countries it may be more readily accepted as a business norm (particularly where **gifts and hospitality** are concerned). One of the greatest concerns is that it is a barrier to fair competition, so responsible procurement professionals must reject all forms of bribery, including gifts and hospitality. They should seek advice when they know or suspect bribery.

Code of conduct
A series of rules set by an organisation that define suitable behaviours and values that should be used and applied by a member of that organisation, for the purpose of acting in a suitable manner, as well as demonstrating uniformity and upholding the standards of the organisation

Bribery
When someone gives something of value to another party in order to influence a more desirable outcome from that party. The difference between a bribe and a standard transaction is that this action is corrupt

Fraud
When an individual deliberately misleads or tells lies to someone to achieve the outcome they desire at their victim's expense

Gifts and hospitality
Material goods, money or entertainment that may be given from one party to another. In the context of business, the giving and receiving of gifts from one organisation or individual to another may be perceived as giving and receiving a bribe

Gifting and hospitality

Bribery is not always an explicit act and is often justified as being a one-way transfer of something desirable to another party, i.e. a gift. The person giving the gift claims to want nothing in return, instead just expressing their gratitude to the receiving party, or demonstrating their generosity to a host. The gift may be a physical object such as luxury stationery or vehicles, or could instead take the form of hospitality including restaurant meals, tickets to sporting events or paid holidays.

In many cases, the person giving the gift may be doing so to gain the favour of the receiver. They hope that it will lead to another form of preference such as a biased awarding of a contract during the tender process, ignoring human rights violations or accepting any other unethical act.

In some cultures, giving gifts is considered to be a normal business practice and the people giving them do not always intend for this to be a form of bribe. This may surprise procurement professionals if this is not normal in their home country, and it may put them in a difficult position. They may decide that if they reject the gift or hospitality, they risk offending the person offering the gift. This could damage the relationship between the parties and may make conducting future business awkward and difficult. However, if the buyer accepts a gift they are offered, there is a chance that their colleagues may view this as accepting a bribe (particularly if the gift or hospitality is high value). This could lead to an accusation of accepting bribery, potentially resulting in an investigation, disciplinary action or dismissal of the procurement professional. The accusation could be from an internal stakeholder but could also be from an unhappy supplier who lost out in a competitive tender against the winning supplier, whom they know to have given gifts.

As you can see, being a procurement professional requires a great deal of tact, a strong knowledge of cultural norms and a good understanding of what is and is not viewed as ethical by the buying organisation and by law. To protect their procurement team and other employees, organisations may choose to adopt a gifting and hospitality policy. This policy would include the following areas.

- The situations in which it is acceptable to accept a gift (i.e. where it would cause offence to refuse it).

- What types of gifts are or are not acceptable (for example, drugs would not be acceptable).

- How to proceed, depending on the value of the goods. An example is given below.

  - Gifts or hospitality at a value of less than $20 may be acceptable as long as they are formally documented in the gifts and hospitality register.

  - Gifts or hospitality with a value of $21—$100 must be documented and the recipient's manager must give their consent for these to be accepted.

  - Gifts or hospitality with a value of $101—$500 must be documented and the recipient's functional director must give their consent for these to be accepted.

  - Gifts or hospitality at a value greater than $500 must not be accepted by any employee.

- How gifts should be used when received, i.e. used by the person receiving it, donated to a charitable cause, etc.

- How gifting should be treated in line with other conflicts of interest that are known or may arise.

Apply

Imagine that a colleague in one of your buying teams has just returned from a business trip to country A where they met with a potential supplier. They returned feeling that they had a very positive experience meeting the supplier and believe that this supplier would be capable of providing the product your organisation requires. They also told you that they were invited to look around the managing director's sister's designer clothing factory, and were given various expensive items as gifts to take back to the office for their colleagues to share.

You suspect that your colleague has been influenced by the experience and the gift they received. You believe that this will unfairly affect the outcome of a competitive tender that the supplier is going to be invited to take part in. None of your colleagues take any action, and you know that your manager is not aware of the situation.

- What action would you take to highlight your concerns?
- What action would you take to ensure the competition is fair?
- What action could be taken for the clothing that has been received?
- What action can you take to mitigate or prevent future occurrences of this?

All of the 44 countries that form the OECD Anti-Bribery Convention[2] have laws that lead to imprisoning anyone found guilty of carrying out bribery. The Convention notes that this may also lead to an organisation being banned from tendering for public sector procurement contracts. This could be far more damaging for an organisation than being issued a fine, as reputational damage may lead to losing other business.

Fraud

Fraud is a crime that can be carried out by any individual. It involves someone unlawfully obtaining funds or resources for their own benefit and it can be hugely damaging to the success of businesses. It can originate from external stakeholders (such as suppliers) and even from employees at a company as **workplace fraud**.

Workplace fraud covers a number of types of fraud (listed below) that may be committed within a company, where a series of smaller thefts that are hard to detect may build to become large losses for an organisation. Individuals committing fraud make efforts to conceal their actions. In cases of **embezzlement**, rather than obvious theft of money, individuals misuse funds or resources that they have authority over, using them in a way that benefits themselves.

Why do individuals commit fraud?

Given the penalties for those found guilty of committing fraud, it can be difficult for many people to understand why some people do it. It is useful to know what motivates individuals to commit fraud, to try to avoid the factors that lead to it. In the field of criminology, Sutherland and Cressey defined three key influences that cause individuals to commit workplace fraud. Over time, these have been

Workplace fraud
Small-scale thefts taking place within the workplace that are difficult to detect and could collectively cause large financial or resource losses. An example of this could be taking inexpensive stationery home, which could cause losses on a larger scale if colleagues do the same

Embezzlement
The misuse of assets or items entrusted to a person for a particular purpose. The ownership of these items is wrongly transferred on purpose to the person entrusted with them, meaning that they are no longer assets of the original owner. An example of this may be a buyer selling a company laptop for their own monetary gain after their company has issued them with a new one

considered by other fraud theorists, and are generally represented as a triangle such as that shown in figure 4.1.

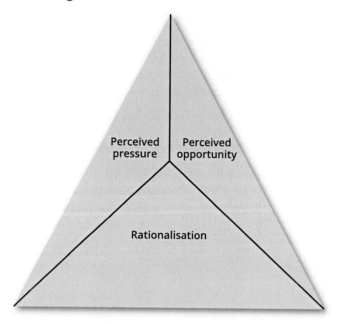

Figure 4.1 The fraud triangle (Source: Wells, J. (2011), Corporate Fraud Handbook: Prevention and Detection, John Wiley and Sons Publishing, Hoboken, NJ.)

- **Perceived pressure (on the individual committing fraud):** for example, personal debt problems that the individual believes they will not be supported in resolving in a legitimate manner.

- **Perceived opportunity (to carry out fraud):** any situation or vulnerability in a system or organisation that the individual believes they can exploit in order to satisfy the perceived pressure.

- **Rationalisation (of the fraud):** the individual's internal dialogue that justifies (from their point of view) carrying out the fraud, such as 'it's only going to be one time and it's not that bad' or 'I need to support my family and this is the only way I'll be able to'.

What forms can fraud take?

There are many types of fraud but the following are the most common.

- Advance fee fraud: where the victim is asked to provide an up-front payment for goods or services that are never delivered.

- Corporate fraud: fraud that targets an organisation.

- Identity fraud: fraud where a false identity is created and used by a person to commit a fraudulent act, or when another person's identity is stolen and used to commit further fraudulent acts.

- Individual fraud: fraud that targets one specific person.

With the widespread use of electronic devices (such as computers, tablets and smartphones) the variations in online fraud as an act of cybercrime are increasing and adapting to trap unsuspecting victims. The following are some examples of cybercrime.

- Phishing is particularly common as it can be easy to get a user to access a link from a convincing e-mail or website, potentially exposing them to the activities of expert cybercriminals.

- Account takeover, where a person fraudulently uses someone else's details to make unauthorised transactions online, for example, placing orders, creating subscriptions or accessing private information.

- Money muling, where people are targeted and chosen to receive stolen money, withdraw it and then forward it on to another person or company's bank account. The victim may comply with this request because they believe that they will get to keep some of the money, but in reality they will probably only receive a small amount (or nothing), in proportion to the risk they take. In this case, the criminal's intention is to break the traceability of the stolen money so that it can be used without suspicion.

- 'Official' request, where victims are sent seemingly official correspondence from an agency of authority (the police, local government, industry regulators, etc.). The message says that they must take a particular course of action in order to be compliant with a law they may be told they are breaking. By clicking a link in e-mails of this nature, the participant may unknowingly activate malware or trigger some other harmful effect.

How does fraud affect supply chains?

Transparency of both the buying and supplying organisation is essential for building trust and for successful procurements. Not all parties may want to be so transparent as to reveal their strategic intentions to the other party and many organisations accept this. Trust can be low or high, but it is up to the buyer to understand the extent to which this will affect the delivery of the contract by the supplier.

Problems arise, however, where trust is exploited by fraudulent behaviours. If either party deliberately deceives the other by exaggerating its capabilities, working under false identities or by telling lies in any form, this party is committing fraud according to the law.

The party committing the fraud may not think it is very serious, particularly if it felt that it was only slightly twisting the truth to win a contract or to win favour with a buying organisation. While it may feel that it is not breaking any law, it is likely that this defence would not be successful in court.

Where a party is suspected or found guilty of committing an act of fraud, its relationship with the other organisation is likely to be permanently harmed. Once again, it will not be able to demonstrate effective corporate social responsibility and so is likely to lose existing customers or fail to attract others, potentially leading to a huge loss of earnings.

Procurement professionals must not tolerate or accept fraud. If someone feels that fraud has or is taking place, they should attempt to resolve this through whatever means are available to them. This could be carried out internally, if the organisation employs staff who are responsible for managing business ethics cases, alternatively they could seek further advice from organisations, such as the following.

- Attorney-General's Department (Australia)

- Corrupt Practices Investigation Bureau (Singapore)

- National Crime Agency (UK)

- Serious Fraud Office (UK)

- Financial Conduct Authority (UK)

- Department of Justice (USA)

Apply

Do you know which organisation in your country you can speak to for guidance with cases of fraud? Look this up on the Internet and familiarise yourself with the support these organisations can provide.

Check

According to the fraud triangle, what are the three key influencers of fraud? Give one example of each of these.

What forms can fraud take and why may these affect supply chains?

Human rights
Rights or principles, based on shared values that are accepted as belonging to every person, regardless of background

Zeitgeist
The 'spirit' of an age/time, meaning the cultural norms, values and behaviours from a particular period in history

Human rights

The Universal Declaration of Human Rights[3] was adopted by the United Nations (UN) in 1948 and today it still contains 30 articles prescribing **human rights** that apply to citizens of all countries within the UN. This is the first modern document of its kind that is comprehensive and accepted by many countries, demonstrating their **zeitgeist**. Examples of these articles include the following.

Article 1: The right to freedom.

Articles 2 and 30: The right to have human rights and for these not to be removed (though these may be restricted if a person has broken the law or if it is essential to preserve national security).

Article 7: The right to be treated equally and receive equal protection of the law.

Article 18: The right to belief and changes in belief.

Article 19: The right to free speech and expression.

Member states must not deprive their citizens of any of the 30 rights listed in the Declaration (under Article 30), but this does not apply to non-member states. Procurement professionals must be aware of this, and understand that selected suppliers may be based in a country that does not recognise these rights.

Human rights are not guaranteed in every country, meaning that the citizens of some countries may be subject to punishments, imprisonment and unfair treatment that would be considered to be a breach of their human rights elsewhere. A responsible buyer's primary concern is the potential mistreatment of people living in the country in question, which could include the staff of a supplier, or its **sub-tier suppliers**. However, there is of course the secondary concern of negative media coverage if the organisation is found to be purchasing from these regions, potentially perpetuating the abuse of human rights (unintentionally, or otherwise).

Sub-tier supplier
An organisation supplying into the suppliers that are contracted directly into a buying organisation's supply chain. This supplier's activities, stability and reputation can all affect the buyer's supply chain

The CIPS Code of Conduct states that procurement professionals who are members of CIPS should promote the eradication of human rights violations by learning about them, carrying out due diligence with potential suppliers, and by taking action to appropriately remedy any such violations. The following organisations may be able to support with this.

- Local law enforcement organisations based in the country where the human rights violation is believed to have occurred. This support may not be available in countries where human rights are not acknowledged.

- Amnesty International[4]: a global not-for-profit NGO dedicated to the promotion of human rights that campaigns for them to be recognised, guaranteed and protected all over the world. This organisation carries out research into human rights, lobbies governments and carries out campaigns to highlight human rights violations using donations from supporters worldwide. Where international business is concerned, Amnesty International is also calling for a global requirement for corporations to do the following.

  o Be required by law to prevent human rights violations by reporting them.

  o Be held accountable for human rights violations that they commit.

  o Provide suitable remedy and justice to victims of human rights abuses, through a proper legal process.

  o Abide by international human rights laws to reduce the chance of violations occurring when the corporation is operating in foreign countries.

- Human Rights Watch[5]: a global not-for-profit NGO that investigates cases of suspected human rights abuses, as well as promoting and defending human rights across the world.

- Equality and Human Rights Commission (UK)[6]: a regulatory body, dedicated to enforcing The Human Rights Act 1998 and the Equality Act 2010 in the UK, both of which are key pieces of legislation in protecting human rights and promoting diversity within the UK. The Commission supports companies in ensuring that their operations do not infringe on human rights by encouraging ethical practice, clarifying ambiguities in the law, and by challenging unethical industry practices.

- Australian Human Rights Commission (Australia)[7]: an organisation that promotes human rights to individuals and companies in Australia, while also working closely with similar organisations that are members of the Asia Pacific Forum of National Human Rights Institutions.

Throughout history, one of the most significant abuses of human freedom has been the use of slavery. While this may have begun long before the concept of human rights had matured, it is important to understand the impact this continues to have on the freedom of individuals, as well as how this affects supply chains.

> *Check*
> In 1948, which document was released by the UN describing human rights?
>
> How many human rights are listed in this document?
>
> Are human rights guaranteed in every country?
>
> Which organisations exist to provide support regarding potential human rights violations?

Modern slavery

In modern society, slavery is thought to be a cruel, outdated practice. However, despite the abolition of slavery in the UK in 1833, and later in the USA in 1865, it is still widespread throughout homes and businesses across the globe. In 2016, the number of modern day slaves was estimated to be 40.3 million (International Labour Organization and Walk Free Foundation, 2017[8]).

Modern day slaves are people who are forced into carrying out labour against their will, often through threats of violence against them and their families. This may be the result of a perceived debt owed to an 'employer' or individual, which they must work to pay off (potentially with no end). Or individuals may be promised a life with better prospects in other countries but are then captured and enslaved through human trafficking networks. Modern day slavery is not just limited to adults; nearly a fifth of such slaves are children.

Slavery within businesses allows companies to offer products or services at a very low cost to buyers, allowing them to submit attractive bids. It is easily hidden beneath tiers of supply and can take place anywhere, which is why it is important for a buyer to be vigilant, looking for signs that slavery may be taking place in its supply chain. Some of these may include the following.

Fair Trade Foundation
An international charity dedicated to encouraging countries and organisations to ensure that their workers are paid a fair salary for the work that they do

- Suppliers based in nations with poor scores in the Corruption Perceptions Index (CPI) (see earlier in section 4.1).

- Suspiciously low labour costs in sub-tier suppliers; suppliers who are not accredited by the **Fair Trade Foundation**.

- Variations in the quality of purchased products (due to labourers being unskilled).

- Evidence that workers live on-site or are held against their will elsewhere.

- Unwillingness of workers to communicate or make eye contact with buyers' representatives who are viewing shop floor areas.

- Poor quality workstations and workshops.

- Few labourers, but long shifts or 'round-the-clock' working taking place (possible breach of the UK Working Time Regulations).

- UK-based supplier who does not have a published anti-slavery statement.

Case study

The worldwide reach of slavery
In 2014, *The Guardian* newspaper exposed a large network of Thailand-based commercial fishermen with ships crewed by a huge number of slaves. The prawns harvested by these slaves were sold straight into the $33bn corporation CP Foods, which then distributed them worldwide to prominent retailers, such as Tesco and Walmart.

The managing director of the UK branch of CP Foods defended the company, stating that they did not have visibility of the problem. Despite this, the company has since faced several lawsuits and has suffered significant reputational damage. Tesco was quick to state that they believe slavery is 'unacceptable' and looked to make their supply chain slavery-free; other retailers publicly shared similar pledges.

(Source: adapted from Hodal, K et al. (2014), www.theguardian.com/global-development/2014/jun/10/supermarket-prawns-thailand-produced-slave-labour, Lawrence, F (2015) www.theguardian.com/global-development/2015/aug/19/costco-cp-foods-lawsuit-alleged-slavery-prawn-supply-chain)

Though the above are not guaranteed indicators of slavery happening at a business or home, it may be enough for a buyer to raise questions that challenge slavery. This could save lives, in addition to mitigating risks relating to product quality and consistency of supply. A procurement professional with modern slavery concerns could act in the following way.

- Carry out due diligence checks for new and current suppliers (discussed later in this chapter).
- Check code of conduct documents provided by suppliers; do they explicitly reject slavery?
- If based in the UK, contact the Modern Slavery Helpline[9] for advice.
- Stay alert and look for evidence of the indicators listed above when interacting with suppliers or visiting a supplier's premises.
- Introduce themselves to workers on the shop floor when visiting suppliers.

In the UK, Part 6 of the Modern Slavery Act (2015) contains provisions for transparency in supply chains and requires UK-based companies with an annual turnover of more than £36m to publish an anti-slavery statement on their website. This should be an assurance that the company does not and has not worked with companies that are known to use or perpetuate slavery.

Apply

Choose five UK-based suppliers with a turnover of more than £36m (for example, companies such as Tesco or Marks & Spencer).

- Access each company's website to see if it prominently displays an anti-slavery statement.
- Do the statements look similar?
- Does the company pledge to mitigate or prevent the existence of slavery within its entire sub-tier supplier network?

For an organisation with which you are familiar and whose suppliers themselves have a turnover greater than £36m or on international supply chain, research whether the sub-tier suppliers in the chain have anti-slavery statements.

For an organisation with which you are familiar, check if it has an anti-slavery statement. If not, do you think such a statement is required or could be beneficial?

Choose a country different to your own. Research whether the government publishes legislation for anti-slavery. Have a look for any applicable regulations on the Internet and familiarise yourself with their requirements.

4.2 Identify practices that support ethical procurement

Supply chains may operate across cultural boundaries, meaning that individuals and organisations from different backgrounds will come into contact with one another. One party may demonstrate values and practices that conflict with those of the other organisation. The same may also happen with sub-tier suppliers and these conflicting values may be accepted by the suppliers at a higher tier of the supply chain. These conditions make it possible for unethical practices to enter into a buying organisation's supply chain, introducing risk.

In this environment, the procurement professional needs to be resilient, confident and clear in its understanding of what is and is not ethically acceptable. Firstly, the procurement professional must know their organisation's values, policies, processes and any other requirements that the organisation may have in place to support procurement activities.

Secondly, it is important that procurement professionals are prepared with knowledge of best practice from within their profession, either by a professional body such as CIPS or from other organisations for example, reading this study guide. Learning this information is useful, but a procurement professional will develop their skills and business acumen by undertaking continuous professional development.

Thirdly, a procurement professional should use whatever tools are available to them in order to understand more about the suppliers they intend to invite to tender and choose to award contracts to, and current suppliers, who are already in contract with the buying organisation. The information available from tender documents and external sources such as databases can alert the procurement team to any risks that are already known, and identify areas of potential future risk, thereby protecting the organisation from reputational and financial harm.

> *Remember*
> Ensuring that ethical values are upheld is not just the responsibility of an organisation's managers. It is also the procurement professional's responsibility, as well as that of any stakeholders the procurement professional interacts with, to challenge unethical practices and to promote sustainable practice where suitable. If a procurement professional does not feel confident in challenging inappropriate practices themselves, they may need to ask for the assistance, of a team leader or manager, an external organisation such as a professional body (for example, CIPS) or a relevant government department.

Application of the CIPS Code of Conduct

The learning you are undertaking now is not intended *just* to enable you to pass assessments. It is designed to help you understand what is required of an effective procurement professional, regardless of which culture you come from, which company you may work for and what services or goods you may purchase. This learning should be supported by Continuing Professional Development, where you meet with other professionals in the CIPS network, attend presentations from subject matter experts and get involved in the work CIPS carries out worldwide, in order to keep your knowledge up to date.

CIPS learners who go on to achieve their Professional Diploma in Procurement and Supply may apply to become a full member of CIPS (MCIPS). To maintain this status, they must follow the CIPS Code of Conduct (available online through the CIPS website) which influences the curriculum. This document is a set of values, behaviours and actions that CIPS requires its members to uphold in the delivery of their professional practice. The main benefit to following the rules set out in the Code is that you will have a better understanding of how to carry out ethical, effective business that meets the needs of your organisation without negatively affecting the needs or rights of others. The secondary benefit of following the code is that it allows you to continue holding CIPS membership.

The CIPS Code of Conduct comprises five sections that outline what CIPS requires of its members and, more importantly, what they should do to meet these requirements. You should take some time to familiarise yourself with these requirements, as shown in figure 4.2.

Chartered Institute of
Procurement & Supply

CIPS Code of Conduct

The purpose of this code of conduct is to define behaviours and actions which CIPS members must commit to maintain as long as they are members of CIPS.

AS A MEMBER OF CIPS, I WILL:

Enhance and protect the standing of the profession, by:

- never engaging in conduct, either professional or personal, which would bring the profession or the Chartered Institute of Procurement & Supply into disrepute
- not accepting inducements or gifts (other than any declared gifts of nominal value which have been sanctioned by my employer)
- not allowing offers of hospitality or those with vested interests to influence, or be perceived to influence, my business decisions
- being aware that my behaviour outside my professional life may have an effect on how I am perceived as a professional

Maintain the highest standard of integrity in all business relationships, by:

- rejecting any business practice which might reasonably be deemed improper
- never using my authority or position for my own financial gain
- declaring to my line manager any personal interest that might affect, or be seen by others to affect, my impartiality in decision making
- ensuring that the information I give in the course of my work is accurate and not misleading
- never breaching the confidentiality of information I receive in a professional capacity
- striving for genuine, fair and transparent competition
- being truthful about my skills, experience and qualifications

Promote the eradication of unethical business practices, by:

- fostering awareness of human rights, fraud and corruption issues in all my business relationships
- responsibly managing any business relationships where unethical practices may come to light, and taking appropriate action to report and remedy them
- undertaking due diligence on appropriate supplier relationships in relation to forced labour (modern slavery) and other human rights abuses, fraud and corruption
- continually developing my knowledge of forced labour (modern slavery), human rights, fraud and corruption issues, and applying this in my professional life

Enhance the proficiency and stature of the profession, by:

- continually developing and applying knowledge to increase my personal skills and those of the organisation I work for
- fostering the highest standards of professional competence amongst those for whom I am responsible
- optimising the responsible use of resources which I have influence over for the benefit of my organisation

Ensure full compliance with laws and regulations, by:

- adhering to the laws of countries in which I practise, and in countries where there is no relevant law in place I will apply the standards inherent in this Code
- fulfilling agreed contractual obligations
- following CIPS guidance on professional practice

USE OF THE CODE

Members of CIPS worldwide are required to uphold this code and to seek commitment to it by all the parties they engage with in their professional practice.

Members should encourage their organisation to adopt an ethical procurement and supply policy based on the principles of this code and raise any matter of concern relating to business ethics at an appropriate level within their organisation.

Members' conduct will be judged against the code and any breach may lead to action under the disciplinary rules set out in the Institute's Royal Charter. Members are expected to assist any investigation by CIPS in the event of a complaint being made against them.

CONTACT US

UK: +44 (0)1780 756777
Africa: +27 (0)12 345 6177
Australasia: +61 (0)3 9629 6000
MENA: +971 (0)4 311 6505
Singapore: +65 6808 8721
             +65 6808 8722

E-mail: info@cips.org

This code was approved by the CIPS Global Board of Trustees on 10 September 2013.

www.cips.org

Figure 4.2 CIPS Code of Conduct

Where it is believed that members are not fulfilling the requirements of the CIPS Code of Conduct, their conduct will be measured against it as per the disciplinary rules that are outlined in the Institute's Royal Charter. If required, other members may be asked to assist in investigations against members in these cases. If it is determined that a member of CIPS has broken this code, they may have their membership revoked, leaving them without this prestigious badge to promote their supply chain acumen. As job applications become more competitive, this could exclude them from consideration, and may prevent the individual from working as a procurement professional.

In addition to promoting the requirements of the CIPS Code of Conduct, an organisation may choose to demonstrate that it supports ethical conduct by publishing an ethical code of practice.

> *Remember*
> In agreeing to hold any level of membership with CIPS, you are confirming that you will uphold the values and behaviours set out in the CIPS Code of Conduct. To help your managers, colleagues and suppliers understand the commitment you have made, you can direct them to the CIPS website where the code is shown in full.

> *Check*
> What are the benefits of holding a CIPS accreditation?
>
> What are the benefits to an organisation of having CIPS-accredited staff?
>
> What are the five sections of the CIPS Code of Conduct and what are CIPS members required to do?

Ethical codes of practice
A document outlining an organisation's accepted behaviours and principles of working

Ethical codes of practice

Developing an **ethical code of practice** allows an organisation to demonstrate its commitment to carrying out ethical business and rejecting corrupt practices. This is especially important for a supply chain department in an international organisation, as procurement staff may be exposed to a lot of situations, both internally and externally, where they may witness corrupt practices. So, it is important that procurement professionals understand what behaviours are required of them. From the buying organisation's perspective, it may also be reassuring to see that a supplier publishes its own code of ethics, meaning that it may be viewed more favourably in due diligence activities.

These codes could take the form of a stand-alone code or could be incorporated into a code of conduct. Either way, they may be in place at a number of levels across organisations, including the following three key levels.

- Profession level: an organisation that provides governance to individuals within a given profession, such as CIPS, which publishes a code of ethics on its website for procurement professionals to follow.

- Sector level: an organisation that provides governance for companies providing a specific service or product, such as the International Diamond Manufacturers Association (IDMA)[10]. The IDMA ethical considerations are incorporated into a code of practice, but they include provisions that uphold human rights and condemn the use of practices that produce 'conflict' diamonds in the international diamond trade.

- Company level: an organisation may choose to publish its own code of ethics to govern the actions of its staff with regards to ethical conduct. This is useful for both supplier and buyer, as each organisation can use this to gain insight into how the other organisation conducts business and what its attitude is towards acting in an ethical manner.

> *Remember*
> Ethical codes of practice may vary greatly between different professions, sectors and companies. At times, there may be conflicts between different organisations' adopted practices. Practice may also vary between the country each organisation is operating from. Whatever the differences, it is useful to discuss these up-front so that the procurement professional can determine what will and will not be accepted as ethical practice, preferably before awarding any contracts to suppliers.

Compliance with codes of practice from professional and sectoral bodies is voluntary, though some elements, such as bribery and corruption, may be governed by local laws. However, if an organisation is found not to be supporting an applicable ethical code of practice, there is the potential that the individual responsible or the organisation itself could lose their membership. This could lead to an individual not being able to practise, or even a company not being able to provide a particular product or service as each would no longer have the prerequisite credentials.

> **Case study**
>
> *The Samsung C&T code of ethics*
> South Korea was ranked 51st out of 180 countries in the Corruption Perceptions Index 2017. South Korean electronics company Samsung C&T supplies to consumers worldwide. It publishes a detailed code of ethics on its website, including the following provisions.
>
> - Management ethics
> - Employee ethics and responsibilities
> - Responsibility to country and society
>
> This code of ethics covers aspects of fairness, ethical practice, environmental protection and contributing to society. In addition to supporting the cultural direction of Samsung C&T's workforce, it will also likely appeal to potential customers of the organisation.
>
> *(Sources: information from www.samsungcnt.com/eng/governance/ codeofEthics.do, www.transparency.org/news/feature/corruption_ perceptions_index_2017)*

Pre-qualification and assessment criteria

Whether a buyer is looking for a supplier to provide a product or service on a short- or long-term basis, it must be possible that the supplier can meet its requirements. The supplier's ability to produce products or deliver services is

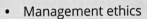

crucial and requires pre-assessment, but the buyer needs to understand whether or not the supplier's organisation shares certain ethical values. The extent of this compatibility can be tested by assessing key criteria through a pre-qualification questionnaire. This allows the buyer to determine, at an early stage, whether or not a potential supplier shares particular values or practices, and allows any unsuitable tenderers to be eliminated.

At the request for quotation (RFQ) or invitation to tender (ITT) stage, the buyer may choose to further assess the supplier in this area, specifically looking at how the supplier's approach to ethical practice is embedded in its delivery of contracts. This could include confirmation that the supplier will adhere to contract clauses, laws and performance terms that support sustainable and ethical practice throughout the delivery of its obligations under the contract.

As will be discussed later in this chapter, contemporary ethics are concerned with topics and factors that belong to social, environmental and economic categories. A supplier can be assessed on its commitment to supporting good practice within these categories, using criteria specified by the buyer. Examples of these criteria are shown in table 4.1, though this list is not exhaustive, and should be adapted to meet the needs and values of the purchasing organisation.

Social	Environmental	Economic
Are the supplier's employees asked to work to a code of conduct?	Are the impacts of the product understood throughout its life cycle, from manufacture, throughout its life and in its disposal?	Has the supplier produced this product before?
Are the supplier's employees part of a trade union and if so, how is this supported in the workplace?	Does the manufacturing process have any environmental impacts (effluvia, spillage, waste, etc.)?	Does the supplier have the time and production line capacity to produce the product?
Do the supplier's employees have a good understanding of their rights?	Is the product composed of materials that may cause harm or are not recyclable?	Is the supplier able to offer any changes or improvements to the product's design, if required?
Do the supplier's employees have a good understanding of their responsibilities in their role?	How are products transported when moved around the supplier's site or delivered to the customer?	Does the supplier take a risk-based approach to quality management, holding accreditations for international standards such as ISO 9001:2015?
Are the supplier's employees trained to work with the safety of themselves and others in mind?	Does the supplier possess an accreditation for working to a recognised international standard, such as ISO 14000:2015?	Has the total life-cycle cost of the product been considered?
Does the supplier have a good understanding of its sub-tier suppliers' workplace conditions and practices?	Do the supplier's products pose a harm to health that should be explained by accompanying material safety data sheets?	What other customers or sectors does the supplier deliver to, and what percentage of its order book do these make up?

Social	Environmental	Economic
Has the supplier declared that it has been convicted of a breach of the law regarding human rights, slavery corruption, etc., (if recognised by its home country)?	Has the supplier declared that it has been convicted of a breach of the law regarding environmental damage, illegal disposal of waste, etc., (if recognised by its home country)?	Has the supplier declared that it has been convicted of a breach of the law regarding fraud, contractual disputes, etc., (if recognised by its home country)?

Table 4.1 Pre-qualification criteria that may be used to pre-assess suppliers on their attitude towards ethical and sustainable practice (Source: adapted from www.cips.org/Documents/About%20CIPS/CIPS_Ethics_Guide_WEB.pdf)

The responses to the criteria shown in table 4.1 will give a greater insight into how well a potential supplier aligns with the buying organisation's values and product/service requirements. At this early stage, a buyer may discover that there are potential risks (both financial and reputational) in working with the supplier, allowing it to instead look to alternative sources of supply. Even if the buyer receives favourable responses at this stage, it is important that these are added to more detailed due diligence activities, which will allow for a more detailed review of potential and current suppliers.

> *Remember*
> If a supplier is found to be acting unethically or unsustainably while it is in the process of delivering against a contract, this may become an issue. Carrying out pre-assessments will allow the buyer to identify potential risks early, giving it the opportunity to filter out unsuitable suppliers before these enter the supply chain, protecting the organisation against the following.
>
> - Reputational damage from having a relationship with an unethical supplier that could negatively affect the organisation's revenue.
> - Money wasted in resolving conflicts, either business-to-business or in a court of law.
> - Time wasted in resolving conflicts or in re-launching sourcing to find an alternative supplier.
> - Late deliveries to customers as a result of sourcing delays and supply interruptions.

Due diligence on suppliers and risk assessment

Due diligence

Due diligence is highlighted as one of the key principles of the UK Bribery Act 2010 and under principle 4, UK-based companies should have a process for carrying this out. In addition to this, the CIPS Code of Conduct specifies that it should be undertaken by procurement professionals worldwide when conducting business with potential (or current) suppliers in supply chains. By carrying out effective due diligence, a procurement professional can improve their understanding of the supplier's quality, performance and ethical make-up, revealing any risks that may be present.

Due diligence may be carried out in the following ways.

- Asking the supplier to provide information on a template (along with supporting documents).

- Visiting the supplier's premises to see its facilities, processes and products in person.

- Carrying out a desktop assessment to see if there is any information about the supplier available online to support its appraisal.

Due diligence can be carried out in great detail by assessing a large number of factors, or a lesser check can be done, where only one factor (such as financial performance) is assessed. Whatever the factors to be assessed, these should be researched to give a better understanding of the supplier's previous and current practices. Some examples of common due diligence factors are given below.

- **First impressions of the supplier:** how responsive it has been so far, if it appears to have values or standards that complement those of the buying organisation, and how capable it appears to provide the goods or services the buying organisation requires.

- **Product or service quality:** appraising (by inspection or test) the perceived level of quality in the product or service, to be supported by data, if possible.

- **Qualifications of product or service providers:** assessing the individuals who are providing the product or service based on how qualified they are.

- **Background check:** research into any of the following factors.

  - **Adverse media:** press reports on negative behaviours of the supplier.

  - **Criminal convictions:** convictions served for breach of law, or wanted notices posted by local police organisations or INTERPOL (International Police Organisation).

  - **Corrupt practice:** practices revealed in adverse media or criminal convictions. It is also important to review any cases where suppliers are suspected or known to have a history of bribery, fraud and other corrupt practices.

  - **Financial performance:** whether the supplier is financially stable and if this has affected its ability to deliver on contracts in the past.

(Source: adapted from Goldman and Schmalz (2005)[11])

Due diligence may be an expensive activity (especially when conducted on many potential suppliers) but it can give enough information on a potential supplier to either give the buyer confidence or to highlight unacceptable risks, preventing such risks from coming into contact with the buying organisation. This allows the buying organisation to demonstrate its consistently ethical conduct and could prevent a loss of income by avoiding relationships with suppliers that do not align with the buyer's principles and conduct.

As with all international business, the key barrier to successful due diligence is language. Suppliers may provide documentation in a language that the buyer cannot interpret, making it difficult to truly understand and appraise. This could result in an otherwise suitable supplier being removed from selection.

Due diligence is carried out by procurement professionals, but this can be supported with the use of purpose-made tools, database subscription services, and best practice guidance. However, these only produce a report taken from a fixed point in time, and the information will only be current at the date it was checked. It is also worth noting that some of these may be costly to purchase or subscribe to, but they may save time and money, as well as reducing risk.

> *Check*
>
> How can due diligence be undertaken?
>
> According to Goldman and Schmalz (2005), what kinds of factors could be assessed when carrying out due diligence?

Risk assessment

Risks identified with potential and current suppliers may be found through due diligence, audit findings, information shared during contract reviews or other monitoring methods. These risks should be scored in terms of 'likelihood' and 'potential impact'.

Risks should be recorded, regularly reviewed and maintained in a risk register. This register allows risks to be recorded and displayed in a consistent format and enables the easy ranking of risks from highest to lowest. The risk register can be used to inform decision-making within a business, and this may help to mitigate or eliminate situations that may cause financial, reputational or other risks if risks are left unrecorded and unchallenged.

Supporting information on ethical practices in supplier quotations and tenders

The best time to further assess a supplier is during the tender/RFQ stage. At this point, it will be asked to submit information in support of the tender bid or quotation, and it is likely to give as much information as possible, to increase its chances of winning the business.

When a procurement professional compiles the invitation to tender or request for quotation, they will ask the supplier to say whether or not it can meet the requirements of the product or service the organisation wishes to buy. A buyer can use 'pass/fail' or scored questions as part of a pre-qualification questionnaire to assess this. Suppliers that do not meet the agreed criteria should be eliminated from the tender process.

This is a good opportunity to include any other questions relevant to the organisation's values in order to make the purchase more ethical, taking social and environmental considerations into account. This is important, as it showcases the buying company's commitment to procuring sustainably, and makes it clear to the supplier that it is expected to demonstrate the same care and behaviours, if it is successful. This also allows the buyer to lead the supplier to show its commitment to sustainability, allowing comparison with the buying organisations' values and those of other potential suppliers involved in the tender process.

CIPS[12] recommends that questions such as the following are asked of suppliers, if a detailed assessment is undertaken.

- Do your organisation's leaders continuously work to improve conditions in the workplace to meet staff needs?

- Are your staff part of a trade union and if so, do the staff have their own representative?

- What practices do you employ when hiring staff?
- Do you employ migrant workers and if so, what is their legal status?
- What is your company's process for handling cases of bribery or corruption?
- Have you encountered any cases of bribery and corruption in your operation and if so, how did you respond to this?
- How can fraud be prevented?

It is important that the 'pass/fail' condition for each criterion is set out before releasing these questions, to make sure that failures lead to disqualification. This condition allows the buyer and other stakeholders to carry out a fair, objective assessment of each supplier's responses, making results easy to compare. These conditions should not be released to the supplier with the questions as this could cause the supplier to answer questions in such a way that it says what the buyer wants to hear. An example of pass conditions is shown in table 4.2.

Question number	Question	Pass condition – award a pass if:	Number of points awarded for 'pass'
1a	Have you encountered any cases of bribery and corruption in your operation?	If 'Yes', the supplier should be assessed with question 1b. A response of 'No' could be because the supplier does not carry out effective monitoring and therefore should not be positively scored.	N/A
1b	If you answered 'Yes' to 1a, how did you respond to this?	If the supplier has encountered bribery or corruption, it can articulate the steps it took to identify and stop the behaviour. The supplier should also explain any new processes, systems or practices that it has since put in place to prevent this from happening again.	1
2	How do you prevent fraud in your operations?	If the supplier has active measures in place to prevent this, and it provides details about these.	1
3a	Are your staff part of a trade union?	If the supplier's staff are members of one or more trade unions.	1
3b	If you answered 'Yes' to 3a, what is the name of this trade union?	Details of trade unions used by the supplier's employees should be listed (where known). Ideally, these unions should be official organisations that can be researched further by the buyer if required to check their legitimacy.	1
3c	If you answered 'Yes' to 3a, do your staff have their own trade union representative?	An answer of 'Yes' is sufficient, details of this person are not required.	1

Table 4.2 An example extract from a section of a pre-qualification questionnaire

As different stakeholders in the organisation want to know different information about the supplier's capabilities, you may find that these stakeholders submit very different quantities of pre-assessment questions. If one section has ten questions in it but another has 55, the latter would heavily influence the overall score the supplier receives, meaning that success in this section is more important if it wishes to score highly. This can create problems as the section with fewer questions may be of far higher importance (i.e. safety requirements, product specification/capabilities, etc.,) than the section with more questions.

With this in mind, it is important that before the RFQ or ITT is released, the buyer works with other stakeholders in the organisation to determine which requirements are more important than others, i.e. hold more 'weight'. Stakeholders can allocate percentage weightings to each criterion, so that any success or failure in the most important sections will have a greater impact on the supplier's score. This means that in each section, scores are treated as percentages, meaning that a maximum score of 100% is achievable. Each section's scores are then adjusted by the weightings applied at a higher level in a weighted evaluation matrix, so that balanced scoring is shown. An example of how sections may be weighted is shown in table 4.3. Only the final column of this table shows the weighted score, which reflects the importance given to each section and is more meaningful than the unweighted scores.

Section	Section weighting	Supplier *X* score per section (unweighted)	Supplier *X* weight-adjusted Score
Commercial	15%	20/25	12%
Engineering	5%	5/20	1%
Ethical and sustainable practice	20%	7/8	18%
Manufacturing capability	40%	67/100	27%
Quality	20%	49/49	20%
Overall score per supplier:		148/202	78%

Table 4.3 A basic example of a summary of all sections of a weighted evaluation matrix

Apply

You have been given the task of developing a pre-qualification questionnaire that will be used to assess potential suppliers. In the context of an organisation with which you are familiar, answer the following questions.

- Who will compile the questionnaire's questions?
- Which stakeholders will need to be involved in developing their own questions and sections?
- From a procurement point of view, what questions do you think need to be included to assess the supplier's values and competence with regards to ethical and sustainable practice?

- What sources could you refer to if you need inspiration for questions?
- Who will be the final authority on the suitability of questions, prior to release?
- Do you expect that the weighting applied to each section will be fairly equal, or is it likely that some stakeholders will want their section to hold the most weight?
- There may be many questions from a number of stakeholders; who will be the point of contact with the supplier if any queries are raised?
- Will your stakeholders be responsible for reviewing the responses to their sections when they are returned, or will you carry this out?

Contractual clauses that support ethical procurement

The contract agreed with a supplier is an important document that sets the basis of the legal relationship between both organisations. This is also one of the best places to record the requirements for work carried out by the supplier to be ethical, giving specific details of what this means, so that the instruction is not misinterpreted. This helps the buying organisation, as a supplier bound by these should act in a manner that complements the buyer's own ethical standards. This means there should be a low risk of a negative impact on the buying organisation's reputation. Though contractual terms can be developed by experts within an organisation, 'boilerplate' terms (in the case of the laws of England and Wales) and CIPS Standard Terms & Conditions[13] are available for use (these can be found within the CIPS knowledge resources). The supplier is expected to conform to local laws, including those that relate to human rights, bribery, corruption and other ethical concerns.

As with other aspects of supplier performance management, suppliers can be contracted to a number of key performance indicators (KPI) to ensure that the organisation fulfils the contract requirements. KPIs are specific measures of different parts of a contract where suppliers are assessed on an agreed regular basis, so that the supplier can learn how well it is performing in its delivery of the contract. In this context, requirements for ethical and sustainable manufacture may be included in the contract, focusing on the value they deliver.

The ethics questions outlined in the pre-qualification questionnaires are natural starting points for outlining KPIs, as they already outline the buying organisation's concerns for the supplier. From here, these could be formally incorporated into any contracts that follow. As contract terms, they would be considered a measure of contractual performance, and if the supplier is found not to be meeting these, it may be considered to be in breach of contract. Importantly, this would give the buying organisation the right to terminate the contract and break off the relationship if it felt that the supplier's continued poor performance would lead to reputational or economic harm. Alternatively, the buying organisation may consider some failings against KPIs to be minor, and may choose to give the supplier an opportunity to improve its performance before taking further action.

Examples of sustainability KPIs

In order to demonstrate its commitment to corporate social responsibility, developing KPIs that encourage sustainable practice benefits the whole organisation. Examples of sustainability KPIs that could be written into supplier contracts include the following.

- Measurement of waste sent to landfill, e.g., 'Waste generated by manufacturing should not be sent to landfill and should instead be recycled where possible.' This could be measured by the number of tons of waste sent to landfill.

- Consumption of energy on an annual basis, e.g., 'The supplier should commit to reducing energy consumption by 5% across the next year.' This could be measured in electrical kilowatt hours, for example.

Though KPIs support the organisation in getting what it needs from the contract, the buyer must be careful to ensure that KPIs are not too much of a burden on the supplier. If it is costly or time consuming to meet the requirements, suppliers may struggle to meet them, putting them at risk of losing the contract due to failure to meet them. The buying organisation may choose to foster a relationship with a supplier where the supplier is able to be open and honest about how it regards the organisation as a customer. This will give the supplier the opportunity to discuss the requirements of the KPIs, discuss adjustments or considerations, and better understand the reason for the conditions of the KPIs.

Supplier monitoring

As discussed, before a contract is awarded, it is important to understand the extent to which a supplier is capable of delivering the product or service required. Even with the best due diligence processes and tools, it is not possible to accurately predict how a supplier will perform once it has been awarded a contract, and it is possible that it may not be able to deliver on time, in full and to the quality required.

Traditionally, supplier monitoring has been focused on the fact that a supplier may be financially unstable, only have a few customers or may be affected by some factor that commercially weakens it, and which may result in its inability to operate or deliver. This could badly affect the supply of goods or services, causing delays to production or interruption of ongoing activities. More recently, concerns about suppliers' ethical performance have been under increased scrutiny. The processes and tools of due diligence allow the buyer to understand how a supplier is currently operating (without having to ask questions directly) and to carry out ongoing monitoring of a range of suppliers. This is preferable as it gives a more accurate, continuous perspective that can be reviewed frequently.

Buyers may also carry out regular contract status reviews with suppliers, enabling both parties to maintain two-way communication, supporting an objective discussion. This method of monitoring may be consistent and frequent, and if the supplier is properly engaged, it may help it better understand the buying organisation's intentions and requirements.

Whichever way an organisation chooses to monitor a supplier, it the buyer's responsibility to ensure that the contract with the supplier is managed to its full delivery.

4.3 Compare the use of audits and other feedback mechanisms to evaluate ethical standards in the workplace

In many cases, the buyer may need to work closely with suppliers to ensure that the goods and services it delivers are being provided as required. The buyer should use the same thoroughness when promoting the use of ethical practices in its suppliers' workplaces (as well as its own). This may be challenging when working with suppliers where some of these practices are not governed by the supplier's home nation's national law. In these cases, the buyer can support the supplier in learning more about the importance of ethics in international (and local) trade, in a non-patronising or imposing manner, highlighting the benefits of demonstrating its agreement with these values.

In the past decade, many organisations have taken a strong stance in upholding ethics, for the sake of ethically concerned customers, as well as compliance with the legal requirements. If a supplier will not comply, the buyer should view this as a serious warning of ethical issues that may arise while working to deliver the contract.

Buyers hope to work with suppliers that already want to demonstrate ethical behaviours and operate in a sustainable manner, as these suppliers will be more likely to be compatible with the buying organisation's way of working. This may be determined during pre-assessment, where a supplier describes its organisation, or could be detected during due diligence, though this would more likely be negative information.

While suppliers may state verbally that they are committed to ethical and sustainable practice in the way they work, they may also explicitly demonstrate this commitment through the attributes shown in figure 4.3.

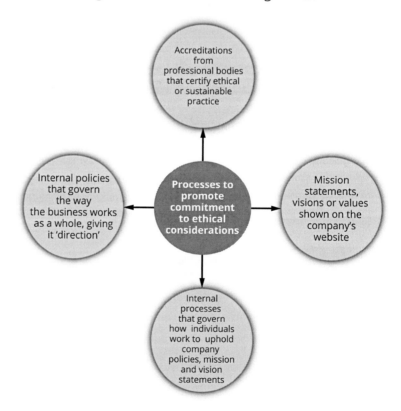

Figure 4.3 Types of processes that promote a company's commitment to ethical and sustainable practice

A buyer should check that the policies and processes in figure 4.3 exist and are kept up to date as, in addition to quality requirements, these also govern ethical and sustainable behaviours. If a supplier is unable to demonstrate these attributes, this should be treated as a risk by the buyer because ethics and sustainability are not clearly embedded into the supplier's processes. When these are in place, however, they may be used as a benchmark of the level the supplier claims to be operating at, enabling the buyer to investigate further and verify the truth of the claims made.

You may already have direct experience of being audited by an external organisation or be aware of an organisation that you are familiar with being asked to prove its competence in a particular practice. By positively responding to these requests or requirements, an organisation demonstrates transparency and effectively promotes the values it claims to stand for. However, the supply chain introduces external risks. Where a supplier is found to be acting unethically (by using slave labour, for example), this may result in an audit failure for the buying organisation, as it has either knowingly or unknowingly been purchasing from the supplier while this practice was taking place. So, it is essential to monitor suppliers to ensure that they are working to a mutually compatible standard of ethics and sustainable practice, where appropriate.

The following are three key ways of ensuring that activities are ethically and sustainably undertaken.

- Monitoring suppliers' ethical performance
- Encouraging dialogue with suppliers to encourage improvements to processes
- Identifying and addressing potential conflicts of interest

Monitoring supplier performance

Monitoring suppliers' ethical performance through auditing

One of the most objective, fair and repeatable methods of measuring a supplier's performance in upholding ethical standards and practices within its workplace is through an **audit**. This is carried out by the buying organisation, which acts as the auditor. As already discussed, while due diligence is an effective way of carrying out ongoing monitoring of suppliers from an ethics perspective, it relies on the use of limited sources of information. These sources are generally 'reactive', waiting for information to become available, rather than seeking it. This means that while negative media reports about an organisation may be picked up by due diligence monitoring, anything happening within the supplier's premises that is not known to the press will not be reported and therefore, not highlighted to the buyer. Audits in contrast can be carried out in much greater depth.

Buyers can use questionnaires to gather information on the supplier's attitude to ethical concerns and sustainable practice, but the responses may be biased and reflect what the supplier thinks the buyer wants to hear, rather than the actual truth. Audits may be a more suitable means of assessing a supplier's true values. By physically visiting the supplier's premises, the auditor is able to make their own assessment of whether or not they believe the supplier operates in an ethical and sustainable manner, while also assessing the supplier on its manufacturing processes, product quality, etc. To further reduce the risk of being misled, the buyer may give the supplier very little or no warning that the audit is taking place, so the supplier does not have time to prepare for what it believes the auditor *should* see, rather than the potentially undesirable or unacceptable things they *could* see.

Audit
An official inspection conducted, either by the procurement organisation itself or by an independent third party, to ensure compliance with requirements and standards

Audits can also be carried out internally (either the buying organisation auditing itself or the supplier auditing itself). However, an external audit carried out by the buyer on the supplier allows the buyer to have more control over it. If either party highlights a conflict of interest, it may be possible to have an impartial person or organisation take the role of auditor on the buying organisation's behalf.

Audits are generally ongoing, occasional activities that are scheduled, at least by the buying organisation. In other cases, they may take place following a failure of some kind (in quality, ethical standards, etc.,) and audits of this type will be more investigative, focusing on the problem and the elements that are believed to contribute to it, for example, not having a process in place or staff not being suitably trained.

Audits can be carried out in a number of ways, but they are generally conducted with some or all of the following features (though this is not a comprehensive list of methods).

- Face-to-face at the supplier's premises, either moving around independently or with a non-participant escort from the supplier's staff. If the auditor is being escorted, the escort must not interfere with the audit by leading the auditor to areas or people they believe will 'pass' the audit, or by prompting participants to give 'acceptable' responses to the auditor's questions.

- A structured series of questions that are aligned to contract requirements, internal process or policies, or international standards (such as ISO 14001:2015, Environmental Management Systems).

- A tour of the supplier's workplace, with the auditor's observations recorded and compared to standards, policies and processes.

- Interviews with members of staff in any relevant position. These may be chosen at random or may be deliberately chosen if there is good reason for this.

> *Remember*
> Although audits can be conducted in much greater detail than due diligence, supplier monitoring and pre-assessment activities, they are likely to require more resources. They will require more staff, take more time and cost more to carry out, but will generate valuable information if the audit is carried out effectively. Despite this, the information received is only correct at one point in time and is limited because in-depth monitoring does not continue. In some cases, it may be possible to 'benchmark' audit findings by comparing the results against those of other organisations, allowing for wider analysis and understanding of the supplier's performance in an industry-wide context.

Scope
The defined boundaries that limit the extent of a study, to ensure that it is focused on the specific situation or problem

Audit planning and scope development

Before starting the audit, the lead auditor should make a plan for it, setting a clear **scope** of how it should be carried out (seeking the advice of other auditors or relevant internal stakeholders where required). When defining the scope, the following elements should be considered.

- How long the audit will be expected to take (an hour, one day or one week – adjustable to meet the needs of the audit).

- The period of time to be reviewed (limiting the documents to be reviewed to those that were completed within a given time period, e.g., no more than three months ago). This may be useful if quality problems occurred during one continuous period and other factors from this time may have caused this.

- The teams or functions the audit will focus on.

- The extent of work or activities that the audit will focus on.

- Which processes will be looked at.

- Any other elements required for the audit to have clearly defined boundaries.

The purpose of defining the scope to this extent is to ensure that all parties involved in the audit are aware of the content it covers and the limits of this coverage (such as just individuals from a particular team, or from within a particular three month period). It is important that this is clearly outlined before the audit begins and it is essential that this plan is followed as closely as possible. If audit plans are not followed, there is the potential for **scope creep** to occur, where elements that are not relevant are covered by the audit (either purposefully or accidentally).

Scope creep can negatively affect the outcomes of audits and other activities in the following ways.

Scope creep
When the original scope of a study (or a specification for example) has been exceeded either deliberately or accidentally, meaning that the study is now focused on elements that were not originally intended to be included

- Time wasted observing the wrong things.

- The audit not being properly completed due to wasted time.

- Money wasted observing other things or carrying out unnecessary checks/analysis.

- The audit findings and conclusions not understanding the true root cause of problems that are identified, instead attributing them to 'false' causes.

- Over-burdening the supplier's resources if many interviews, documents reviews or access to areas are requested by the auditor.

- Disruption to the supplier's operations or production processes if operations are halted during the audit.

Spending time properly planning audits is essential. Without a clear, agreed plan, the audit risks being ineffective, costly and giving an inaccurate picture of the situation. Though the lead auditor has discretion to change the plan, it should be kept to as closely as possible until its full delivery.

Audits can be complex, involving a lot of stakeholders and a wide-ranging scope in some cases. The audit plan and scope should contain details of the following (along with any additional requirements).

- The name of the lead auditor, supporting auditors and others required to support the audit's operation.

- The names of any individuals who will be specifically audited.

- Teams or functions that will be focused on.

- The audit's timescale (preferably with milestones for key activities).

- The period in the past from which information will considered as part of the audit.

- Any relevant activities or tasks.

- Processes that govern the activities in question.

Audit execution

Where possible, audits should be unannounced, meaning that the participants receive no warning that it will take place (though this may not be practical or appropriate in some circumstances). This will mean that a supplier does not have the opportunity to take precautions to 'protect' itself from the suspected scope of the audit, particularly in areas where it is not performing to requirements. This would give the lead auditor an inaccurate, 'unnatural' representation of the way the business operates. Such precautions or preparations could include the following.

- Fraudulently creating new documents that the supplier believes the auditor will want to see, purely for the purposes of 'passing' the audit. For example, processes, policies or records of hours worked by staff.

- Cleaning facilities and equipment, to give the auditor the impression that the workplace is always clean and well maintained.

- Suddenly mandating the wearing of personal protective equipment (PPE) by all staff in manufacturing environments where this should be worn but usually is not, to convince the auditor that health and safety is a priority for the organisation.

- 'Coaching' staff to ensure that if they are chosen to participate in the audit, they give a particular response, lie or do not speak at all.

> *Remember*
> Companies being audited will be anxious to give a good impression to the auditor to prevent failure. In the supplier-customer relationship, this may be especially common if suppliers do not want to be seen as under-performing or lacking in some way. It is the responsibility of the lead auditor to ensure that the findings of the audit reflect reality as much as possible. It might be that this can only be achieved by keeping the supplier unaware of the buyer's intention to audit them.

Attempting to mislead an auditor in order to appear to be performing well is unethical practice. This can distort the audit results, giving the buying organisation an inaccurate representation of the supplier's practices. This could mean that improvements are not made in areas where they are required, as they are deliberately hidden from the auditor.

During the audit, the lead auditor should lead the activity. As this will take place on a supplier's premises, the audit team will need the support of the supplier's senior employees to ensure the team has access to any required areas, employees and documents that it needs (where safe and possible). If the supplier's representative attempts to lead the auditor to information or obstructs them from accessing something without good reason, the audit may be compromised.

Non-conformance
Where an audit finds that something does not work or is not carried out in line with the rules that govern it. These generally require action to fix the problem

Similarly, allowing a representative of the supplier or an agency supporting it to audit the supplier's process or premises on behalf of the buyer would be highly likely to reduce the integrity of an audit. This would be regarded as a conflict of interest as the audit may not be carried out with the same level of scrutiny (with potentially serious **non-conformances** being deliberately overlooked, or problematic areas or topics being avoided) or may lead to the production of a falsified report. In either case, the audit would be flawed, ineffective and unreliable, meaning it cannot truly be used to assess the ethical performance of the supplier.

Often, individuals become nervous or anxious when they are audited. While in some cases this may be because the individual is aware that they are not acting appropriately (and might be expecting to fail the audit), in many cases, they are just nervous because their work is under scrutiny.

To best put them at ease, auditees should be treated objectively and with respect, giving them a fair opportunity to answer questions, give evidence and demonstrate their knowledge.

Encouraging dialogue with suppliers on process improvements

After an audit, the auditor generally prepares a report of their findings, which may or may not be shared with the supplier, at the auditor's discretion. However, it is good practice to communicate any non-conformances or **opportunities for improvement** to the supplier using a simple, recognised format, such as a corrective action plan. This plan should state specific non-conformances and the requirement that they relate to. It should also include the action to take to fix the problem, ensuring that it is SMART (Specific, Measurable, Achievable, Relevant and Time bound) so that it can be effectively executed. A named person should then take responsibility for and complete this action, to ensure accountability is maintained. Opportunities for improvement may be recorded in the same way, but these are generally seen as recommendations, rather than required improvements.

The auditor, supplier and action owners will regularly monitor the progress of any actions recorded in the corrective action plan, to ensure that they are properly completed on time. Even if they have not been involved until this point, it would be a good idea to at least brief senior members of the supplier's staff on the findings and actions arising from the audit. This will help them to understand its purpose and will give the lead auditor an opportunity to highlight the importance of ensuring that the actions are fully completed on time. Hopefully, the senior staff will then provide the authority and support necessary to help the action owners complete their actions.

Where the requirements of actions are not met or are not met on time, this should be taken as a warning sign by the buying organisation, as it may suggest that the supplier does not share its values.

Exchanging two-way feedback is particularly important for encouraging suppliers to make improvements, by request or through their own continuous improvement activities. It encourages suppliers to better meet the buying organisation's contractual requirements or other standards.

Opportunity for improvement
Where an audit identifies potential improvements to a process or ways of working and highlights them for future consideration. These do not always require action, but may be treated as suggestions

> *Remember*
> Feedback is a key aspect of improvement in many areas of business. In order to get the best possible result, audit findings should be shared with suppliers, preferably face-to-face so that any misunderstandings or ambiguity can be addressed at that time. When actions are agreed, suitable stakeholders should take ownership of them, making sure they are fully completed on time.

Apply

You work for a car manufacturer that prides itself on protecting the wellbeing of its employees; this is clearly embedded into the policies and processes that govern its operation.

One day a colleague shares their concern that your reliable, exterior panel supplier (that only has a small number of employees) has been putting on extra shifts to meet increasing manufacturing demands from new customers. By her calculations, this means the supplier's staff would have to work very long shifts in order to produce the required supply. In addition to this, she has received reports that a number of the supplier's staff are on leave following injuries reportedly received in the workplace within the last three months. When she asked the supplier how these injuries occurred, the supplier advised that they were the result of machine operators' carelessness and dismissed the idea that they might be serious accidents.

You have asked the supplier to share records of its employees' working times and accident records, and the supplier said that it would send these as soon as possible. Seven days have since passed and you have not received them. Your colleague is concerned that these records do not exist and believes that this is quickly developing into a risk to your organisation.

You decide that an audit would be the best way of objectively assessing the situation, in order to understand the situation yourself.

Outline the following as a plan in preparation for your audit.

- Who will lead the audit?
- Who should support the lead auditor?
- What is the expected timescale for the audit?
- What is the full scope of the audit, including:

  ○ How far back will information be reviewed?
  ○ Will the audit focus on any teams or functions in particular?
  ○ Will any specific tasks or activities require focus?
  ○ Which processes are expected to cover all of the above elements?
  ○ Any other elements that you believe should be covered.

Check

What are the benefits of carrying out supplier audits?

What are the constraints or limitations of carrying out supplier audits?

What are the benefits of not announcing planned audits to suppliers before carrying them out?

Recommending remedial actions where appropriate

When working with suppliers over a period of time, issues may arise during the relationship, which can be caused by the suppliers' extended supply chain. It is necessary to have formal processes in place that allow for timely remedial and corrective action and address all of the root causes of the problems.

For example, a raw materials supplier may be subcontracting to an organisation that exploits child labour. This is a clear CSR performance issue, and one that can cause serious reputational damage for the purchasing company.

Within the purchasing company's quality management system, there will be formal corrective action plan policies and procedures that provide both parties with a step-by-step, closed-loop formal plan of action for communicating, resolving and closing out any problem that arises or any error that is identified. The supplier will be responsible for identifying the root cause of the non-compliance that the buyer has recognised and raised, and for developing corrective and preventative actions against it.

Figure 4.4 below shows an example of a corrective action plan.

CORRECTIVE ACTION PLAN			
Non-compliance with CSR audit	Root cause	Corrective action	Preventative action
When reviewing supply chain, raw materials supplier found to be subcontracting to a company that exploits child labour	The subcontracting of services by the raw materials supplier – clause on subcontracting was omitted from the buyer–raw materials supplier contract	Terminating the contract would cause disruption throughout the supply chain – so took decision to vary the contract to include a subcontracting clause	Regular reviews with raw materials supplier to ensure future prevention Training programmes on CSR (with supplier and subcontractors)
Comments (from purchaser's quality manager)			
Proposal accepted			
Factory verification			
Date of verification			
Verified by		Joe Bloggs	
Verification results		Conform to plan	

Figure 4.4 A sample corrective action plan

Root cause analysis and corrective action

Remember the reason for the root cause analysis is to allow the buyer not only to address the issue but to ensure it does not occur again.

Taking timely, effective and direct action

Buyers want positive relationships with suppliers. However, it is necessary to resolve issues quickly when they do arise, because continuing non-performance or non-compliance by suppliers will harm the business.

Supplier development programmes

As well as having formal supplier corrective action policies and procedures in place to address issues and errors through a quality management system, buyers can also establish proactive supplier development programmes.

Supplier development programmes are carried out to strengthen relationships with suppliers, and to strengthen their capabilities and competences. A collaborative approach can be much more effective for solving problems and improving performance. In many cases, suppliers can offer innovative solutions to resolve issues and increase performance, due to their specific breadth and depth of knowledge.

In terms of remedial actions, the supplier must be given time to implement and maintain the corrective actions and improve performance. However, if the supplier's performance does not improve despite the best efforts of the buyer, then the buyer will need to decide whether the relationship with the supplier continues or whether it is time to exit the relationship and find a new supplier.

If the buyer decides to terminate the relationship, they need to mitigate supply disruption by managing an effective exit strategy and bringing up a new supplier. It is important to recognise that this can be costly and takes effort, time and multiple resources.

> *Remember*
> Supplier development programmes are effective for maintaining relationships with a current supplier, as well as for helping them to improve performance (provided the supplier is willing to co-operate).

Identifying and addressing potential conflicts of interest

Nepotism
Using actual or perceived power to give an unfair advantage to friends or family members

In all aspects of business, there is the potential for conflicts of interest to arise. The relationships that people form in both their social and professional lives have the potential to make someone behave differently in a given situation. This is known as a **conflict of interest**, as a person may choose to satisfy a particular person in a given situation, rather than do something fairly, in line with processes or in a manner that does not bring risk. **Nepotism** is a common type of conflict of interest, which specifically describes someone giving preference to family members or friends in a situation where they should not (e.g., choosing to hire a family member or friend for a job instead of a more suitable applicant).

The following relationships could be seen to cause a conflict of interest if they are given preferential treatment.

- Partners, such as wives or husbands

- Former or current business partners of an external business (such as a manufacturer)

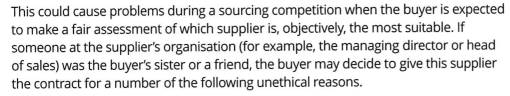

- Shareholders in another company
- Close friends
- Children

This could cause problems during a sourcing competition when the buyer is expected to make a fair assessment of which supplier is, objectively, the most suitable. If someone at the supplier's organisation (for example, the managing director or head of sales) was the buyer's sister or a friend, the buyer may decide to give this supplier the contract for a number of the following unethical reasons.

- The buyer feels that they *should* be awarding contracts to family members, rather than 'strangers'.
- The buyer knows and likes their sister more than the stakeholders they have met from the other suppliers.
- The buyer believes that they can trust a family member to deliver to a good standard.
- The buyer may want to start the supplier off with smaller contracts and gradually build up to higher-paying contracts when they have built up a good reputation.
- The buyer may expect the success of the supplier to lead to personal gains for themselves, such as a financial return to their family.

> *Remember*
> Obviously not every person with a conflict of interest is guaranteed to behave in a corrupt way. Everyone's individual nature will decide how they act, but conflicts of interest can leave decision-makers open to potential accusations that they have acted or will act unethically.

Remember, conflicts of interest do not always relate to the buyer working with the supplier. Those in authority (CEO, head of department, managers, etc.,) may have their own relationship with a supplier or other figure and they might make a deal of their own outside of official tendering and negotiations. This person may then put pressure on the buyer to choose the supplier that the individual wants, rather than through the result of fair competition.

Conflicts of interest may not always be from one business to another but could be internal, where family members or friends both work at the same company. There is no guarantee that something corrupt will happen, but there could be a perception of the potential for unfair advantages or corrupt practice resulting from the close relationship. So even if individuals are not behaving in a corrupt manner, there is a chance they could be accused of this.

It is also possible for two people whose relationship is not a known conflict of interest to act in a corrupt way. Sometimes, it can be difficult to avoid conflicts of interest within organisations. They may be more common when organisations are based in smaller communities where a lot of family members work for the same organisations, or where there are few organisations that employ large numbers of people from the local area.

For example, a member of staff might need an amendment to their timesheet. They may have a relative who can make this amendment but if they were to ask them to make the changes, other staff may accuse both of them of committing fraud. They could be suspected of adding, removing or changing worked hours to benefit the staff member, particularly if they haven't worked the extra hours that they will then be paid for. Though this could be innocent, with no fraud taking place, both parties are open to the accusation by suspicious colleagues.

One of the most effective ways to prevent issues arising from a perceived conflict of interest is to openly declare it. By doing so, both parties publicly acknowledge that their relationship may give others reason to accuse them of acting in their joint interests. However, this is not the same as accusing themselves or admitting to acting fraudulently. In these cases, both parties may actively avoid working together on particular projects, or may inform their colleagues that a conflict exists if they are asked to work together.

In some cases, individuals may not recognise or perceive that a conflict of interest exists between themselves and another person. Then it may be down to that person's manager or another suitable person to declare that they believe a conflict of interest exists. Ideally, the people who have the conflict of interest should be included in any discussion.

If there was ever a legal dispute as a result of a damaging behaviour, such as fraud arising from a conflict of interest, a good audit trail of information would be required to support the case. To cover themselves from liabilities, many organisations now have a conflicts of interest log or register, in which all known or declared conflicts of interest (both internal and external) can be recorded. Being on this register does not mean or imply that the parties have done anything wrong.

A conflicts of interest register would contain the following information.

- The date the conflict of interest is raised
- The names of the people the conflict of interest pertains to
- Details of their roles and teams
- Details of the relationship between them and the reason the conflict of interest was raised
- The boundaries or conditions to be set if the individuals in question should ever be asked to work together

Entries on the conflicts of interest log should be reviewed regularly (in proportion to the risk) to understand if the conflict still exists. These should be treated the same as other risks identified by the organisation.

Remember
Conflicts of interest are not declared to incriminate individuals. Instead, they are a good way for both parties to positively and openly declare the limits of their professional relationship. This mean that others are able to support them in making sure activities are carried out fairly, while still ensuring both employees are not under suspicion.

Conflicts of interest between businesses (for example, between supplier and contracting organisation) must still be declared and understood. As a part of the sourcing process, a buyer may ask a supplier to complete a 'Declaration of No Conflict of Interest'. This form is the supplier's written positive confirmation that it is not aware of any conflict of interest existing between both businesses, and the employees communicating between them. It is particularly important that there are no conflicts of interest between members of the buying team of the contracting organisation and the sales team of the supplier. This could lead to unethical practice or reputational harm if either party is accused of acting unethically due to a conflict of interest (generally by other suppliers that did not win a contract).

Case study

HS2 contract potential conflict of interest
Conflicts of interest can cause reputational harm to organisations, along with other costly consequences. In 2017, US engineering firm CH2M withdrew its interest from a UK HS2 rail network contract it was awarded because a competitor identified a potential conflict of interest between the buying and supplying organisations. In this case, the Chief Executive of HS2 was a former employee of CH2M, leaving both organisations open to accusations that the contract award was unfair due to this conflict of interest (whether that was proven to be the case or not).

As a result of this, CH2M lost a £170m contract, HS2 was affected by a delay in the sourcing and both parties suffered reputational harm in the press.

(Source: adapted from www.ft.com/content/de63f8aa-1481-11e7-80f4-13e067d5072c)

Apply
A procurement professional may see various conflicts of interest and it is important to be able to identify these with confidence, and to declare them in line with the company policy, if they are not already declared. For the following scenarios, decide whether or not you believe that there is a conflict of interest and give reasons for your choice.

- One of the contractors invited to tender is located in the same town or industrial zone as the buying organisation.
- A married couple work in two teams within an organisation. The two teams do not work with each other.
- A mother based in a team where her daughter is her line manager.
- An accountancy firm operated by a relative of the managing director is contracted to manage the organisation's financial accounts.
- A contract is awarded to a supplier that also supplies to a competitor.
- A stakeholder involved in down-selecting suppliers is a shareholder with one of the companies that has submitted a bid.

Check

Give three examples of situations that may be considered potential conflicts of interest.

What information would you expect to be recorded in a conflict of interest register?

What damage could arise from a conflict of interest not being raised between two businesses?

4.4 Contrast processes and practices that the organisation could adopt to meet the requirements of corporate social responsibility (CSR)

What is corporate social responsibility?

By now, you should have a general understanding of what corporate social responsibility (CSR) is. It is the demonstration of ethical behaviours carried out by an organisation, and can be closely scrutinised by external stakeholders. It recognises that the organisation has additional responsibilities, for which it should be held accountable, beyond the main considerations such as making profit.

Stakeholders' perceptions of an organisation's CSR can be key to whether or not inter-organisational relationships are successful, and whether or not contracts are won. This means that not being able to demonstrate CSR could cause irreversible harm to an organisation's reputation.

One of the best ways to display a strong commitment to CSR is an organisation's understanding of **sustainable development** and the ways it applies these principles.

Sustainable development in supply chains

During the industrial revolution, the UK thrived as some of the most advanced and economically successful manufacturing of the time was taking place on a scale that had never been experienced before (encouraging other nations to quickly follow). The industry involved extracting and consuming a huge amount of natural resources, such as coal, iron ore and water. These are known as 'common' resources because they are unregulated and freely available.

In 1863, the rapid consumption of these resources in the UK concerned economist William Forster Lloyd who wrote the *Tragedy of the Commons*: an influential essay discussing the future problems that could be caused by over-exploitation, extraction and pollution of natural resources. He attempted to encourage industry leaders and the government to understand the negative impact that industry may be having on the natural environment. Damage caused to common resources may be irreversible, meaning that the activities that require them may no longer be able to continue. This concept was one of the main influences of the report *Our Common Future*, which was published over a century later in 1988.

Sustainable development
Development that meets the needs of the population in the present without negatively affecting the resource needs of future populations

Our Common Future[14] (also known as the *Brundtland Report*) discussed the importance of carrying out sustainable development in all aspects of life. Sustainable developments are those that meet the requirements of the people using them at this point in time, but also take care that this does not have a negative impact on future generations. This was a further development on the concept of the *Tragedy of the Commons*, as it began to recognise the importance of protecting people, or socio-cultural preservation, in addition to economic and environmental factors.

4.4 L04

Case study

How much water is enough?

An example of this concept is the case of a drinks manufacturer extracting large amounts of water from a lake or aquifer that a town depends on for water. If the drinks manufacturer extracts too much, the population of the town may not have enough drinking water and local wildlife may not have a suitable habitat to thrive in. There may also be by-products from this company's processes, such as effluvia released into the air, or polluted water that harms ecosystems or is absorbed into crops that are later consumed by people living in the area. If the negative effects of activities are not properly considered, understood or assessed, people may die, natural resources may be damaged and local ecosystems may collapse and never be restored.

If, instead, the drinks manufacturer monitors its water extraction rates, taking only as much water as it needs and actively working to protect the local population and fauna, it *may* be possible for it to continue operating there without harm. Or if the company finds that it needs more water than is sustainably available, it may try to improve its recipe or process to reduce the amount of water required, or may relocate the manufacturing plant to a place that offers greater access to more water, or will not have a negative effect on local populations of humans and wildlife. The company would also need to monitor any waste emissions released from the site (including their composition, transmission pathways and the potential health impacts to humans and other animals) to prevent lasting damage.

Sustainable development and the sustainability of activities in general is often described as being made up of three main 'pillars'. These three pillars, shown in figure 4.5, are all required to uphold the holistic principals of sustainability.

Social: how an activity affects people, relationships, cultures, laws and political situations.

Environmental: how an activity affects ecosystems, environments and the abundance of natural resources.

Economic: how an activity affects the finances or resources of individuals, organisations, markets and national economies.

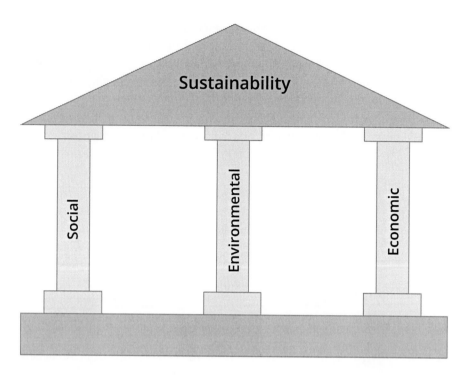

Figure 4.5 The three pillars of sustainability

The decisions a procurement professional makes can help to influence whether or not procurement activities are sustainable. With the products purchased, there is potential for impacts at different stages of the process (shown in figure 4.6). It is important for a buyer to consider what effects their purchases may have on the environment and on people, by asking questions such as those in figure 4.6.

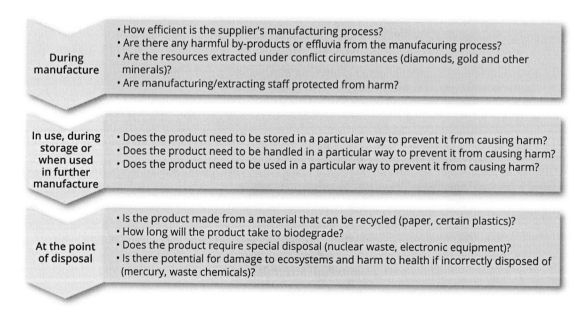

Figure 4.6 Potential sustainability impacts throughout different stages of the product life cycle

The importance of sustainable development is now widely recognised, and in 2015, the United Nations[15] set 17 Sustainable Development Goals for its member nations. All of the goals are designed to provide targets in achieving positive social, economic and environmental improvements. These improvements are scheduled to be met by 2030, but these targets can only be met if people from all aspects of society are involved, meaning that governments, industry, communities and individuals all have a role in supporting this. Organisations worldwide are beginning to recognise the importance of working to implement policies, processes and practices to work towards these goals. This demonstration of corporate social responsibility to external stakeholders may contribute to an organisation winning more business.

The triple bottom line – profit, people and planet

The financial term 'bottom line' is often used in connection with trading profit and loss accounts. This refers to the profit made by an organisation, which is the lowest line on this document. In the private sector, success depends on being profitable, and staff in these organisations may be challenged to save money while also trying to maximise income to the company. While economic gain is the primary driver for many organisations, there are some that take a more philanthropic approach to business by incorporating the principles of CSR into their objectives or visions. This could involve a company setting itself targets to improve its social and environmental impacts, both inside and outside the organisation. While the organisation must consider the affordability of meeting these targets, the targets are not necessarily intended to support financial gain.

These additional targets might seem intangible, meaning measuring the success of the activities may not be straightforward compared to more obvious measures of economic profit. One way of incorporating these measures is to create a **triple bottom line**. This is where organisational performances against social and environmental factors are considered to be important value streams, in addition to economic performance. The triple bottom line is an economic term, developed by John Elkington[16] (a leading authority on sustainable development and CSR), that follows the principles of sustainability shown in figure 4.6 and is made up of the **3 Ps**.

Profit: an organisation's economic focus on generating financial wealth from the products or services it sells.

People: an organisation's socio-cultural focus on those it directly and indirectly affects, including the people it employs, the communities it operates in and the markets of customers it sells to.

Planet: an organisation's focus on its impact on the environment, which could include ecosystems, ground water contamination and over-extraction of resources.

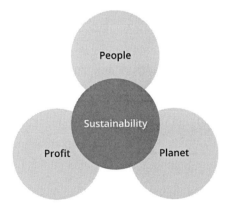

Figure 4.7 Sustainability can be expressed as being at the intersection of profit, people and planet

If a company actively monitors and promotes the factors that make up its triple bottom line, it will be able to more easily understand its financial, social and environmental performance. This will also allow the organisation to demonstrate its commitment to CSR, which may be attractive to investors and customers. This has become especially important recently as many customers have become more socially and environmentally conscientious, expecting the same values from the companies they buy from.

Adopting sustainable practices, standards and specifications in the supply chain

When an organisation is aware of the benefits of sustainable practice, it may choose to implement standards that its workforce can follow, to support the organisation in achieving sustainability. As discussed, an organisation's supply chain is one of the areas that can best benefit from sustainable practice, as well as being vulnerable to practices that are not sustainable.

ISO 20400:2017[17] is an international sustainable development standard that specifically covers the process of sustainable procurement. It gives guidance for stakeholders involved in procurement activities and the processes that govern them. Importantly, it contributes to achieving eight of the 17 UN Sustainable Development Goals, which include the following.

- The provision of decent work and the driving of economic growth
- Reducing inequality in the supply chain
- Responsible production
- Supporting communities

ISO 20400:2017 (International Organization for Standardization), the Sustainable Agriculture Standard (Rainforest Alliance) and the Standard for Hired Labour (Fair Trade International) are just a few of many standards that exist to support organisations in acting ethically and sustainably. If an organisation requires its suppliers to follow a particular standard, it can include this in a specification. The specification will contain details that the supplier must adhere to in order to meet the performance requirements of the contract and fulfil its obligations. Within the specification, the buyer can include more specific details of standards that a supplier must follow, including requirements for ethical practice and sustainable development.

One of the major benefits of being accredited to a standard is that standards are recognised globally by other organisations, which may make the organisation more attractive to potential customers. However, a company may choose to develop its own set of ethical or sustainable practices and policies in order to best suit its own needs and vision. An excellent example of this is the case of Marks and Spencer, which enacts its sustainable practice and ethical cognisance through 'Plan A'.

Plan A – because there is no Plan B
UK retailer Marks and Spencer operates over 1400 stores worldwide, across 56 international territories. It recognises that operating on this scale can have lasting negative external and internal impacts on people and the environment, and to demonstrate its commitment to mitigating this, the company has

Case study »

4.4 LO4

developed its 'Plan A' strategy. Named 'Plan A', because the company believes that there is no 'Plan B', this strategy outlines the company's commitment to being sustainable in all aspects of its operation. This includes the supply chain and by 2025 the company has committed to the following.

- Support the physical and mental health and wellbeing of employees

- Introduce produce from smallholders into the supply chain

- Carry out 'ethical' assessments of suppliers

- Lead on understanding more about in-work poverty and human rights violation across the supply chain

- Understand more about the socio-economic background of staff and improve social mobility

- Combat gender discrimination within the supply chain

- Encourage 'circular economy' by ensuring that no waste is sent to landfill

- Implement water stewardship plans

(Source: information from Marks and Spencer (2018) corporate. marksandspencer.com/plan-a, Marks and Spencer (2018) corporate. marksandspencer.com/aboutus/key-facts, Marks and Spencer (2018) corporate.marksandspencer.com/documents/plan-a/plan-a-2025-commitments.pdf)

Check

Which influential report was released in 1988 and why is it important?

How has sustainable development been defined?

What are the three pillars of sustainable development?

How do these pillars relate to the triple bottom line?

Give two examples of standards that can be adopted to promote sustainable development-focused practice.

Considering the social impact of the organisation's behaviours

As we have already explored, the behaviours of organisations are closely watched by the media and are at the mercy of a more socially conscious, well-connected network of consumers. Many consumers are quick to criticise a company if they believe the organisation has had a negative social impact on any group of people, but especially disadvantaged people. A buying organisation could be under scrutiny for this, or it could be that a supplier is creating a negative social impact. This could harm the buying organisation's reputation too, as it may be seen to be partly responsible, by implicitly supporting the behaviour.

Social impacts can be positive or negative, and can include some of the following elements.

- Health-related effects
- Splitting communities
- Causing unsustainable population influxes
- Attracting highly affluent and/or skilled people
- Cultural changes as the composition of communities change

It is important to remember that the social impacts of organisations are not always intentional, meaning that an organisation is not always aware of the **direct** and **indirect** impacts it has. Where an organisation carries out an activity with the intention of imposing a positive or negative social impact, this is a direct impact. Examples of this could include making certain changes to human resources policies, implementing a sustainable procurement policy, making a conscious effort to employ local, unemployed job seekers or banning smoking on site. These all directly impact (either positively or negatively, depending on the individual's perspective) employees and in some cases, the wider public.

In the case of banning smoking on a work site, this may be viewed differently by different people. The organisation's occupational health and safety teams may see this as a success, believing that this promotes stopping smoking and a healthy lifestyle, as well as reducing the potential for a fire starting on site originating from a discarded cigarette. Employees who smoke are likely to see this as a negative social impact and may feel that the organisation has challenged their right to enjoy smoking. This could lead to a couple of important indirect social impacts. Firstly, the smokers may ignore the ban and find a hidden place to smoke on site, increasing the potential for a fire to start from discarded cigarette butts (which would have been far less of a risk if smoking was limited to designated smoking areas).

Secondly, smokers may instead leave the site to smoke, as the company's policy does not apply there. The company may see an effect on productivity due to staff leaving the site. It may also receive complaints from members of the public who are concerned about the effect that second-hand smoke could have on their health, as a result of seeing staff smoking in public areas surrounding the site, rather than in designated smoking areas.

There can be many indirect social impacts such as these for organisations, and they can come from a huge number of behaviours, activities, processes and policies carried out by employees, their managers and their leaders. As they are very likely to be unintentional impacts, they can be difficult to predict. Where negative indirect social impacts occur, their effects may not be understood until it is too late. This makes it hard to plan for these and mitigate any potential problems.

Depending on the organisation's operations, these impacts could be either **external** to the organisation (affecting people based outside the organisation) or **internal** (affecting employees). Organisations can interact with and affect individuals, communities and organisations on a global scale. On an international scale, this can affect people in other countries, either positively or negatively. Table 4.4 shows some social impacts an organisation can have internally and externally.

Internal social impacts	External social impacts
• The organisation does not meet the requirements of employment law. • Human rights are violated. • Employees are asked to work very long hours. • Employees work in unsafe conditions or are not protected from physical harm, e.g., no provision of personal protective equipment, machine guarding or safe walkways. • Unethical behaviours are not properly challenged. • The organisation's leaders tolerate any of the above.	• Suppliers secretly using slave or low-paid labour to satisfy a contract where an unsustainably low price was negotiated and agreed. • Employees who cannot park their vehicle on site instead park elsewhere in surrounding areas, taking up space designated for residents. • Suppliers resort to using conflict materials in order to meet product costs for a contract where an unsustainably low price was negotiated and agreed. • If the organisation closed its on-site canteen facility, staff may purchase food from external vendors, which could lead to increased waste and rubbish in the surrounding area (which may be residential) if suitable waste bins are not available.

Table 4.4 Examples of possible internal and external social impacts of an organisation's activities

> *Remember*
> Different individuals perceive and experience the social impacts of an organisation in different ways. This means that the social impact of a particular activity may be considered to be trivial by one person but may be unsettling to or affect the health and wellbeing of another.

Designing procurement processes to deliver social outcomes as well as, or as an alternative to, normal economic measures of value

Processes are used by organisations to maintain consistent quality across employees' activities. To external observers, such as suppliers and customers, this consistency demonstrates a commitment by employees to follow the company's vision with uniformity. As we have already explored, there are a number of advantages to including socio-environmental targets in an organisation's vision or strategy. However, to achieve these it is essential that the organisation's processes are complementary.

One of the problems with socio-environmental factors in an organisation's operation is that they are often intangible. They may be less well understood (requiring expert advice) and are not as easy to relate to as more traditional economic measures of value, e.g., how much money is wasted due to an activity failing. To help employees to understand their personal contribution to socio-environmental targets, processes can be assessed on the nature of the ethical, socio-environmental impacts they have. Where these exist, the processes can be adapted to include tailored **control points**. These control points can take many forms, but should cover how an important part of the process should be carried out.

At each of these control points, a linked measure can be added, allowing observers outside of the process to know how effective that control point has been in preventing negative social or environmental impacts. For this measure, the organisation should also state the following.

- What will be measured *or* the scope (this should directly link with what the control/process step asks the user to do or provide).

- Whether or not there is a tolerance for an acceptable number of failures against this control in a given period of time.

- How often this measure should be reviewed and the person or group responsible for this.

An example of a simple control is a buyer asking a supplier to complete a questionnaire about its attitude to sustainable practice during the ITT/ RFQ stage. There are then two measures to assess how well this control is performing, as shown in table 4.5.

Measure scope	Tolerance	Action to be taken for failure	Period covered	Frequency of review	Measure owner/ reviewing group
Buyer sends sustainable practice questionnaire to supplier with each ITT/RFQ.	100% required to be sent as this forms part of the supplier assessment.	Establish root cause of failure. Procurement professional and their manager made aware. Questionnaire to be sent as soon as possible and buyer to confirm when sent.	Previous 30 days.	Daily – procurement team meeting.	Head of procurement and procurement managers.
The supplier returns a completed sustainable practice questionnaire with ITT/ RFQ response.	100% required to be returned as this forms part of the supplier assessment.	The supplier may not be accepted for down selection if this is not delivered with its quotation or tender. The supplier should be informed if this is the reason for its exclusion from the remainder of this activity.	Previous 30 days.	Weekly – managers' meeting.	Head of procurement and due diligence team manager.

Table 4.5 Control performance criteria

Controls at one point in the processes generally feed into other controls through a series of **inputs** and **outputs**. In the example in table 4.5 above, the buyer being required to send the questionnaire is an output of this control. The returned questionnaire is also an output of this, but it becomes an input into the next controls. If the input into these controls was not satisfactory or did not exist, then it may not be possible to properly satisfy subsequent controls.

In the example shown in table 4.5, if the buyer fails to send the questionnaire, it will not be possible for the supplier to submit a response, automatically excluding it from down selection. This could lead to the unfortunate exclusion of a supplier that could have been the best candidate. On the other hand, if the supplier has been sent the questionnaire but fails to return a fully completed response to it, it may also be removed from the competition on these grounds. The fact that the supplier does not choose to return a response, or returns one that is incomplete, may suggest that its involvement with or commitment to sustainable practice is limited or non-existent. This allows information about suppliers' attitudes to sustainable practice to pass further through the buyer's process, and allows for the fair and objective rejection of suppliers that do not meet this criteria. This potentially saves the buying organisation from working with a supplier that does not have complimentary organisational values and instead helps to cut down the selection of suppliers to determine which are most suitable.

This is why both controls and measures are important. In addition to protecting an organisation, they provide structure and a monitoring system for that structure. These can be used to monitor the success rate of employees' actions, but could also be used to understand what the **root cause** of any failure of an individual control is. In the example in table 4.5, looking at the measure alone may show that only 70% of the buyer's staff are sending the form to suppliers. However, when the root cause is analysed, it may be discovered that the buyer's staff have not read or understood the process, have not been trained in this activity or simply do not have access to the form – all of which result in failure.

In cases such as these, it is important that if employees do not feel they understand or can work to a particular process, they should seek further support. This may lead to improvements being made to the process or additional employee training. Either way, processes are essential in supporting employees in delivering quality outputs throughout the organisation and the supply chain. This consistency is designed to protect the organisation from intolerable risk and supports the supply chain in awarding contracts to only suitable, compatible suppliers where possible.

Where failures are reported, staff should work with process owners and users to make improvements to the process itself. This should meet any higher-level requirements (usually embedded in a process) but should also reflect the way employees actually work. This will allow the process update to be more effective, easier to implement and brief, and should encourage employees to become more actively involved in making process improvements.

> *Apply*
> Choose an organisation with which you are familiar. Buyers in the organisation may follow internal processes in the course of their duties. Review one of these processes and write answers to the following questions.
>
> Are there requirements explicitly relating to sustainable or ethical practice?

What do these requirements ask the buyer to do?

Is it clear which of the organisation's recorded risks are mitigated by requirements relating to sustainable or ethical practice?

Is the performance of these requirements monitored?

Based on your findings, do you believe that improvements could be made to this process?

Expanding reporting frameworks to include ecological and social performance

An organisation may choose to begin monitoring other aspects of its performance, including its ecological and social impacts.

The benefits of this could include the following.

- Reduced wastage during manufacture

- Less waste sent to landfill

- A reduction in time lost to sickness

- Money saved as a result of any combination of the above

Implementing and maintaining reporting frameworks and targets will require additional resources. However, if implemented correctly, this monitoring could save the organisation money due to more carefully managing the impacts of activities on staff, suppliers, the local community and the environment. These could be added to the agenda of contract management reviews to ensure that they are given proper focus and monitored on a regular basis. As for other targets, those with social or ecological impacts should be stated as early as possible to ensure that the supplier agrees to these and can support them. This focus could lead to the improved ability to demonstrate the supplier's commitment to CSR, and if it is proud of its results, the supplier may choose to publish these on its website for customers and other organisations to see.

While these reporting frameworks will benefit the buying organisation, it can be a good idea to ask suppliers if they have a similar approach. Where a supplier does not, it may be open to adopting new practices if it benefits them. Where a supplier already has a similar approach, it may be able to offer suggestions of good practice for the buying organisation to consider for its own operations.

Apply

Choose an organisation with which you are familiar. Review the organisation's reporting framework and write answers to the following questions.

Is the reporting framework easily accessible to staff within the organisation?

Is the reporting framework easily accessible to people outside of the organisation?

Is the reporting framework purely focused on delivery, or does it also report on ecological and social factors?

Are there clear targets for each element of the framework and are these being achieved?

Defining organisational value for money to include social outcomes

As with all procurements, various relationship styles can be used with suppliers. This could be anywhere from arms-length, where the buying organisation remains distant from the supplier, or it could be a much closer relationship that ultimately results in a collaboration.

In some instances, a government or a government-related organisation may contract a supplier from a foreign country to supply products. These contracts are often high value contracts, and if carried out as a traditional procurement, the government will receive its product and the supplying organisation will receive its payment. Though the government will receive the deliverable, it may still be dependent on foreign organisations to provide what it needs in future purchases. In order to support its nation's economy and capability, the government may impose **offset** or **industrial participation** requirements on foreign companies that it procures from.

Offset/industrial participation
An agreement that a foreign organisation will invest into the country of the procuring government as part of its contractual obligations

Use of local labour

Industrial participation, or offset, is when an organisation that is supplying to a foreign government makes an effort to ensure that its process of manufacturing the supplied goods in some way directly benefits the economy of that country. The requirements of industrial participation should be clear and concisely mapped out by the government of the host country, so that it is clear to potential suppliers that this must be met in order to win a contract.

The requirements for offset fulfilment will vary from country to country but, generally, they are expressed as a value in proportion to the value of the procurement. For example, a supplier may be asked to offset 50% of the contract value, meaning that if the contract is worth an equivalent of $1 million, $500,000 of the value should somehow circulate back into the contracting economy. Clearly, the least effective way of achieving this would be the supplier directly paying that money to that government or country. Instead, other routes can be used that allow the supplier to meet offset requirements while supporting the production of its product for that particular government.

The following are some examples of offset categories that may be considered for use by some countries.

- Procurement of products or services.

- Investment into improving local infrastructure (building houses, improving condition of roads, access to electricity, telecoms, etc.).

- Contributions or investment into research and development through sharing knowledge and, potentially, intellectual property.

- Investments into improving local access to education for people of different age groups and backgrounds.

It is clear that the supply chain plays an important part in meeting offset requirements when supplying to foreign governments. At a high level, a strategy is required to give guidance on which areas procurements will be focused on. This could include a breakdown of different sectors (i.e. infrastructure, education, etc.,) or could instead focus on sourcing suppliers that meet the organisation's manufacturing requirements.

The following are some benefits of using local sub-tier suppliers.

- Supporting local economies.

- Providing or securing jobs for local workers.

- Providing the supplier with an opportunity for portfolio diversification.

- Providing an opportunity of becoming an international supplier.

- Providing an opportunity to promote the sub-tier supplier's work, based on its work with the supplying organisation, which may help the sub-tier supplier to secure future contracts with other organisations.

- The buyer learning more about the culture of the country the supplier is based in, including business and cultural norms and expectations.

> *Remember*
> The procuring government will provide requirements that state what will and will not be accepted as suitable for fulfilling offset. Before selecting suppliers, the buying organisation should confirm with the government that either the potential supplier or the package of work it may produce qualify as acceptable offset opportunities. Where this is not done, unsuitable suppliers may be selected and alternatives may need to be chosen, or another route to satisfying the offset requirements may need to be explored.

To execute the strategy, procurement processes may need to be adapted to include instructions that enable the effective delivery of offset requirements. These processes ensure that, where required, contracts are designed to support the accrual of offset-qualifying value, which should be well documented so that it is easy to justify.

While the enforcement of offset would benefit any economy, it is especially beneficial to emerging economies (formerly known as developing countries), where manufacturing and industrial capabilities may be growing. This may also have the multiplying effect of attracting other organisations to carry out business in these countries, after seeing other companies embedding themselves there.

One of the criticisms that multi-national organisations have faced in the past is that they establish a plant in a country, hire local people (usually at low rates of pay) and subsequently abandon them and the plant when there is an opportunity to establish a more economically advantageous plant and workforce elsewhere in the world. While some organisations would argue that this is essential for the organisation to remain profitable and offer its products at a lower price to the customer, this could be seen as harmful to the community it affects. Behaviours such as this may cause social, economic and even environmental impacts to communities, potentially drawing the attention of the press.

> *Check*
> Define offset (also known as industrial participation).
>
> What are the benefits of using local labour to the following groups?
>
> - The workers
> - The suppliers
> - The local economies
>
> What are the criticisms of the ways international organisations have previously used local labour?

Participation of disadvantaged groups

Another important way of looking at an organisation's value is the extent to which it proactively supports vulnerable or 'disadvantaged' groups. Procurement strategies, decision and actions should take these groups into consideration, whether they are from within the organisation, part of the supply chain or within local communities. The World Health Organization[18] identifies the following categories of people under this term.

- Children
- The elderly
- People with disabilities
- Pregnant women
- People living in poverty
- Immunocompromised people

In E/C.12/GC/19 (2008)[19], the UN stated that citizens in all its member countries have a right to social security. Essentially, this means that vulnerable or disadvantaged people should be supported by their government in securing their health, wellbeing and way of life where possible.

In some countries, there are schemes in place that support disadvantaged people in finding work, and sometimes, companies are given quotas (or set their own target) to hire a particular proportion of disadvantaged people as employees. Initiatives such as this are fantastic social interventions that help many people secure employment, develop new skills and foster relationships with others, reducing the potential for individuals to become isolated as a result of their disadvantage.

Organisations welcome a greater range of diversity into their workforce, boost staff's awareness of how to support disadvantaged colleagues and as a result are able to demonstrate that they have a strong commitment to CSR.

Chapter Summary

This chapter has covered the following topics.

- The impact of international ethical standards on procurement and supply
- Which practices support ethical procurement
- How audits and other feedback mechanisms can be used to evaluate ethical standards in the workplace
- How an organisation could use processes and practices to meet the requirements of corporate social responsibility

Recommended reading

Elkington, J. (1998), *Cannibals with Forks: The Triple Bottom Line of 21st Century Business*, Capstone Publishers

UN (1988), *Report of the World Commission on Environment and Development: Our Common Future* [online]. Retrieved from: www.un-documents.net/our-common-future.pdf [Accessed on: 05 February 2019]

Transparency International, www.transparency.org.uk

Amnesty International, www.amnesty.org/en

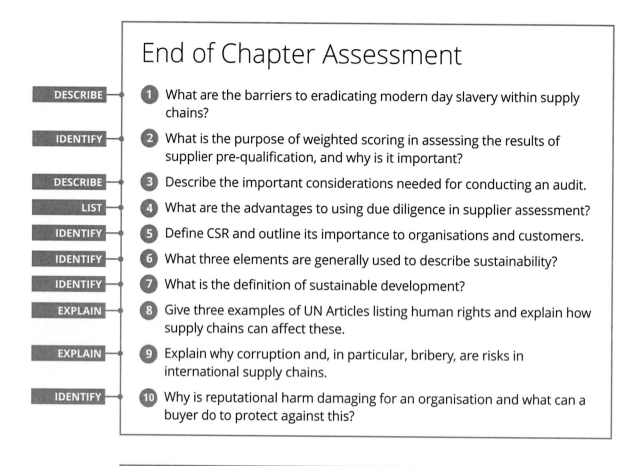

End of Chapter Assessment

DESCRIBE — ① What are the barriers to eradicating modern day slavery within supply chains?

IDENTIFY — ② What is the purpose of weighted scoring in assessing the results of supplier pre-qualification, and why is it important?

DESCRIBE — ③ Describe the important considerations needed for conducting an audit.

LIST — ④ What are the advantages to using due diligence in supplier assessment?

IDENTIFY — ⑤ Define CSR and outline its importance to organisations and customers.

IDENTIFY — ⑥ What three elements are generally used to describe sustainability?

IDENTIFY — ⑦ What is the definition of sustainable development?

EXPLAIN — ⑧ Give three examples of UN Articles listing human rights and explain how supply chains can affect these.

EXPLAIN — ⑨ Explain why corruption and, in particular, bribery, are risks in international supply chains.

IDENTIFY — ⑩ Why is reputational harm damaging for an organisation and what can a buyer do to protect against this?

References

1 OECD (n.d.), *Foreign Bribery Factsheet* [online]. Retrieved from: www.oecd.org/daf/anti-bribery/Foreign_Bribery_Factsheet_ENGLISH.pdf [Accessed on: 5 February 2019]

2 OECD (n.d), *OECD Convention on Combating Bribery of Foreign Public Officials in International Business Transactions* [online]. Retrieved from: www.oecd.org/corruption/oecdantibriberyconvention.htm [Accessed on: 5 February 2019]

3 UN (1948), *Universal Declaration on Human Rights* [online]. Retrieved from: www.un.org/en/universal-declaration-human-rights/ [Accessed on: 5 February 2019]

4 Amnesty International [online]. Retrieved from: www.amnesty.org/en/ [Accessed on: 5 February 2019]

5 Human Rights Watch [online]. Retrieved from: www.hrw.org/about [Accessed on: 5 February 2019]

6 Equality and Human Rights Commission [online]. Retrieved from: www.equalityhumanrights.com/en/human-rights/human-rights-act and British Institute of Human Rights (2018) www.bihr.org.uk/my-human-rights [Accessed on: 5 February 2019]

7 Australian Human Rights Commission [online]. Retrieved from: www.humanrights.gov.au/about-commission [Accessed on: 5 February 2019]

8 International Labour Organization and Walk Free Foundation (2017), *Global Estimates of Modern Slavery: forced labour and forced marriage* [online]. Retrieved from: www.ilo.org/wcmsp5/groups/public/@dgreports/@dcomm/documents/publication/wcms_575540.pdf [Accessed on: 5 February 2019]

9 Modern slavery helpline [online]. Retrieved from: www.modernslaveryhelpline.org/ [Accessed on: 5 February 2019]

10 International Diamond Manufacturers Association (2018), *Code of Conduct* [online]. Retrieved from: idma.co/code-of-conduct [Accessed on: 5 February 2019]

11 Goldman, K. D., Schmalz, K. J. (2005), "Doing Due Diligence! Vetting the vendors", *Health Promotion Practice*, Volume 6, Issue 4, pp. 360-362

12 CIPS (n.d.), *Ethical and Sustainable Procurement* [online]. Retrieved from: www.cips.org/Documents/About%20CIPS/CIPS_Ethics_Guide_WEB.pdf [Accessed on: 5 February 2019]

13 CIPS (n.d.), Developing and Managing Contracts [online]. Retrieved from: www.cips.org/Documents/Knowledge/Procurement-Topics-and-Skills/10-Developing-and-Managing-Contracts/T-and-Cs-and-Developing-of-Contracts/1/Standard_T_Cs_Goods_Guidance_Notes.pdf [Accessed on: 5 February 2019]

14 UN (1988), *Report of the World Commission on Environment and Development: Our Common Future* [online]. Retrieved from: www.un-documents.net/our-common-future.pdf [Accessed on: 5 February 2019]

15 UN (n.d.), *Sustainable Development Goals* [online]. Retrieved from: www.un.org/sustainabledevelopment/sustainable-development-goals/ [Accessed on: 5 February 2019]

16 Elkington, J. (1998), *Cannibals with Forks: The Triple Bottom Line of 21st Century Business*. Capstone Publishers

17 International Organization for Standardization (2017), ISO20:400 2017 [online]. Retrieved from: www.iso.org/standard/63026.html [Accessed on: 5 February 2019]

18 WHO [online]. Retrieved from: www.who.int/environmental_health_emergencies/vulnerable_groups/en/ [Accessed on: 5 February 2019]

19 UN (2007), *Committee on Economic, Social and Cultural Rights* [online]. Retrieved from: socialprotection-humanrights.org/wp-content/uploads/2015/06/CESCR-General-Comment-19.pdf [Accessed on: 5 February 2019]

4.4 L04

Glossary

ABC analysis
A categorisation process dividing the subject matter into three levels of value

Ad valorem
An estimated value of goods that are imported, based on the value of the goods plus a number of other factors (insurance, freight and other costs) that is calculated to give a total value

Assets
Items of value owned by an organisation, which can be used to meet debts

Audit
An official inspection conducted, either by the procurement organisation itself or by an independent third party, to ensure compliance with requirements and standards

Binding origin information (BOI)
A legally binding decision on the origin of goods provided by an EU member state

Bottleneck
A specific stage in a process which slows down the flow of production and limits the overall output rate

Breach of contract
A situation where one party fails to deliver against the agreement made

Bribery
When someone gives something of value to another party in order to influence a more desirable outcome from that party. The difference between a bribe and a standard transaction is that this action is corrupt

British Standards Institution (BSI Group)
An institution that produces the technical standards that products must conform to in the UK

Business case
A justification for a proposed project or undertaking on the basis of its expected benefits

Call for competition
A notice released by a buying organisation through the Official Journal of the European Union (OJEU) to make potential suppliers aware that they may participate in a sourcing competition, in line with the organisation's requirements

Cartel
A group of organisations that work together to prevent competition, raise prices and gain control of a market

Cash flow
The money moved in and out of an organisation

Centralised procurement
A structure where procurement for the whole organisation is carried out by a centralised function often from one central location

Code of conduct
A series of rules set by an organisation that define suitable behaviours and values that should be used and applied by a member of that organisation, for the purpose of acting in a suitable manner, as well as demonstrating uniformity and upholding the standards of the organisation

Commodity pricing
The market average price charged for a product

Components
A part that makes up a product

Conflict of interest
Where an individual is unable to remain impartial due to a personal, professional or public interest

Consumables
A commodity that is used up quickly or requires replacing frequently

Consumer
The end user of a product or service

Continuous improvement
A concept based on constantly improving processes to eliminate waste

Core activities
Activities that are key to an organisation's success

Corporate social responsibility (CSR)
The responsibility of an organisation to act favourably towards the environment, contribute to the community and behave ethically

Corruption
Abuse or misuse of a person's entrusted position, power or authority for personal gain. In procurement, this could include a person with authority agreeing to give a specific supplier a contract before a fair competitive tender has been carried out (making it unfair)

Credit check
A process to evaluate an organisation to determine its financial stability

Cross-functional team
A team made up of people from different departments all working towards a common goal

Cultural relativism
The idea that the way a person behaves, what they believe and what they consider to be normal are not universally applicable, but may be different from culture to culture

Currency
A monetary system used within a country, for example, the rand in South Africa (ZAR) or Australian dollars (AUD)

Currency hedging
A method of purchasing foreign currency ahead of an expected payment in order to prevent the financial loss caused by market fluctuations

Cyberattack
A malicious act attempting to disrupt or steal information using computers

Cybercrime
Crime that involves computers or networks

Cybersecurity
The protection of computers and networks against cybercrime and cyberattacks

DDP
Delivery duty paid – goods are delivered to the buying organisation's location of choice with all associated costs included and paid for by the supplier

Demographics
Data relating to trends within the population

Devolved procurement
Devolved or decentralised procurement is a purchasing structure whereby individual locations are responsible for their buying activity

Dual sourcing
Sourcing from two suppliers

Due diligence
Appraising a supplier to ensure that it is a suitable match for an organisation

E-auctions
Auctions where the bidding takes place on the Internet

E-catalogues
Online catalogues

E-requisitioning
Sending a requisition via electronic methods

E-tendering
An electronic approach to tendering using e-mails or portals

Economies of scale
Saving costs by increasing the levels of production

Economy
The state of a region, country or the world in relation to its production and consumption of goods and services

Embezzlement
The misuse of assets or items entrusted to a person for a particular purpose. The ownership of these items is wrongly transferred on purpose to the person entrusted with them, meaning that they are no longer assets of the original owner. An example of this may be a buyer selling a company laptop for their own monetary gain after their company has issued them with a new one

Equity
The amount of shareholders' funds and retained earnings is the difference between the value of the assets and the value of liabilities

ERP
Enterprise resource planning system, a multi-functional electronic system that combines work flows both in and out of the business from all functions

Ethical codes of practice
A document outlining an organisation's accepted behaviours and principles of working

EXW
Ex works – goods are required to be collected by the buying organisation from the suppliers' premises

Facilitation payment
A type of bribe where a payment is made to enable something to take place or to speed up its progress. This corrupt practice may also be known as a 'grease payment'

Fair Trade Foundation
An international charity dedicated to encouraging countries and organisations to ensure that their workers are paid a fair salary for the work that they do

Financial statements
A company's formal financial statements are their published year end accounts – in most countries it is a legal requirement for companies to publish these statements soon after their year end accounting date

Fit for purpose
Being good enough to do the job it was designed for

Five Rights
The key objectives of procurement: the right quantity, the right quality, at the right time, delivered to the right place and at the right price

Fixed-price contract
A contract where the price remains the same for the agreed period

Fraud
When an individual deliberately misleads or tells lies to someone to achieve the outcome they desire at their victim's expense

FTSE 100
The United Kingdom's stock exchange

Functional fit
Be able to work with an organisation on the same technical level

Futures exchange
A marketplace where the seller of a commodity agrees to sell or buy a certain amount of the commodity to a buyer at a particular price on a specific date in the future

GDPR
The European Union's General Data Protection Regulation

Gearing
A measure of how the business is being funded, based on its ratio of debt to equity

Gifts and hospitality
Material goods, money or entertainment that may be given from one party to another. In the context of business, the giving and receiving of gifts from one organisation or individual to another may be perceived as giving and receiving a bribe

Hedge
A form of risk management in investing used to reduce any potential losses

Human rights
Rights or principles, based on shared values that are accepted as belonging to every person, regardless of background

Imperfect competition
A situation in the marketplace where one supplier has complete control

Import duty
A payment made to allow the entry of goods into the destination country. The payment is made to the local customs agency of the receiving country

In-house
Within an organisation

Incoterms®
International commercial terms of sale that assign costs and responsibilities between the buyer and seller when delivering products

Indices
The plural of index – a statistical measure used within economics

Insource
To bring a function of activity back in-house after previously being outsourced

Intellectual property
An idea or creative work, which can be treated as an asset

Inter-trading
Trading between companies that are owned by different entities

International Labour Organization (ILO)
A United Nations organisation uniting governments, employers and workers with the common goal of improving labour standards for all

International sourcing
Sourcing goods or services from all over the world

Internet
A worldwide system of interconnected electronic networks

Intra-company trading
Business conducted within a company, i.e. between two departments or locations

Intranet
A private network within an organisation or group of organisations

Investment
A measure of the attractiveness of an organisation to a potential investor

Invitation to tender (ITT)
A formal invitation sent to suppliers inviting them to make an offer to supply goods or services

ISO 9001
An international standard for quality management

Key performance indicators (KPIs)
A measurable value that generates feedback on performance

Lead time
The amount of time from placing the order to the goods/services being delivered

Lease
A contract between two parties – the lessee and lessor – where one party agrees to pay a sum of money for the use of an asset such as a car or a machine

Letter of credit
A document issued from one bank to another to act as a guarantee of payment against agreed terms and conditions, including the presentation of compliant documentation

Life-cycle costs
The total cost involved in items of inventory, including purchasing price, inward delivery, receipt and handling, storage, packing and preparation, dispatch costs, insurance and overheads

Liquid
Having enough money to pay for short- to medium-term liabilities or debts

Liquidity
A solvency measure to determine whether an organisation is able to meet its liabilities (short-term debts) when they come due from net current assets

Logistics
The movement of something from one place to another

Low cost countries
Countries that have a slow-growing economy and where rates of pay are significantly lower than in countries with more affluent economies

Market share
The portion or percentage of a market owned or controlled by a supplier or product

MEAT
Most economically advantageous tender

Modern slavery
Individuals being forced to work for little or no pay, or humans who are trafficked to work in foreign countries

Modified re-buy
A product/service that has been sourced before but requires a slight change prior to sourcing again

Monopoly
A situation where one supplier has the entire market share and there is no competition

Multiple sourcing
Sourcing from many suppliers

Named destination
The final destination goods should be delivered to. This should be clearly defined from the start

Negotiated tendering
When only a single or a few suppliers are approached based on a previous relationship or track record

Nepotism
Using actual or perceived power to give an unfair advantage to friends or family members

New buy
A brand new requirement – the first time the product/service has been sourced

Non-conformance
Where an audit finds that something does not work or is not carried out in line with the rules that govern it. These generally require action to fix the problem

Non-disclosure agreement (NDA)
An agreement between two or more parties to agree not to disclose any information in relation to a project or contract

Non-governmental organisation (NGO)
A nonprofit organisation that operates independently of any government

Offset/industrial participation
An agreement that a foreign organisation will invest into the country of the procuring government as part of its contractual obligations

Offshoring
The relocation of one part of a business, usually an operational function, to another country in an attempt to reduce cost

Open tendering
The opportunity is widely advertised allowing any supplier to make a bid

Opportunity for improvement
Where an audit identifies potential improvements to a process or ways of working and highlights them for future consideration. These do not always require action, but may be treated as suggestions

Original equipment manufacturer (OEM)
The producer of own-branded parts or equipment which are sold to other manufacturers for production and retail

Origin
The economic nationality of goods in international trade (European Commission definition)

Pareto principle
A theory that states that 80% of events are generated from 20% of the causes

Patent
A way of protecting intellectual property, excluding other parties from using, marketing or making products that relate to it

Post tender negotiation (PTN)
Negotiation that occurs after the best value supplier has been chosen. This is to see if any further improvements can be made before the contract is awarded

Pre-qualification questionnaire (PQQ)
A document sent to potential suppliers to assess their suitability against the buyer's minimum standards of performance – generally based on experience, capacity, financial standing and insurances

Primary data
Data that comes directly from the source and constitutes new data for a specific purpose

Prior information notice
A notice released by a buying organisation through the OJEU to make potential suppliers aware of a sourcing competition that it intends to run in the future

Profitability
The organisation's revenues minus its total costs

Profit margin
The amount of profit made on a sale, i.e. profit expressed as a percentage of sales or revenues

Prototype
An early sample of a first attempt at making a product

Public sector
A sector of the economy that provides services to the people and is funded through taxes

Pure competition
A situation in the marketplace where there is plenty of competition

Qualitative
Measured in terms of quality

Quantitative
Measured in terms of numbers or quantity

Quota
A quantity of something. In international trade, the quantity of a commodity being imported or exported

Raw materials
The base material from which a product is made, e.g., steel

Request for information (RFI)
A document used to gather information about suppliers and their capabilities prior to a formal procurement process

Request for quotation (RFQ)
An invitation to suppliers to ask them to give a quotation to supply goods or services

Restricted tendering
A two stage tendering process

Revenues
Income to an organisation

Reverse auction
An auction where the bidding decreases over time to ensure the buyer gets the lowest price

Samples
Examples of the product that is required

Scope creep
When the original scope of a study (or a specification for example) has been exceeded either deliberately or accidentally, meaning that the study is now focused on elements that were not originally intended to be included

Scope
The defined boundaries that limit the extent of a study, to ensure that it is focused on the specific situation or problem

Secondary data
Data that already exists

SENSEX
India's stock exchange

Service level agreements (SLA)
An agreement to deliver and maintain an accepted and expected level of service

Shareholder
An individual or organisation that legally owns part (a share) of a business

Shareholder equity
The owner/s of the organisation's residual claim once all debts have been paid

Single sourcing
Sourcing from one sole supplier

Specification
A detailed description of the product or service required

Staff churn
The turnover of employees in an organisation

Stakeholder
Anyone with an interest in or who is impacted by decisions made by an organisation

Stock markets
A place where public limited companies' stocks and shares are traded (bought and sold)

Straight re-buy
Exactly the same product/service as sourced previously

Strategic sourcing
High level sourcing for core products or services

Sub-tier supplier
An organisation supplying into the suppliers that are contracted directly into a buying organisation's supply chain. This supplier's activities, stability and reputation can all affect the buyer's supply chain

Supplier appraisal
A process of evaluating a supplier's ability to carry out a contract in terms of quality, delivery, price and other contributing factors

Supplier pre-qualification
An early process within procurement to find out if potential suppliers meet the buying organisation's criteria on capability, capacity and financial stability

Sustainability
The ability to meet the needs of the present without compromising the needs of the future

Sustainable development
Development that meets the needs of the population in the present without negatively affecting the resource needs of future populations

Tactical/operational sourcing
Low level sourcing for low risk or routine items

Tangible
Something that you can see or touch

Tariff
Rules regulating the type of goods, their volume (determined by quota) and their import duty when imported from specific countries. Tariffs may have a unique code, making them easy to identify and reference

The public interest test
The test used by public sector organisations to determine whether or not information should be released to the public when it is requested. Information will not be released if it is not seen to be in the public interest

Total cost of ownership
A structured approach to calculating the full costs associated with buying and using an asset or acquisition over its entire life cycle

Total quality management (TQM)
A management approach linked to organisational culture and attitudes, which aims to gain complete customer satisfaction

Trade bloc
An economic group, formed by different countries in a geographical zone, to create preferential trade conditions

Transfer of ownership
The point where title to the goods passes from one party to another

TUPE
Legislation to protect employees when outsourced contracts are moved between suppliers

Wearing parts
Parts within equipment that have a limited life and require replacement regularly

Weighted score
A score calculated by using a scoring system that emphasises the areas with the highest level of importance

Win-win
The best solution to a negotiation; where both parties are satisfied

Workplace fraud
Small-scale thefts taking place within the workplace that are difficult to detect and could collectively cause large financial or resource losses. An example of this could be taking inexpensive stationery home, which could cause losses on a larger scale if colleagues do the same

Zeitgeist
The 'spirit' of an age/time, meaning the cultural norms, values and behaviours from a particular period in history

Index